"*Lively Oracles of God: Perspectives on*
contribution to twenty-first century liturgical scholarship. This
deals with the various ways that the Scriptures function in liturgical prayer including proclamation, anamnesis, drama, and of course, the Lectionary itself. The scholars in this volume are so careful in treating historical, systematic, and pastoral concerns together. This volume is not only necessary reading for scholars. It is a gift to the ecumenical Church who journey together in remembering the mystery of salvation in the context of late modernity."

— Timothy P. O'Malley, Director of Education, McGrath Institute for Church Life, University of Notre Dame

"Scripture's anamnetic function makes sense only if remembrance (of the past) and encounter (towards the future) are maintained in balance. This observation, drawn from O'Loughlin's essay, suggests a theme which unites these bold and insightful new investigations into the Bible's liturgical presence. Many contributors expose the inherent ritual and interpretive tensions when full account is taken of Scripture's multiple roles—pedagogical, kerygmatic, and doxological, while others reveal the challenges, as well as the potential, of the inherited modes of biblical reading. Although drawing upon history, liturgical traditions, and a wealth of earlier scholarship, the main focus of these essays is to make sense of the ways in which the dynamic interplay between the biblical text, the ritual act, and contemporary contexts drives liturgical change and creates meaning. Liturgical ministers, as well as students and scholars, will be inspired by this tantalizing array of ideas and approaches."

— Juliette J. Day, University of Helsinki

"The Word of God has always provided rich fare for worshipers. Many Christian denominations consider it the central feature of assembling. In a sense, we Roman Catholics were late for dinner, reforming our liturgy after coming to a renewed awakening into the value of the Scriptures that have always guided our prayer. In this lively volume, all believers may celebrate together at the various ways that the Bible has fed our faith, anchored our worship, and opened our vision."

— Father Paul Turner, Pastor, Cathedral of the Immaculate Conception

"'Biblical' worship is a term used by some writers to claim superiority for their worship tradition over so-called 'liturgical' worship. This rich collection of essays demonstrates that 'liturgical' worship is drenched in Scripture to its core and is deeply evangelical in all senses of this word. This book is a joy to read."

— Bryan D. Spinks, Bishop F. Percy Goddard Professor of Liturgical Studies and Pastoral Theology, Yale University

The Alcuin Club: Promoting the Study of Liturgy

Founded in 1897, the Alcuin Club seeks to promote the study of Christian liturgy and worship in general with special reference to worship in the Anglican Communion. The Club has published a series of annual Collections, including *A Companion to Common Worship*, volumes 1 and 2, edited by Paul F. Bradshaw; *The Origins of Feasts, Fasts and Seasons in Early Christianity* by Paul F. Bradshaw and Maxwell E. Johnson (SPCK 2011) and, by the same authors, *The Eucharistic Liturgies: Their Evolution and Interpretation* (SPCK 2012); and a new completely revised 4th edition of R. C. D. Jasper and G. J. Cuming, *Prayers of the Eucharist: Early and Reformed* (Liturgical Press Academic, 2019); also *The Cross and Creation in Christian Liturgy and Art* by Christopher Irvine (SPCK, 2013), *Eucharistic Epicleses Ancient and Modern* by Anne McGowan (SPCK, 2014), *Dean Dwelly of Liverpool: Liturgical Genius* by Peter Kennerley (Carnegie Publishing, 2015), *Ancient Christian Worship* by Andrew B. McGowan (Baker Academic, 2016), *The Rise and Fall of the Incomparable Liturgy: The Book of Common Prayer 1559–1906* by Bryan D. Spinks (SPCK, 2017) and, by the same author, *Scottish Presbyterian Worship* (St Andrew Press, 2020); also *The Pilgrimage of Egeria* by Anne McGowan and Paul F. Bradshaw (Liturgical Press Academic, 2018); and *Introduction to Eastern Christian Liturgies* by Stefanos Alexopoulos and Maxwell E. Johnson (Liturgical Press Academic, 2022).

The Alcuin Liturgy Guide series aims to address the theology and practice of worship, and includes *The Use of Symbols in Worship*, edited by Christopher Irvine, two volumes covering the celebration of the Christian Year: *Celebrating Christ's Appearing: Advent to Christmas*; and *Celebrating Christ's Victory: Ash Wednesday to Trinity*, both by Benjamin Gordon-Taylor and Simon Jones, and most recently *Celebrating Christian Initiation* by Simon Jones.

The Club works in partnership with the Group for the Renewal of Worship (GROW) in the publication of the Joint Liturgical Studies series, with two studies being published each year.

In 2013 the Club also published a major new work of reference, *The Study of Liturgy and Worship: An Alcuin Guide*, edited by Juliette Day and Benjamin Gordon-Taylor (SPCK, 2013).

Members of the Club receive publications of the current year free and others at a reduced rate. The President of the Club is the Rt Revd Dr Stephen Platten, its Chairman is the Revd Canon Christopher Irvine, and the Secretary is the Revd Dr Gordon Jeanes. For details of membership and the annual subscription, contact The Alcuin Club, 5 Saffron Street, Royston, Herts, SG8 9TR United Kingdom; email: alcuinclub@gmail.com; or visit the Alcuin Club website at: www.alcuinclub.org.uk.

Alcuin Club Collections 97

Lively Oracles of God

Perspectives on the Bible and Liturgy

Edited by
Gordon Jeanes
and
Bridget Nichols

Foreword by
Paul F. Bradshaw

LITURGICAL PRESS
ACADEMIC

Collegeville, Minnesota
www.litpress.org

Cover design by Tara Wiese. Image courtesy of Wikimedia Commons. *The Hand of God from Sant Climent de Taüll*. Circa 1123. Museu Nacional d'Art de Catalunya.

1 2 3 4 5 6 7 8 9

Library of Congress Cataloging-in-Publication Data

Names: Jeanes, Gordon P., editor. | Nichols, Bridget, 1963– editor.
Title: Lively oracles of God : perspectives on the Bible and liturgy / edited by Gordon Jeanes and Bridget Nichols.
Description: Collegeville, Minnesota : Liturgical Press, [2022] | Series: Alcuin Club collections ; 97 | Includes index. | Summary: "A collection of essays re-examining how Scripture is heard by regular worshipers and by those with little experience of the church. Contributors also consider how the relationship between Scripture and liturgy is tested by new priorities—the climate crisis, the honoring of children and those on the margins of the church, and the significance of gender and identity"— Provided by publisher.
Identifiers: LCCN 2021042636 (print) | LCCN 2021042637 (ebook) | ISBN 9780814667224 (paperback) | ISBN 9780814667231 (epub) | ISBN 9780814667231 (pdf)
Subjects: LCSH: Bible—Criticism, interpretation, etc. | Liturgics. | Preaching to non-church-affiliated people.
Classification: LCC BS511.3 .L583 2022 (print) | LCC BS511.3 (ebook) | DDC 220.6—dc23
LC record available at https://lccn.loc.gov/2021042636
LC ebook record available at https://lccn.loc.gov/2021042637

Contents

Foreword

Is the inclusion of extensive Bible reading in church services nothing more than a hangover from times long ago when most congregations were largely illiterate and so had no other means of accessing the contents of Scripture? And does the custom that can be observed in many congregations today, where worshippers read from their own copy of the Bible or from the relevant texts printed in a service leaflet at the same time as those same texts are being read aloud by ministers or others, spring from a confusion between the two practices, or perhaps from an inability among people today to *listen* without *viewing*? Or is there a much more profound reason behind the regular public proclamation of scriptural passages in Christian worship?

The contributors to this collection of essays argue that not only is there such a reason but that there are more than one, that Scripture can fulfil a number of different functions in relation to the liturgy of which it is a part. This does not just apply to Bible readings properly so described, but also extends to the use of biblical material as songs and hymns or prayers, as well as to allusions to particular scriptural passages and texts in other parts of the liturgy. These other liturgical uses, in particular, may not simply replicate the meaning that the passage was understood to have in its original setting—still less the meaning assigned to it by modern biblical scholarship—but can convey distinctive meanings of their own through the new context within the act of worship.

That context includes the nature of the specific rite, but also the occasion on which it is being celebrated, and equally the particular people participating in it. It will make a difference to the meaning, to take an obvious example, if they are largely strangers to one another and unfamiliar with the ritual of the event, or if they are a close knit community who regularly celebrate together in this way, and who therefore already share a liturgical "language" or "script" of which the Bible texts or allusions are an integral part. And, of course, there can always be a difference in meaning between that intended by those who compiled the rite and those who experience it, and also between the experiences of ministers and of the congregation.

The richness and variety of this interplay between liturgy and Scripture also raises new questions in what may fairly be described as a secular, or at least much less biblically knowledgeable, age. People in general are much less likely to recognize an allusion to, or even a quotation from, a passage in the Bible than they were a generation or two ago. Does it matter that the same is true when it appears in liturgy rather than in literature? Do modern lectionaries with their multi-year cycles of readings place too much emphasis on the maximum coverage of the Bible and too little on the roles that passages of Scripture might play within the context of worship? Is familiarity with the contents of the Bible necessary in order to enter more fully into the experience of Christian worship? Did it matter, for instance, that for years in my youth I had no idea that the hymn, "Bright the vision that delighted once the sight of Judah's seer," was referring to Isaiah 6?

It is issues like these that lie behind the essays that make up this volume, issues that were often taken for granted in the heyday of the twentieth-century movement of liturgical renewal, but which now return to challenge us in the changed atmosphere of the current age. The contributors approach the relationship of liturgy and Bible from a variety of angles and with their own perspectives, but always with probing questions in mind. Thus, the commissioning of a collection addressing this topic is a timely initiative by the Alcuin Club.

Paul F. Bradshaw
Emeritus Professor of Liturgy
University of Notre Dame

Preface

Worship is the main place where we meet the Bible, either read or heard. It was where the Bible came into being (the origin of the canon) and it is where it comes most alive. The psalms, obviously, and prophecies like those of Isaiah and Jeremiah are full of songs, laments, and a variety of poetic forms, but even "historical" books contain hymns and prayers (e.g., Exod 15:1-18; Deut 32, 33; 1 Sam 2:1-10; 1 Kgs 8:23-53). Luke's gospel contains the canticles of Zechariah, Mary, and Simeon, and numerous passages in the New Testament letters and the book of Revelation are used as hymns—indeed, some are thought to have begun their life as hymns. The Bible, then, is a collection of books to be prayed and sung as much as to be read.

The liturgy, for its part, is permeated by the Bible. Psalms and canticles make up the bulk of daily prayer across the ecumenical spectrum. Readings from Scripture form part of every act of worship and are treated with reverence and attention in every tradition. Prayers of all genres are full of biblical allusion, sometimes with an additional layer provided by patristic commentary on Scripture. Paraphrases of Scripture are used as the central verbal focus in the action of baptism and Eucharist.

Such natural reciprocity is a check on any attempts to treat Scripture and liturgy as separate subjects, or as participants in a competition for dominance. It would be more accurate to say that the liturgy is the primary means by which the Bible lives in the life of the church. This book sets out to explore more of what this involves, and the contributors have brought a proper consciousness of tradition, developments in scholarship, practice, performance, and pastoral efficacy to their probing of some of the prominent areas of encounter.

When the Trustees of the Alcuin Club invited us to edit a collection of essays on the Bible and liturgy, we set out to determine how it might contribute to a field already populated by the work of distinguished scholars. Jean Daniélou had illuminated the role of biblical typology in the shaping and symbolism of liturgical rites in *The Bible and the Liturgy* (1956), and if this approach is less fashionable in contemporary scholarship, his work richly repays attention, not least as a form of hermeneutics which engages the liturgical imagination as well as the intellect.[1] In Geoffrey Wainwright's words, the book's exploration of the "continued presence of the Scriptures in the liturgy . . . allows the originating realities of salvation history to perpetuate themselves as permanent archetypes, rather than as mere prototypes on which later generations might be tempted to 'improve.'"[2] Victoria Raymer's study, *The Bible in Worship*, has done much to bring together disparate approaches to the proclamation of Scripture in the liturgical setting, the way it is encountered, and the kinds of responses it evokes. Her work is particularly valuable for its ecumenical approach, which provides comparative insights for anyone hoping to gain a perspective informed by the use of the Bible in different ecclesial traditions.[3] Gordon Lathrop's rich and fruitful discussion in *Saving Images* encouraged us in the conviction that the place where Scripture comes to life is the liturgical assembly. This has consequences for the formation of a canon, for the interpretation of Scripture, and for identifying records of liturgical practice within Scripture. It also requires attention to a subject that features prominently in Lathrop's scholarship—the liturgical *ordo*. Here the relationship in juxtaposition of word and meal becomes immensely significant. The book also gives welcome space to the role of the imagination in creative response to both verbal and visual images, a task which Lathrop believes to be all the more urgent "in a time of often murderous religious literalism."[4]

Underpinning all these works are questions about the way Scripture works on those who encounter it when they gather to worship.

[1] Jean Daniélou, SJ, *The Bible and the Liturgy* (Notre Dame, IN: Notre Dame University Press, 2014).

[2] See also Geoffrey Wainwright, "'Bible and Liturgy': Daniélou's Work Revisited," in *Worship with One Accord: Where Liturgy and Ecumenism Embrace* (Oxford: Oxford University Press, 1997), 35–44, 43.

[3] Victoria Raymer, *The Bible in Worship: Proclamation, Encounter and Response* (London: SCM Press, 2018).

[4] Gordon W. Lathrop, *Saving Images: The Presence of the Bible in Christian Liturgy* (Minneapolis: Fortress Press, 2017), 24.

To use a term which has come to be prominent in the liturgical lexicon, they are questions about the formation of worshippers. Two scholars addressed this topic from complementary perspectives in the journal *Studia Liturgica* in 1992. Paul Bradshaw considered the historical evidence for the use of the Bible in the liturgy, while Louis-Marie Chauvet asked what makes the liturgy biblical, with close attention to texts. It is Bradshaw's proposal of four principal functions of the Word in worship—the kerygmatic, the anamnetic, the paracletic, and the doxological—that has provided the thematic architecture of the first section of this collection of essays. Cally Hammond, Normand Bonneau, and John Baldovin ask how Scripture is presented to worshippers and how it is heard, especially by those with little experience of the life of the church. David Kennedy, Anne McGowan, and Thomas O'Loughlin reflect on Scripture's role in mediating the great narratives of incarnation and redemption at the high points of the Christian year, and supremely in the celebration of the Eucharist. Lizette Larson-Miller and Catherine Reid show how Scripture meets people in ritual transition, in discussions of funeral and marriage liturgy. Bridget Nichols considers the Bible as source of the language of much public prayer and praise, alongside its overt presence in the lectionary.

We realised, however, that we did not have categories to describe how the relationship between Scripture and liturgy is tested by new priorities, and the final four contributions begin to explore the territory defined by the shifting relationship between the conventional, if notional, centre of liturgical activity and its margins. Thus, Léon van Ommen attends to those who, on account of their personal circumstances, gender identity, sexual orientation, neurodiversity, or physical disability find themselves on the margins of the church and its worship. Christopher Irvine writes on the environment and the climate emergency, pointing both to emerging liturgical resources and forms of prayer already in the tradition of the churches. Ann Loades explores the meaningful inclusion and nurture of children in the whole ecology of Christian worship, with striking indications for the use of biblical narrative in this endeavour. Stephen Burns tackles the complex topic of gender, bringing together developments in society and sometimes parallel, sometimes convergent developments in ecclesial life. His essay might stand as a prolegomenon to any act of worship.

It falls finally to Gordon Jeanes to reflect on the large and multifaceted question of what it means to read the Bible through the liturgy. This, as he shows, is a task that can be well done or badly done, and the temptation to impose our own views and prejudices and in that way to foreclose interpretation is always present. While he performs the important task of drawing together the perspectives offered by other contributors, it is always with a sense of provisionality. As he points out, the ongoing encounter between Scripture, liturgy, and the Christian life is also a journey with no predeterminate path.

Paul Bradshaw writes that "liturgy is not only the place where the word of God is received, but also the locus of its transmission, where we must do justice to the Bible as an inheritance from the past and also engage with it as the creative force in our Christian life and worship today."[5] It is in this spirit that we offer the title, *Lively Oracles of God*. For as the New Testament writers who spoke of these *logia* (Acts 7:38, Rom 3:2, Heb 5:12, 1 Pet 4:11) and the generations of English translators who have found "oracles" to be the closest rendering have recognised, the words of God are living and active, and speak with new eloquence and urgency in every age and to every liturgical community which holds them in trust.

These essays have been written during the Covid-19 pandemic to which some of the authors refer. A trivial result of the appalling loss of life worldwide and the economic damage has been the closure of research libraries, which has hindered some contributors, but we are proud of the scholarship which is evident throughout this work.

We gratefully acknowledge the advice and guidance of Hans Christoffersen and Michelle Verkuilen of Liturgical Press, and the careful copyediting of Mary Carol Kendzia. The support and interest of the Alcuin Club Trustees have made this project possible.

Gordon Jeanes and Bridget Nichols

[5] Paul F. Bradshaw, "The Use of the Bible in Liturgy: Some Historical Perspectives," *Studia Liturgica* 22 (1992): 52.

Contributors

John F. Baldovin, SJ, is professor of historical and liturgical theology at the Boston College School of Theology and Ministry. His most recent publication is "Mass Intentions: The Historical Development of a Practice [Part One]" (*Theological Studies* 81 [December 2020]).

Normand Bonneau, OMI, is retired professor of New Testament studies, Saint Paul University, Ottawa, Canada, former dean of the faculty of theology and former editor of Theoforum, and author of *The Sunday Lectionary: Ritual Word, Paschal Shape* (Liturgical Press, 1998) and *Narrative Time in the New Testament* (Peeters 2020).

Stephen Burns is professor of liturgical and practical theology at Pilgrim Theological College in the University of Divinity, Melbourne, Australia. His recent publications include *Twentieth Century Anglican Theologians* (co-editor with Bryan Cones and James Tengatenga; Wiley 2021).

Cally Hammond is dean of Gonville and Caius College, Cambridge, where she teaches early Christian history, New Testament Greek, and classical Latin. Her publications include *Caesar: The Gallic War* (Oxford World's Classics, 1995); *Passionate Christianity: A Journey to the Cross* (SPCK, 2007); *Joyful Christianity: Finding Jesus in the World* (SPCK, 2009); *Glorious Christianity: Walking by Faith in the Life to Come* (SPCK, 2011); Augustine: *Confessions*, vol. 1, 1–8 (Loeb Classical Library; Harvard, 2014), vol. 2, 9–13 (2015); *The Sound of the Liturgy: How Words Work in Worship* (SPCK, 2015).

Christopher Irvine is chairman of the Alcuin Club. He is the author of *The Cross and Creation in Christian Liturgy and Art* (SPCK, 2013), and more recently has contributed to *Oneness: The Dynamics of Monasticism* (SCM Press, 2017), *Pilgrimage and England's Cathedrals* (Palgrave Macmillan, 2020), and the forthcoming *T&T Clark Handbook of the Doctrine of Creation* (Bloomsbury, 2021).

Gordon Jeanes has recently retired as a parish priest in London. Previously he taught liturgy in the Universities of Durham and Cardiff. He is the author of *The Day Has Come! Easter and Baptism in Zeno of Verona* (Liturgical Press, 1995) and *Signs of God's Promise: Thomas Cranmer's Sacramental Theology and the Book of Common Prayer* (T&T Clark, 2008).

David Kennedy is vicar of Corbridge in Northumberland. He was previously vice dean and canon precentor of Durham Cathedral. He served on the Liturgical Commission of the Church of England from 2001 to 2011. He teaches liturgical modules for the Department of Theology and Religion, Durham University, Cranmer Hall, Durham, and the Lindisfarne College of Theology.

Lizette Larson-Miller is the Huron Lawson Professor of Liturgy at Huron University College and canon precentor for the Anglican Diocese of Huron (Canada). She has published in the areas of sacramental theology and rites with the sick, dying, and dead, and has served as president of Societas Liturgica as well as chair of the International Anglican Liturgical Consultation.

Ann Loades, CBE, is professor emerita of Divinity University of Durham and honorary professor in the School of Divinity, University of St Andrews. She is currently preparing a book of essays, including some previously unpublished (selected and edited by Stephen Burns). Her most recent publication is *Grace Is Not Faceless: Reflections on Mary*, edited by Stephen Burns (Darton, Longman and Todd, 2021).

Anne McGowan is assistant professor of liturgy at Catholic Theological Union in Chicago. A graduate of the University of Notre Dame, she is the author of *Eucharistic Epicleses, Ancient and Modern* (2014) and co-author (with Paul F. Bradshaw) of *The Pilgrimage of Egeria* (2018), both published by Liturgical Press.

Bridget Nichols lectures in liturgy and Anglicanism at the Church of Ireland Theological Institute in Dublin. She is the author of *Liturgical Hermeneutics* (Peter Lang GmbH, 1996) and editor of *The Collect in the Churches of the Reformation* (SCM Press, 2010). She is a past president of Societas Liturgica.

Thomas O'Loughlin is professor emeritus of historical theology in the University of Nottingham. He is currently writing a book of discipleship and liturgy in early Christianity. His most recent publication is *Eating Together, Becoming One*, published in 2019 by Liturgical Press.

Catherine Reid is Anglican chaplain to the University of York, UK. She also teaches liturgy and other subjects at the York School of Ministry. Prior to her current post, she was vicar of the Ampleforth Benefice and Initial Ministerial Education (part 2) and training adviser for Cleveland Archdeaconry in the Diocese of York.

Armand Léon van Ommen is lecturer in practical theology and codirector of the Centre for the Study of Autism and Christian Community at the University of Aberdeen. He is the author of *Suffering in Worship: Anglican Liturgy in Relation to Stories of Suffering People* (Routledge, 2017).

Chapter 1

"Today This Scripture Has Been Fulfilled in Your Hearing"

Cally Hammond

The most habitual aspects of liturgical performance often deserve the closest attention yet receive comparatively little.[1] The performance of Scripture in public worship is a case in point. A reading from the Bible is mandatory at almost every service from Morning Prayer to Holy Matrimony; and from confirmation to Holy Communion.[2]

Luke 4:16-21 stands at one end of the third canonical Gospel, marking the beginning of Jesus' ministry; while Luke 24:13-35 stands at the opposite end, as an icon of the early days of The Way (Acts 19:9, 23, etc.) in the aftermath of the ascension. But they both show the man Jesus—before *and after* his resurrection—reading a recognised form of Scripture and then explaining it to his hearers. These two narratives capture in microcosm the approach used in modern reading and interpretation of Scripture in collective worship. They shift between the written word and the proclaimed w/Word; and in both cases their ultimate target is the living Word—through the breaking of bread through which Christ is made known.

[1] The language of "performance" carries no taint of insincerity.

[2] There is no Scripture reading in the Churching of Women or the Commination (both *BCP* 1662); but there is a magnificent ministerial address in the latter, woven out of scriptural strands—and plenty of psalmody in both.

From within the faith, it can be difficult to recognise those aspects of the performance of holy Scripture within worship which carry encoded, value-added, meaning for what they really are. They are so regular a part of divine service as to feel "natural" or seem to be "common-sense," or "mere (*sic*) habit." In collective worship, we learn how to move and behave by watching and imitating others. At the same time we are also absorbing attitudes of thought, in particular, as to what Scripture is: why it matters; how it works; and what to do with it. At one end of the wide spectrum of usages is Scripture as a teaching tool—a rule book of propositions about the nature of God-humankind relations, requiring study, consent, and obedience. This can be reinforced through repetition—of the Decalogue, or the Lord's summary of the Law, for example. In that case the text shifts from the category of the written word or proclaimed (preached) word, becoming in effect an additional text for the ordinary.

At the other end is Scripture as a sacred object transmitting holiness through four of the five senses—predominantly sight, hearing, and touch, but sometimes also smell (through the use of incense). This can be reinforced by the placing and reverent treatment of, say, a large Bible on the lectern; or the rituals accompanying use of a book of the Gospels. No Christian is ever left in doubt that the use of Scripture within worship is high-profile, or that it deserves reverence and makes demands of worshippers. But the "why" and "how" of those convictions produce a wide range of responses.

Jesus is recorded in all four gospels as having made use of what were for him holy writings, both in public worship and in private prayer. This fact gives us an indicator, if not that later Christian worship was in conscious imitation of his example, then at least that it looked to that example for endorsement of its methods. Luke 4 shows the man Jesus first proclaiming and then interpreting Scripture in worship. Luke 24:35, with its unmistakeable eucharistic overtones, shows how a Liturgy of the Word (including exposition of chosen scriptural passages) might give way to a liturgical action of a clearly sacramental kind. Teaching gives way to explanation and then to understanding and experience, as a value-added action[3] emerges from that understood teaching.

[3] An action which transmits or *realises* an encoded meaning—a sacrament, in other words.

This process begins and ends with human beings. The catalysts are words and (in the case of the Emmaus story) bread. To call Scripture in worship a "catalyst" is, from one theological viewpoint, entirely proper: the words of the text have no power or value in themselves; they are vessels or carriers or stimuli of divine truth, as Mary was (in one interpretation) a vessel for the incarnate Son.

At the opposite extreme are those Christians of the early centuries, for whom the Scripture was powerful in itself, rather than only as a container for factual and propositional truths. This was a consequence of the belief that "holiness," like, say, radioactivity, was a real power transmissible through touch or other physical contact. It might not be visible, but it was *real*. The proof of that reality was in its effects. Jesus transmitted holiness to his mother from the moment of his incarnation within her (thus setting in train—from a very early period—the development of supreme veneration for her, culminating in the title *Theotokos*, Mother of God). In a similar way, the semantic content (meaning/message) of the words of Scripture transmitted the holiness of its subject matter to the physical objects and materials which recorded it. In Judaism this is evident from the belief that Scripture is defined as that which "defiles the hands."[4] One reason why some books of the Hebrew Bible/Christian Old Testament caused arguments about inclusion when the canon was emerging is that their holiness was in question. This was not on account of their message or morality, but because the ultimate holy thing (the divine name YHWH) was not contained within the text. This understanding of holiness is tied more to a written than an oral form of the individual elements of "the books" (the Bible), though some of them may have been transmitted through memory and recitation before they were written down. It is difficult to imagine how this understanding of holiness could apply to words about God before the emergence of the book (scroll or codex) as a physical object.

The highest form of this regard held that every letter of every word of Scripture was holy, sacred (among Jewish as well as Christian

[4] Holding with the hands a scroll for reading aloud is envisaged. This understanding of what is holy ("consecrated/set apart for God") treats that quality of holiness as transmissible; overtly, in Christianity, for sacraments, but covertly in the case of the printed word of Scripture. See Cally Hammond, *The Sound of the Liturgy* (London: SPCK, 2015), 139–41.

commentators). It entailed that those who regarded the contents of "the books" (the Bible) as holy are disposed to transfer that holiness from the semantic content of the words (their meaning, instructions, ideas, teaching) to the actual ink, paper, vellum, or boards by means of which they are transmitted. This renders "the books" a holy object in itself—without reference to how its contents are used, or how they affect the lives and behaviours of hearers and readers.

The concept of words as "vessels" is a metaphor to illustrate how vibrations in air and marks in ink on a page can "contain" meaning (information, truth, wisdom, etc.). That underlying concept is so ubiquitous as to be virtually invisible; and the search for clarity about how to use Scripture in worship is not helped by the risk that, in public prayer and private, the categories of written (Scripture), spoken (kerygma) and living (Jesus Christ the incarnate Son) w/Word will bleed into one another, so that what is predicated of (for example) the living Word (e.g., "No one comes to the Father except through me," John 14:6) can by analogy be predicated of the written and spoken word also.[5]

From early times, the church recognised a distinct "minor order" known as "readers."[6] They were tasked with the public reading of Scripture (except the gospel, reserved to the "holy orders," namely the deacon, if present, and otherwise the priest). The role of reader was assigned to those who had the prized specialist skill of literacy, in a world in which relatively few people could read. Where oral communication was still the basis of most social interaction, people did not learn to read unless they needed to. It cost money to learn, and books cost money to buy. By the time Christianity emerged as a distinct form, the category of "holy writings" was already long understood within its matrix, Judaism. So was the practice of reading (i.e., performing) portions from them at various moments in the religious year, at sabbaths and festivals. Greek and Roman culture had no equivalent of this revering and proclaiming of sacred texts in a public space, with all the reinforcement of a shared identity and values that it imprinted on those who came to hear.

[5] Another example of this blurring of categories: in prayer, especially informal prayer, the word "Lord" is used interchangeably of both God (the Father) and Jesus (the Son).

[6] The first reference to reading of Scripture in a church gathering dates to the mid-second century (Justin, *Apology* 1.67.3–4).

People in holy orders were, and are, expected to be able to read as an indispensable part of their job. It is important to understand that early Christianity was no level intellectual playing field where everyone's interpretations were equally valid. The job of the clergy was to draw on their scriptural learning to proclaim the one true meaning of the gospel to their people; and to exclude "what is falsely called knowledge" (1 Tim 6:20). There survive from this period only a few traces of the idea that different interpretations may be allowed to co-exist. Those who inhabited the role of clergy, and expressed that learning, would be admired and revered for imparting it: both positive ("put on the Lord Jesus Christ") and negative ("make no provision for the flesh," Rom 13:14). The expounding of a passage from Scripture as part of Sunday worship was back then, as it still is today, potentially a small step to tedium for both parties. But to explain Scripture well, each party expecting the best efforts of the other in seeking truth and learning God's will? That was, and remains, a noble endeavour. And just as in the case of human rights, so too when it came to the teaching of a moral life, giving people credit for their desire to live well, and calling them to strive for goodness, *whatever their status*, were distinctive marks of Christianity. They counted as a "unique selling point" for the new Way, in a world in which learning and "the good life" had previously been the preserve of the few, the wealthy, the fortunate. A similar excitement at the prospect of being allowed to engage their brain, credited with having the intelligence to form their own views, and invited to apply ancient stories to modern situations (a particular subtype of intertextuality), has given the reform movements of the sixteenth century and later much of their appeal. In the years after the English Reformation, endowing sermons became a popular way to encourage Christians to learn more and go deeper. This was one response to a demand for the proclamation of the word, followed by exposition, as a form of real education and challenge at different levels of status in society.

It has always been the practice of the Church of England to present copies of the New Testament to deacons, and Bibles to priests, at their ordination. This partly represents the freedom to access and interpret Scripture, which characterised reformed churches from the sixteenth century on; but it is also a visible sign-action that interpretation of Scripture is a core part of those vocations.

The layout and punctuation of *Book of Common Prayer* 1662 make it clear that literacy was not expected of anyone other than the clergy at the Holy Communion; but the manner of public reading was important enough to require its own rubric: for the morning and evening offices the ability to read "*distinctly with an audible voice*" was prescribed, together with a note on appropriate posture for the reading: "*He that readeth so standing and turning himself, as he may best be heard of all such as are present*."

Some years ago, I wrote a book about how words work in worship in which I highlighted four matters in performed liturgy (posture, repetition, rhythm, and punctuation), which seemed to me to receive relatively scant attention.[7] There are, not surprisingly, points of overlap between my focus on the liturgy there, and the subject matter of this chapter. Posture—the bodily stances, movements, and gestures adopted by reader and hearers during the reading of Scripture; and punctuation—in this case the metaphorical punctuation that is the arrangement of the elements (*taxis*) of a service—are of particular importance to the argument here.

Any shift in posture, any bodily movement, can carry a weight of encoded meaning within a liturgy. Some of these postures and movements can be prescribed: standing, sitting, kneeling. Others are absorbed through repetition and imitation: crossing oneself, raising hands in praise, bowing the head or body, etc. Not that the distinction is absolute—a posture or gesture may be carried out not because it features in a rubric but because other people are doing it. This could include: standing when an officiating minister enters, bowing the head at the words "let us pray," responding to one person's spoken "Amen" with an answering "Amen," and the like. So the question here must be: what do worshippers do with their bodies during the public reading of Scripture? And how is the reading of Scripture arranged and practised within the structures of individual liturgies?

If we take the standard pattern of a *Common Worship* 2000 (*CW*) service of Holy Communion Order One, there is almost nothing in the performance directions known as rubrics to guide us as to how the reading of Scripture is to be effected. Unlike in *BCP* 1662, no direction is given within the printed liturgy as to the voice and posture of the reader or to the posture of worshippers. The only stipulation is that either one or two readings from elsewhere in Scripture should

[7] Hammond, *Sound of the Liturgy*.

be followed by the reading of a passage from one of the four gospels. This is supplemented in Note 12 by a longer instruction about the correct order of readings, and about maintaining a good balance between the Old and New Testament for the first reading if only one is used in addition to the gospel. Note 1 gives a direction that posture should follow local custom but does make reference to the practice of standing for the gospel as mandatory.[8]

The arrangement of the readings from Scripture, as well as the performance directions, are examples of an ancient, still enduring, tradition of intertextuality. In other words, the different lections are designed and expected to be in dialogue with each other. For example, the psalm (Note 12 again) speaks to the Old Testament reading and must be kept together with it. Both Old and New Testament readings are expected to speak to the gospel. Sometimes this speaking is associative, like Year B, Proper 13, which links Exodus 16 (manna in the wilderness) with John 6 (Jesus the bread from heaven). Occasionally there is a hint of supersession or contradiction between Old Testament and New Testament/gospel, as in the pairing of Numbers 15:32-36 with John 8:2-11 for the seventh Sunday before Easter in the *Alternative Service Book* 1980 (*ASB*).[9] When the lectionary follows a book or books over several weeks, as is usual in Ordinary Time, the intertextuality depends more on the ingenuity of the preacher, and less on that commonality of subject matter that leads, for example, to the letters to Titus and Hebrews always being read with the gospels of Luke and John at Christmas. The old monthly pattern of psalms in *BCP* 1662 eschewed overt thematic selections entirely, and thus has been felt to fall short in expressing a seasonal element. But there may be a value in letting psalms speak outside their traditional interpretative framework—freeing, for example, Psalm 8 from restriction to the messianic, and Psalms 22 and 69 from confinement to the passion of Christ.

As I mentioned earlier, where the Eucharist is concerned, posture has an aspect that is not shared by any other liturgical performance of Scripture: the congregation stands for the reading of the gospel.

[8] Archbishops' Council of the Church of England, *Common Worship* (London: Church House Publishing, 2000), 332.

[9] General Synod of the Church of England, *The Alternative Service Book 1980* (London: Clowes, 1980).

This is enshrined in *BCP* 1662: "Then shall [the Priest] read the Gospel (the people all standing up)." The people begin the service on their knees and stay there to the end of the collect, at which point, it is usually assumed (it is not stated), they are to sit for the "epistle" (shorthand for "the rest of the New Testament") and then change to a standing position for the gospel. The contrast could not be more marked. Elsewhere I have discussed in some detail the meaning in worship of standing up or being in a standing position.[10] For now it is enough to understand that it is a marker of relative value and honour. The meaning of standing up when a person enters a room may not be openly acknowledged as anything more than unreflective "courtesy," while remaining seated when someone enters is equally likely to appear "rude." But the underlying message is that personal comfort and ease must give way in the presence of something greater than oneself. It is a form of the principle underlying postures in worship more generally; our mental and spiritual exertions, to be fully realised, need to be matched by physical ones. We should not offer to God that which costs us nothing—because "in him we live and move and have our being" (Acts 17:28).

This practice puts emphasis upon honouring the subject of the text (the life of the incarnate person of Jesus), rather than specifically its message (the meaning of that incarnate being's life, which is occasionally reflected in asides from the evangelist such as John 21:25, or Luke 1:1-4; and treated at length in the rest of the New Testament). In fact, the picture is more complicated than this, which is what makes the act of standing for the gospel at the Eucharist so critical. It is not the content, or the message, of the gospel that demands this posture of reverence; rather, it is the content and message *within the context of a sacramental, eucharistic meal*. Thus, if the second (New Testament) reading at Evening Prayer happens to come from one of the gospels, it is heard sitting, not standing. This cannot be because of its content or its message; only the performance-context is different, and it is that which necessitates the change of posture. The stipulated posture of standing acknowledges, in other words, that the worshippers recognise one greater than themselves as being *present in their midst* through the action (hearing a gospel being read is never passive) of

[10] Hammond, *Sound of the Liturgy*, 34–35.

listening to the words of the Christ being spoken aloud, and immediately reflected on (sermon), providing a springboard for declaring faith (creed), prompting and directing prayer for others (intercessions), and culminating in the eucharistic meal in which the worshippers are made one with Christ (communion). At Evening Prayer what usually follows a gospel lection is a canticle, in *BCP* usually the *Nunc Dimittis* and in *CW* the *Magnificat*. Worshippers usually stand for the canticle instead—the contrast here is marked.

In church, it is generally the case that "the last will be first" (Matt 20:16): in a procession the most honoured/high status person goes at the end, not at the beginning. Does this reveal an attempt through liturgy to reorder human priorities in accordance with Scripture through an ascent from the Old Testament through to New Testament to gospel? Hardly. What it definitely does reveal is that the punctuation of a liturgy (its ordering, divisions, and units) has been shaped by unwritten rules and subconscious intuitions, probably based on repeated experience of performance, and through trial and error, in many times and places. The liturgy has a shape, an arc, a trajectory, in the same way that a piece of music or a theatrical entertainment (from stand-up to Shakespeare) does. Writing this during the "lockdown" due to Covid, I have followed daily workout routines, which always start with a warm-up and end with a cool-down. In theory this is about physical preparation for physical action—the literal warming and cooling of the body. In practice it is also a matter of preparing mentally, emotionally, even spiritually, for the oncoming time of exertion, of "getting in the zone" beforehand; and of "coming down" from the high afterwards.

What has this to teach us about the way Scripture works within a liturgy? We must first acknowledge degrees of scriptural presence within any Christian liturgy: from the opening hymn to the final responses or dismissal, the words spoken are saturated with Scripture. In that way, Scripture is omnipresent. What is under discussion here, though, is the set performance of the written word in continuous form (passages, not sentences).[11] Not individual fragments quoted

[11] The encounter with sizeable passages of Scripture is another gift of the Reformation, which in England and elsewhere sought to end the practice of cherry-picking and fragmenting texts in performance in favour of encountering the key words and sentences embedded in their original narrative contexts.

or adapted, but large portions, consisting in some cases of many verses. This performed Scripture, most obviously, comes neither first nor last. This indicates that it has the status of a key element of the action. It needs a "warm-up" period beforehand and a "cooling down" period afterwards. In a service of the word, there is a rite of preparation, including praise and penitence, and there needs to be a postlude of intercession and praise. In the eucharistic liturgies, old and new, there is a point of division (implied or stated[12]) between the Liturgy of the Word and the Liturgy of the Sacrament. And the Liturgy of the Word goes first. In terms of structure, it is placed so as to act as the groundwork for the Liturgy of the Sacrament. Such liturgies are a one-way system: there is no going from the Liturgy of the Sacrament to that of the Word. One may attempt to revise a liturgy so as to change how an element of that liturgy is received;[13] but the performed reading of Scripture is the foundation on which all the rest is built. It is not a lower-status segment but a *sine qua non* for worship of almost every kind.

This may be the principle underlying the usual placing of scriptural reading in worship. But it is easy to see how the Liturgy of the Sacrament might appear to have higher status in both ancient and modern worship. In early Christianity, it was usual for unbaptized worshippers to attend for the Liturgy of the Word, but leave for that of the Sacrament. There was an element of mission in this—hearing and learning Scripture was an attraction, a "draw." The Liturgy of the Sacrament would make no sense until a degree of knowledge of the story of Christianity had been absorbed. But it was also the case that Christians followed the customs, or perhaps shared the outlook, the milieu, of their "pagan" neighbours, whose mystery-cults were closed to the uninitiated. Such mystery-cults had (as far as we can tell, they being so secret and their practices left unwritten) no equivalent of a Liturgy of the Word functioning as a teaching opportunity, or as an historical/anamnetic, kerygmatic, informative, identifying, expressive, or performative opportunity.[14] In practice this seems to

[12] *BCP* 1662: the "Antecommunion" ending with the prayer for the church when there is no communion; *CW* 2000.

[13] Such as moving the *Gloria* of the *Sarum Ordinary* to a place of post-communion praise as *BCP* 1662 does.

[14] Hammond, *Sound of the Liturgy*, 7.

suggest gradations of value, with the "word" being lower grade because of its being open to all; and the "sacrament" being higher grade because of its being restricted. This was the pattern of Augustine's experience of another religious movement, when he was a Manichean "hearer;" this gave him an identity as belonging within the group, but not at the supreme level of the "elect."

The situation becomes more complex, however, when we consider an alternative praxis. In many free churches, the main act of worship each Sunday is always what is now called "a service of the word." The pattern identified as "the Liturgy of the Sacrament" is still practised, and, in the same way as in the early church, by a smaller subgroup of baptized initiates. But the focus, the emphasis, is entirely different. The service of the word is entire in itself, following a fixed Sunday structure. The remembrance of the Lord's Supper ("meeting round the Lord's table") is an optional add-on at the end of the main service, perhaps once a month.

This is a complicated way of saying that the way a service is normally structured sends signals and creates expectations in worshippers. Variations from the regular structure and its dimensions (the extra 15 minutes for a "meeting round the Lord's table;" the truncated liturgy that is a service of *BCP* 1662 ante-communion) shape the participants' perceptions about what matters most and is of highest value.

How do we learn the value of Scripture within liturgy from the encoded/value-added behaviours that accompany it? Posture is one element. There is not only the usual practice in Catholic churches of standing for the (holy) gospel: other actions are also incorporated, such as the processional carrying of a gospel book; censing; raising; turning to face it[15]; kissing it. The sermon that follows is normally expected to include reflection on the gospel, as well as the reading(s) that precede(s) it. That structure sends a message that a sermon proceeds from the Scriptures, that the written word is a natural and necessary precursor to the word proclaimed in a homily. In many free church services, the sermon takes all the spiritual weight of the service. Size may not be everything, but it does matter. This is pointed out by a character in Dorothy L. Sayer's novel, *Busman's Honeymoon*,

[15] Hammond, *Sound of the Liturgy*, 141, on the general treatment of sacred things.

who is employed as cleaner by the murder victim. Her remarks reflect a sense of the glaring inadequacies of the Church of England:

> "Me?" said Mrs. Ruddle, quite affronted. "I'm chapel. They're out and gone by the time we finish. Not but what I *'ave* been to church now and again, but there ain't nothing to show for it. Up and down, up and down, as if one's knees wasn't wore out with scrubbing on week-days, and a pore little bit of a sermon with no 'eart in it."[16]

Worshippers bring their own Bibles, in which to follow the reading. The preacher makes frequent reference to the text, encouraging them to consult their version. Steeping the congregation in the content of Scripture and its interpretation thus becomes the heart of the worship. There may be a fixed pattern of readings for a set period, but there is no equivalent of the formal requirement of an Old Testament → New Testament pattern, or an Old Testament → New Testament → gospel one.[17]

The effect of this difference in performance is not unlike that effected by comparing the Christian arrangement of the Old Testament with the Jewish arrangement of the Hebrew Bible (*Tanak*). The latter is thematic, arranged in order of diminishing importance—from Law to Prophets to Writings. What is most important comes first, because of what it contains. The former is historical; it also begins with the Law, but with a view to starting at the beginning of the story of God-humankind relations, moving through the story of the patriarchs, the exodus and the Promised Land, the monarchy and splitting of the kingdom, and exile from Jerusalem, and ends with the hope of return for God's people. The Christian Old Testament ends with prophecy of the Messiah, the Christ. One turn of a page is all that is needed for the Old Testament to give way to the New, as the genealogy and nativity of Jesus Christ unfold. So the movement from Old to New Testament lessons in the daily Office is broadly historical, because for Christians time is linear, historical; it is going in a direction.

In the Eucharist, by contrast, like the *Tanak*, the reading of the New Testament relative to the Old moves forwards in historical sequence.

[16] Dorothy L. Sayers, *Busman's Honeymoon* (first published by Gollancz in 1937), chap. 9.

[17] Imposed by a centralised church, and underpinned by canon law.

The New Testament part of the Bible-as-book (one-volume codex, not "the books") follows the historical/linear-time arrangement of the Christian Old Testament; and it sets the Gospels first within that corpus of documents, when we consider the arrangement of the individual texts between the covers of the Bible-as-physical-object. But the New Testament → gospel part of the sequence of lections within a liturgical performance goes backwards in time from the epistles. Those epistles are written in response to events centred on Jesus and his life/death/resurrection but focus on the consequences of that narrative of a life for groups of followers of the Way in later years. Modern historical-critical method, with its emphasis on date and milieu of composition of all the Bible documents, complicates the picture still further—as the Gospel of Mark, for example, is generally agreed to have been written before Matthew's, but stands after it in the canonical Christian order; or the letters of Paul to the Corinthians, which describe circumstances later than the life of Jesus but were composed before the gospels, which are the only continuous records of that life. The upshot of all this is that the Old Testament → New Testament → gospel structure of the eucharistic readings is clearly governed by a theological principle (Christ is "all in all," Eph 1:23) not a historical one. Worshippers are being shown a theological truth through a liturgical structure, even if they are entirely unaware of the message being inculcated.

We can conclude, then, that following the principle that what is most important comes last (in the procession, the bishop; in the readings, the gospel; in the Eucharist, the communion), the gospel is the most valuable, perhaps the most holy, part of Scripture. Richard Hooker draws attention to the meaning of this sequence when he remarks: "In ancient times there was publicly read first the Scripture, as namely, something out of the books of the Prophets of God which were of old; something out of the Apostles' writings; and lastly out of the holy Evangelists, some things which touched the person of our Lord Jesus Christ himself."[18] Touching the person of our Lord Jesus Christ himself—even metaphorically so—was an act requiring supreme reverence, more than was required for reading even the most exalted writings about the wider aspects of faith in him (the rest of

[18] Richard Hooker, *Of the Laws of Ecclesiastical Polity* V.20.6. in John Keble, ed., *Works of Mr Richard Hooker*, vol. 3 (Oxford: Oxford University Press, 1836), 95.

the New Testament), or the divine foreshadowings of him (Old Testament).

This content-based hierarchy is at odds with the date-based hierarchy of the daily offices. In these, the Old Testament always precedes the New. The historical exposition of the faith in Scripture is preferred over a hierarchy of holiness like the Old/New Testament/gospel structure of the modern Eucharist. The two become mixed, or muddled, in the newer eucharistic rites in which the performance of Scripture moves from Old to New Testament (historical) then from epistle to gospel, even though the latter is earlier, viewed historically.

During the Covid-19 pandemic, instructions have been issued in the Church of England and other churches that service books should not be used; and that leaflets printed for each act of worship must be provided, and taken away by worshippers afterwards. This is hastening a process already begun, of moving away from books in worship: from the enduring to the disposable. Whether this will lead to a decline in valuing the holiness of Scripture in worship, or a renewal and deepening of the belief that Christ will "mak[e] all things new" (Rev 21:5) remains to be seen.

Chapter 2

"How Are They to Hear Without Someone to Proclaim Him?"

John Baldovin, SJ

The story is told of someone walking into a jeweller's shop in the United Kingdom and asking for a cross. "Sure," says the salesperson. "Would you like a plain one or one with a little doll on it?" Even allowing for the salesperson's not coming from a Christian background, the tale (perhaps apocryphal) is emblematic of the religious illiteracy of a good many people in our contemporary societies. And Timothy Larsen tells the story of British university students who, after a tour of the Uffizi Gallery in Florence, "decided that Italian parents did not value daughters because although they were fond of depicting mothers, the baby was always a boy."[1] Of course, they were talking about Jesus! I could go on giving examples, but I think it is fairly obvious that most people in advanced industrial societies are biblically illiterate. As Stephen Prothero put it rather strongly with regard to the United States: "We live in a Land of Biblical Idiots".[2] Such illiteracy represents a considerable challenge not only for religion in general but particularly for participation in liturgy, a participation

[1] Timothy Larsen, "Literacy and Biblical Knowledge: The Victorian Age and Our Own," *Journal of the Evangelical Theological Society* 52 (2009): 528.

[2] Stephen Prothero, "We Live in a Land of Biblical Idiots," *Los Angeles Times*, March 24, 2007, cited in Larsen, "Literacy," 529.

which presupposes at least some familiarity with the Christian Bible (Old and New Testaments).

In a 2012 article entitled "Is the Liturgy Hitting its Target?"[3] I suggested that one of the ways that the liturgical reforms of the past half century have not been successful (especially but perhaps not solely in the Roman Catholic Church) has been in the area of biblical appreciation. After all, one of the objectives of the Second Vatican Council's Constitution on the Sacred Liturgy (*Sacrosanctum Concilium*) was to provide worshippers with a "richer fare" of biblical readings (51).[4] As we shall see when dealing with the lectionary, that aim has certainly been addressed. To what extent the current lectionaries, which owe a great deal to the Catholic reform, have succeeded is another matter. I am suggesting that even attempts like the laudable efforts to provide richer fare will fail if the Bible is proclaimed in a vacuum.

It is important, however, to avoid an idealised version of the past in which everyone shared a basic religious/biblical literacy. Historians like Jean Delumeau have argued that prior to the sixteenth century most of Europe was barely evangelized.[5] After all, one of the tasks of the Reformations (Protestant and Catholic) of the sixteenth century was to address this situation. But for those areas which had been evangelized, probably cities and towns, we can presuppose the existence of at least some biblical literacy, whether it came from visual sources like stained glass windows or the interior and exterior statues and sculptures of church buildings or from occasional preaching and catechesis.

But as I pointed out above, the problem is rather clear—today by and large we cannot expect people to bring any knowledge of the Bible to their liturgical experience. This difficulty is compounded by the fact that the liturgy itself—and especially the way most mainline churches construct the lectionary and liturgical cycle—does seem to presuppose at least some familiarity with the Christian message. The estimable liturgical scholar Robert Taft frequently contended that

[3] John Baldovin, "Is the Liturgy Hitting its Target?," *The Jurist* 72 (2012): 453–65.

[4] Quotations of Vatican II documents are from Austin Flannery, ed., *Vatican Council II: Constitutions, Decrees, Declarations; The Basic Sixteen Documents* (Collegeville, MN: Liturgical Press, 2014).

[5] Jean Delumeau, *Catholicism between Luther and Voltaire: A New View of the Counter-Reformation* (Philadelphia: Westminster Press, 1977), 225–31.

anamnesis and not kerygma is essential to the way we celebrate liturgy:

> *Kerygma* is preaching the Good News to awaken the response of faith in the new message not yet heard. But the *kerygma* written down and proclaimed repeatedly in the liturgical assembly to recall us to our commitment to the Good News already heard and accepted in faith, even though "we know them and are established in the truth" (2 Pet 1:12), is memorial, *anamnesis*, and that is what all liturgy is about.[6]

Taft is right in claiming that traditional liturgy is based on anamnesis rather than initial proclamation of the gospel (kerygma). That, however, must be regarded as a rather purist or idealised position, for the question today is whether such understanding and practice of liturgy are really effective. I fear that in our dominant secularised culture the practice of liturgy needs to be at least as kerygmatic as it is anamnetic.

Paul Bradshaw makes a credible case for the multiple ways in which the Bible has functioned in the liturgy. He gives examples of the pedagogical or didactic function of the liturgy from the Jewish practice of proclaiming the Torah to Justin Martyr in the second century to the Lutheran, Reformed, and Anglican reform movements of the sixteenth century.[7] His approach is more flexible than Taft's in that he acknowledges that the boundaries between the didactic (kerygmatic) and anamnetic use of the Bible in liturgy are somewhat fluid. He is worth quoting at some length here:

> The boundaries between the first two types of ministry of the word are inevitably somewhat blurred. An anamnetic ministry of the word will exercise a didactic function for those who are unfamiliar with the tradition, and readings which were first intended to be didactic can in the course of time become anamnetic, as they grow in familiarity to the hearers and become associated with particular

[6] Robert Taft, "What Is a Christian Feast? A Reflection," *Worship* 83 (2009): 13.

[7] Paul F. Bradshaw, "The Use of the Bible in Liturgy: Some Historical Perspectives," *Studia Liturgica* 22 (1992): 32–38. I should acknowledge that Bradshaw and I are using the word "kerygmatic" somewhat differently here since he, following Rolf Zerfass, links kerygmatic and anamnetic under the same category.

> occasions. It may be argued that this is in large part what happened to the Sunday eucharistic lectionary in both East and West.[8]

Let us take a classic example: the nativity story from Luke 2 on Christmas. In line with the medieval Roman liturgy, the Roman Catholic missal and several other churches as well provide for three Masses and three sets of lectionary readings for Christmas—during the night, at dawn, and during the day. The gospel readings are respectively: Luke 2:1-14 (night), Luke 2:15-20 (dawn), and John 1:1-18 (day). I submit that in the vast majority of congregations it would be foolish to use anything other than the traditional "Christmas story" as the gospel reading for the day. No matter how theologically rich and appropriate the prologue to John's gospel may be (and it is very much so) there are occasions on which the expectation of a particular reading should take precedence because of people's familiarity. Christmas is clearly one of them. The kerygmatic and anamnetic functions of reading Scripture in church clearly combine in this case. I am not sure that Bradshaw is correct when he goes on to argue that we need to distinguish between occasions on which the use of the Bible is aimed primarily at education or primarily at connection with the rest of the rite and the feast. Sometimes they coincide.

All of the above raises some further questions which I hope to address, even if somewhat tentatively, here, namely:

1. What may be needed to help prepare people to hear the Bible in church?
2. How can the word be proclaimed more effectively in the context of the liturgy itself?
3. Is the Roman Lectionary of Mass or the Revised Common Lectionary adequate for kerygmatic proclamation today?
4. How can liturgical preaching, by nature somewhat kerygmatic, contribute to people's understanding of the Bible?

But before we turn to the lectionary and preaching we need to consider the profoundly biblical nature of the traditional liturgy itself. The eucharistic liturgy contains a great deal of biblical material. As Louis-Marie Chauvet has put it: "the Bible is in the liturgy as a fish

[8] Bradshaw, "Use of the Bible," 41.

in water."[9] Especially in its Catholic and Eastern Christian forms this includes not only the readings, including the responsorial psalm, the entrance and communion chants, the Holy, Holy, Holy acclamation, (a paraphrase of) the eucharistic institution narrative, and the Lord's Prayer. But there are two other factors that need to be recognised. First, the Bible itself has its native home in the Christian assembly, the liturgy; and second, the liturgy recapitulates the formation of the Bible.

Chauvet has ably argued for the first point. The books of the Bible were formed into a canon by being accepted in the assembly of the church.[10] This is an important fact to acknowledge, not only historically but also theologically. Christians have traditionally read the Hebrew Bible precisely as the Old (or First) Testament. That is, in addition to the literal or historical-critical study of the Bible, which is widely if not universally appreciated today, the church has interpreted the Old Testament as a Christian book. This is not to deny a legitimate Jewish reading of the Hebrew Bible, but it is to insist that Christians too have a claim on it, and this claim can be demonstrated by the fact that it has always been read in the assembly as can be demonstrated, for example, by the reference to Scripture in 2 Timothy 3:16 ("all Scripture [i.e., the Old Testament] is inspired by God and is useful") and the second-century description of the Sunday practice of reading the writings of the prophets along with the memoirs of the apostles (Justin Martyr, *I Apology* 67). As Chauvet says: "The Christian Bible is nothing else than a rereading of the Hebrew Bible in light of the death and resurrection of Jesus Christ."[11]

1. What May Be Needed to Help Prepare People to Hear the Bible in Church?

As I noted at the beginning of this chapter most contemporary societies suffer from massive biblical illiteracy. This biblical illiteracy is part and parcel of a more widespread cultural illiteracy, as any

[9] Louis-Marie Chauvet, "What Makes the Liturgy Biblical—Texts," *Studia Liturgica* 22 (1992): 127.

[10] Louis-Marie Chauvet, *Symbol and Sacrament: A Sacramental Reinterpretation of Christian Existence*, trans. Patrick Madigan and Madeleine Beaumont (Collegeville, MN: Liturgical Press, 1995), 190–212.

[11] Chauvet, *Symbol and Sacrament*, 195.

number of contemporary social commentators have lamented.[12] One anecdotal example: I can recall a comment in a graduate-level course evaluation over twenty years ago to the effect that I had used the phrase "between Scylla and Charybdis" in a lecture as though everyone understood it. It was a wake-up call. The common cultural heritage that I simply assumed because of my own classical education was no longer relevant to my students. I could have been speaking a foreign language. I'm not trying to argue here that everyone should read Homer nor am I arguing for a mainly Euro-centric education. I do want to point out, however, that it is no longer possible to assume a basic and common cultural background either in education or *a fortiori* in church. To enable the Bible to be heard, a massive amount of catechesis/proclamation needs to take place.

Traditional means do not seem to be sufficient in order to do this. Modern social media and marketing techniques need to become commonplace among those wishing to evangelize. Of course, evangelicals have known this and practised very public proclamation of the gospel through radio and television for a long time. Luckily, others seem to be catching on. To single out American Roman Catholics, popular figures like Bishop Robert Barron and Fr. James Martin, SJ, have had a significant impact. I can draw other examples from my own religious congregation, the Jesuits, who sponsor various creative means of outreach in the area of religion and spirituality—and therefore Scripture: *The Jesuit Post* and *America Media* (USA), *Sacred Space* (Ireland) and *Pray as You Go* (Great Britain). Of course, these reach certain niche audiences but at least they are an attempt to broaden cultural appreciation of religious faith. Naturally, times of stress and anxiety such as the present coronavirus pandemic produce a great religious hunger, and so perhaps a silver lining in a very difficult situation might be an increase in efforts for greater biblical and religious literacy. This is a task that involves more than religious professionals since, as Pope Francis argued in his programmatic *The Joy of*

[12] I would not want to be classed with authors who simply lament the passing of classical Western culture, but they do describe the loss of a certain commonly held body of knowledge. Some examples are Richard Arum and Josipa Roksa, *Academically Adrift: Limited Learning on College Campuses* (Chicago: University of Chicago Press, 2011), and Allan Bloom, *The Closing of the American Mind: How Higher Education Has Failed Democracy and Impoverished the Souls of Today's Students* (New York: Simon and Schuster, 1987). See also Stephen Prothero, *Religious Literacy: What Every American Needs to Know—and Doesn't* (San Francisco: HarperSanFrancisco, 2007).

the Gospel, evangelization must become a task for all Christians.[13] My point here is that it is unlikely that people will be able to appreciate the Bible as it is read and proclaimed *in* the church unless they have had some familiarity with it *outside* of the church. The liturgy and extra-liturgical biblical literacy have always had a dialectical relationship, extending to lived Christian experience. A great deal of the problem today, therefore, may be that the church has lost so much credibility because of scandals, secularisation, and a host of other causes that the vast majority of Christians are not participants in a liturgy that can be kerygmatic in the precise way that it reads the Bible. As I once put it in an article: liturgy can't do everything.[14] This fact notwithstanding, it will also be helpful to see how the liturgy might enable or at least enhance biblical literacy.

2. How Can the Word Be Proclaimed More Effectively in the Context of the Liturgy Itself?

At this point we can turn to the question of how the liturgy already fulfils a kerygmatic function and—even more important—how such kerygmatic biblical proclamation can be improved.

One of the suggestions made by the Roman Catholic *General Introduction to the Lectionary for Mass* involves brief introductions before the various readings: "There may be concise introductions before the readings, especially the first. The style proper to such comments must be respected, that is, they must be simple, faithful to the text, brief, well prepared, and properly varied to suit the text they introduce."[15] With regard to the psalm that follows the first reading the *General Introduction* goes on to say: "Brief remarks about the choice of the

[13] Pope Francis, Apostolic Exhortation *Evangelii Gaudium* (The Joy of the Gospel), 2013, http://www.vatican.va/content/francesco/en/apost_exhortations/documents/papa-francesco_esortazione-ap_20131124_evangelii-gaudium.html.

[14] See John Baldovin, "Must Eucharist Do Everything?," *Liturgical Ministry* 1 (1992): 98–102. Reprinted in Robin A. Leaver and Joyce Ann Zimmerman, eds., *Liturgy and Music: Lifetime Learning* (Collegeville, MN: Liturgical Press, 1998), 117–27.

[15] *General Introduction to the Lectionary for Mass* 15, 2nd ed., 1981, https://www.ewtn.com/catholicism/library/general-introduction-to-the-lectionary-second-edition-2189. Technically, the *General Instruction of the Roman Missal* limits words of introduction to the readings as a whole to the priest (31), http://www.usccb.org/prayer-and-worship/the-mass/general-instruction-of-the-roman-missal/girm-chapter-2.cfm.

psalm and response as well as their correspondence to the readings may be helpful" (19).

In my experience this is not done frequently, but on occasion the practice can be very helpful. I recall a reader giving a very brief introduction and comment on a lesson from Philemon, not one of the more familiar books of the New Testament. The passage would normally fall on deaf ears—even for the biblically literate. I suppose such introductions can be included in orders of service but the likelihood of their being consulted prior to the liturgy is slim.

Perhaps it goes without saying but the biblical lections must be proclaimed intelligibly. Once again, the *General Introduction to the Lectionary*: "A speaking style on the part of the readers that is audible, clear, and intelligent is the first means of transmitting the word of God properly to the congregation. The readings, taken from the approved editions, may be sung in a way suited to different languages" (14). Apart from the proclamation of the gospel in some churches, singing the readings rarely seems to be done. I imagine that chanting the lessons might be a very effective means of communication in some cultures.

Since the liturgy is by nature an embodied experience, the place where the readings are performed also has an impact on the assembly's ability to hear the word of God as the proclamation of good news. The practice in some churches of proclaiming the gospel in the midst of the assembly can have the visceral effect of God's word alive in the midst of the congregation.[16] In addition, Catholics emphasise the priority of the gospels by the use of a distinctive, well-decorated gospel book. A Dutch Roman Catholic liturgical scholar, Herman Wegman, took another view and suggested that a Bible should replace a lectionary and I presume *a fortiori* a gospel book for reading in church:

> If we use a Bible rather than a lectionary in the Sunday liturgy, we are in fact showing that we want to move in a different direction in our understanding and our carrying out of worship. To summarise, this intended change of direction, we can say that we want to give an equal and independent place to both the Old and the New Testaments. In practice, this means that we do not want to cut the Old

[16] Unfortunately, this does not seem to be an option for Roman Catholics, since the *General Introduction* (16) seems to allow the readings to take place only at the ambo. Understandably the Roman Catholic rationale for this is the unity of the word of God.

> Testament up into little pieces and stick the pieces onto the readings from the Gospel, but that we prefer to read it as an expression of God's covenant with his people in its own right.[17]

I will touch on the implications of how the lectionary deals with the Old Testament below, but for now it is important to acknowledge the reality that tangible materials like Bibles and lectionaries or gospel books have an effect on the gathered assembly. Even when we are concentrating on intelligibility we must give attention to the symbolic/ritual elements of worship. Liturgy is always embodied.

Let me go out on a limb here and speculate further that dramatisation of the lections might be appropriate at least some of the time. This would have to be done without compromising the integrity of the Scriptures or respect for the genre of the particular piece. But one recalls that the passion narratives are (normally) read dramatically in parts during Holy Week. Although they are not officially sanctioned, I have experienced Roman Catholic liturgies in which the three great "scrutiny" gospels of the Third, Fourth, and Fifth Sundays in Lent (John 6, the bread of life; John 9, the man born blind; and John 11, the raising of Lazarus) have been read dramatically as well.

Of course, some so-called "seeker" congregations regularly produce dramatisations in order to render the Scripture intelligible. In these churches the point of biblical readings is primarily, if not exclusively, kerygmatic. Some churches have used dance and/or visual effects to communicate the message of the biblical readings. To anticipate an objection, I do realise that such practices might run the risk of being gimmicky. I would never suggest that they replace the spoken proclamation of the word.

3. Is the Roman Lectionary of Mass or the Revised Common Lectionary Adequate for Kerygmatic Proclamation Today?

We can now turn to the very substantial question of the use of the lectionary. In an extremely useful study, *Scripture and Memory*, Fritz West made use of Walter Ong's *The Presence of the Word* and described

[17] Herman Wegman, "Significant Effects of Insignificant Changes," in *Liturgy: A Creative Tradition*, ed. Mary Collins and David Power, 56 (Edinburgh: T&T Clark, 1983).

and analysed the diverse approaches that Protestants and Catholics have taken to Scripture reading in church.[18] Ong had argued that there are three stages to the transmission of language:

- Oral/aural culture where language is encountered purely as sound.
- Script or chirographic cultures in which language is written down on the page.
- Print or typographic cultures where language is defined by being seen in print.

Obviously the last of these stages presents a challenge—at least to churches with a traditional liturgical culture which do not encourage people to pick up their Bibles and read along. Moreover, we seem to have moved into a fourth stage of linguistic culture, one which is more and more influenced by the digital and screen-visual presentation of language. In some ways this is illustrated by those churches which project the words of the music being sung on a screen often dominating the sanctuary or chancel space. It is probably too soon to know what consequences the digitisation of culture will have on biblical literacy. It might possibly be a boon.

West distinguishes between Catholic and Protestant lectionary paradigms. The Catholic paradigm is far more in line with Ong's first stage of language transmission. It reads the Bible more in the context of a tradition than simply as a text. The Protestant paradigm, on the other hand, corresponds more closely to communication via the written word.[19] One can well imagine that using the lectionary basically favours the Catholic paradigm.

Consistent with this, Paul Bradshaw has pointed out there can be little doubt that using a lectionary favours an anamnetic approach to biblical proclamation.[20] At least this is clear during the major sea-

[18] Fritz West, *Scripture and Memory: The Ecumenical Hermeneutic of the Three-Year Lectionaries* (Collegeville, MN: Liturgical Press, 1997); Walter Ong, *The Presence of the Word: Some Prolegomena for Cultural and Religious History* (New Haven: Yale University Press, 1967); see also Ong, *Orality and Literacy: The Technologizing of the Word*, 3rd ed. (New York: Routledge, 2012).

[19] See West, *Scripture and Memory*, 42–70.

[20] Bradshaw, "Use of the Bible," 39–41.

sons of Advent, Christmas, Lent, and Easter as well as on major feast days, some of which preclude the ordinary Sunday readings. Examples of the latter for Roman Catholics or Eastern Christians would be the major feasts devoted to Mary, the Mother or God, or the Feast of the Holy Cross or Saints Peter and Paul. Thus, a lectionary places a celebration firmly within a church's liturgical cycle with its unfolding of the celebration of Christ and the saints.

I want to address briefly a prior question at this point: why a lectionary at all? The seventeenth century saw a vigorous debate in England over just this subject. The traditional lectionary, adapted by Anglicans for the Eucharist (but not for the Divine Office) from the medieval Western tradition, was seen by those who can be called free church Christians as unduly chaining God's word.[21] This move was part and parcel of the Puritan and Reformed abandonment of feasts and seasons in favour of Sabbatarian (i.e., Sunday) worship.

What of the free church approach characterised by freedom from the constraints of a lectionary? This approach can take one of several forms, usually decided on by the leader of worship or preacher. The minister might select a book of the Bible on which to preach through for a series of Sundays, for example, 1 Corinthians or Jeremiah. A chapter from that book would be the sole lection for the day. I call this the "chapter-a-week" strategy. The advantage of this option is that the congregation can be provided with a biblical education by the consistent exposition of the book in question. It should be noted that this chapter-a-week strategy can be enhanced by the preacher's ability to cross-reference other biblical material in her/his exposition, thus enabling the congregation to appreciate the Bible's intertextuality. Many biblical scholars would be pleased with this strategy since it allows for both an historical-critical and a theological approach to a biblical book in its integrity.

The drawback, as is well known, is that the choice of a biblical book may well depend primarily on the predilections of the minister. I can recall a television documentary in which a professor who had been fired from a Bible school pointed out that the conservative evangelical pastors associated with his denomination shied away from

[21] Horton Davies, *Worship and Theology in England: From Andrews to Baxter and Fox, 1603–1690*, vol. 2 (Princeton: Princeton University Press, 1975), esp. chap. 2, "Calendary Conflict."

preaching about the Synoptic Gospels. The former professor was committed to social justice, an unavoidable theme in Matthew, Mark, and Luke but not exactly the preference for those who let him go.

Another free church strategy is more difficult but closer to the goal of having the freedom to preach to the moment. This would be to choose a passage that seems relevant to the issue(s) of the day. One has to admit, I think, a real kerygmatic value to this practice. From where I sit at the moment the world and particularly the United States is experiencing a massive threefold crisis: the coronavirus pandemic, an economic disaster, and outrage over racial injustice and systemic racism. The use of a predetermined lectionary forces the preacher to adapt the Scriptures to the moment, which may involve shoehorning the issues of the day into what has already been proposed by the church. As a preacher I can recall having to make that adjustment the Sunday following September 11, 2001. Here again, however, the drawback is that the choice of a reading will inevitably involve the minister's predilections.

To summarise—the free church approach has several kerygmatic advantages for biblical literacy. Even in an age in which people may be generally culturally/biblically illiterate outside of the context of worship the free church strategy of choosing lections either by the chapter-a-week or by occasion can serve a catechetical function.

In light of all this, can a case be made for the current three-year lectionaries used by many churches? There are, of course, two basic versions of the three-year lectionary in use. The first is the Roman Catholic *Lectionary for Mass* (1969), which seeks to fulfil the call of Vatican II's Constitution on the Sacred Liturgy for a "richer fare" of Scripture than had been the case with the one-year cycle of the pre-Vatican II liturgy.[22] Briefly, the *Lectionary for Mass* uses the three Synoptic Gospels (Matthew, Year A; Mark, Year B with John 6 included in weeks 17–21; Luke, Year C).[23] For Ordinary Time, that is, the Green Sundays that follow Epiphany and precede Lent and then follow Trinity Sunday and precede Advent, the Old Testament readings are chosen on the basis of typology. They correspond somehow to the gospel readings. The second readings—taken from the non-gospel

[22] Constitution on the Sacred Liturgy (*Sacrosanctum Concilium*) 51; see also 24.

[23] See the extremely helpful online introduction to the *Lectionary for Mass* by Felix Just, https://catholic-resources.org/Lectionary/.

New Testament—are semi-continuous and on a separate track from the gospels. In terms of helping people to understand the Bible it is difficult to say whether these strategies are effective. In the first place, the typological Old Testament readings are read out of context—a practice to which many biblical scholars react rather negatively.[24] Second, the readings from the epistles are somewhat free-floating and often (normally?) overlooked in terms of preaching.

The second version is the *Revised Common Lectionary*, first published in 1992 and popular among Protestant/Anglican churches, which has some variants from the Roman Catholic Lectionary but particularly provides an alternative series of first readings from the Old Testament for the Sundays after Pentecost. These readings provide a semi-continuous series from Genesis in Year A through to the prophets in Year C.[25]

With both schemes we might ask—is the richer fare too rich? Might it cause indigestion? It seems to me that at least part of the answer to this question must be sought in the connection between proclamation of the Scriptures and preaching.

But we might also ask how the lectionary interprets the Bible? Historical and biblical theologians have long recognised that beyond the literal or historical reading of the Bible there are three other legitimate methods of interpretation: the symbolic (allegorical), the moral (tropological) and the eschatological (anagogical).[26] To these need to be added a liturgical hermeneutic. Given the liturgically

[24] For a critical view of how the Old Testament is used in the Roman Catholic Lectionary, see Gerard Sloyan, "The Lectionary as a Context for Interpretation," *Interpretation* 31 (1977): 131–38.

[25] I am omitting comment on the Byzantine and other Eastern Christian Sunday lectionaries that follow a one-year cycle (see https://www.byzcath.org/index.php/resources/faith-worship/lectionary-mainmenu-114). The pre-Vatican II Roman Missal also uses a one-year cycle (see https://catholic-resources.org/Lectionary/Roman_Missal.htm). Both systems employ only two readings—one from the non-gospel New Testament material and the other from the gospels. The Old Testament is virtually absent for readings at the Eucharist. For the Byzantines several Sundays are named after the gospel passage that is read, e.g., the Sunday of the Prodigal Son two weeks before Lent.

[26] As the common Latin ditty put it: *Lettera gesta docet, quid credas allegoria, moralis quid agas, quo tendas anagogia*—roughly "a literal reading tells you the facts, a symbolic reading what you should believe, a moral reading what you should do and an eschatological reading where you're going."

native soil of reading the Bible, the liturgy itself shapes interpretation. As Chauvet has argued, all reading—lection—is *se-lection*.[27] Therefore I contend that hearing the Bible in church is not only constituted by extra-liturgical knowledge and culture, important as they may be, but also by precisely how the church has chosen to interpret the Bible by means of selection. In fact, West makes a helpful point when he distinguishes between the Protestant and Catholic paradigms for the liturgy's interpretation of Scripture. For Protestants it is the Bible itself as a book which is interpreted in the course of the liturgy. For Catholics, on the other hand, selections are made from the books which constitute Scripture. So the Bible and the liturgy are certainly related, but there is a sense in which the lectionary deals not with the Bible considered as a book but with the collection of books that constitute what the churches call the Bible.[28] One more step and we shall see how these observations lead necessarily to the question of biblical preaching in the liturgy.

According to the Lutheran scholar, Gordon Lathrop, the liturgy reveals the same process of composition that we find in the Bible itself. In other words, just as the Bible builds new meanings by applying new situations to older texts, so the liturgy makes the Bible new today by its fresh interpretative reading. For example, Isaiah 43:19-20 on how God is doing a new thing recapitulates Exodus 15 on the crossing of the Red Sea, which in turn had recapitulated the creation story of Genesis.[29] Just so, in its selection of readings for any given day the church practises the same method by applying the past to the present. Lathrop calls this process "juxtaposition." The liturgy as read in a lectionary which combines selections from Scripture does precisely what the Bible has done. Interestingly this is what Taft describes when talking about liturgy as anamnesis rather than kerygma,[30] but I am suggesting that this liturgical hermeneutic of juxtaposition is a kind of kerygmatic proclamation in itself. Ironically in this view the traditional approach of using a lectionary might even be more useful for biblical literacy than the "chapter a week" ap-

[27] Chauvet, *Symbol and Sacrament*, 209.

[28] West, *Scripture and Memory*, 65–66. Note that each tradition has a slightly different selection of books which make up the Bible.

[29] Gordon Lathrop, *Holy Things: A Liturgical Theology* (Minneapolis: Fortress, 1993), 19. I have summarised these ideas in "The Sacramentality of the Word: An Ecumenical Approach," *The Journal of Ecumenical Studies* 53 (2018): 224–44.

[30] Taft, "What Is a Christian Feast?"

proach, or the Anglican practice of reading large sections of the Bible at Morning Prayer and Evening Prayer.

4. How Can Liturgical Preaching, Which Is by Nature Somewhat Kerygmatic, Contribute to People's Understanding of the Bible?

I cannot summarise here the huge number of writings about useful strategies for liturgical preaching.[31] On the other hand, we cannot avoid the issue of preaching in our effort to understand how the liturgy is kerygmatic and to answer the question that the title of this chapter proposes. The liturgical sermon or homily (in churches with lectionaries I believe the terms can be used interchangeably) is by its nature kerygmatic as well as anamnetic. We might like to think ideally that we are simply reminding people of what they already know and believe (anamnesis) but I doubt this has ever been the case in real life—at least outside of communities of consecrated religious.

The Roman Catholic *General Introduction to the Lectionary for Mass* describes the homily in this fashion:

> The purpose of the homily at Mass is that the spoken word of God and the liturgy of the Eucharist may together become "a proclamation of God's wonderful works in the history of salvation, the mystery of Christ." Through the readings and homily Christ's paschal mystery is proclaimed; through the sacrifice of the Mass it becomes present. Moreover, Christ himself is always present and active in the preaching of his Church. Whether the homily explains the text of the Sacred Scriptures proclaimed in the readings or some other text of the Liturgy, it must always lead the community of the faithful to celebrate the Eucharist actively, "so that they may hold fast in their lives to what they have grasped by faith." From this living explanation, the word of God proclaimed in the readings and the Church's celebration of the day's liturgy will have greater impact. But this demands that the homily be truly the fruit of meditation, carefully prepared, neither too long nor too short, and suited to all those present, even children and the uneducated.[32]

[31] For a minor attempt to do something like that, see John Baldovin, "Biblical Preaching in the Liturgy," *Studia Liturgica* 22 (1992): 100–118.

[32] *General Introduction* 24, citing *Sacrosanctum Concilium* 35 and *General Instruction of the Roman Missal* 65.

Leaving aside the fact that the Catholic documents allow for preaching to concentrate on non-biblical liturgical texts, for example, prayers or even the nature of a particular feast or observance, it should be clear that for Catholics at least the expectation is that the homily is able to articulate the relation between the Scripture and the rest of the liturgy. In the case of the section of the *General Introduction to the Lectionary* quoted above with regard to the Eucharist, this would also apply to other liturgical services, for example, baptisms, weddings, and funerals. In fact, the principle should apply especially to those services where, if the preacher does not realise that this must be primarily a kerygmatic opportunity, he or she is most likely whistling in the wind.

For these occasional services it is imperative that the preacher perform the kind of juxtaposition and liturgical hermeneutic described in the last section. For example, 1 Corinthians 13, a biblical passage which is not about marriage but used in a good many church weddings, needs to be contextualised in light of this particular joining of two individuals. Ideally it should also be juxtaposed with the gospel and with psalmody, if not in addition to a lesson from the Old Testament. Otherwise, this notable passage from Scripture runs the risk of being sentimentalised and therefore trivialised (which it no doubt often is).

Perhaps, as I have suggested elsewhere, the point of biblical preaching in the liturgy is not *primarily* exposition of the Scripture according to one or another acceptable methods of interpretation. Rather it is an attempt in faith to interpret the present circumstances in which we live in the context of our faith that the Bible is truly revelatory of what God is doing in us and for us.[33] In other words, what needs interpretation is what God is doing now—in light of the Scriptures. Clearly given general biblical illiteracy this does involve some

[33] Baldovin, "Biblical Preaching," 112–13; on the inadequacy of employing simply a historical-critical approach, see Elizabeth Schüssler-Fiorenza, "For the Sake of Our Salvation: Biblical Interpretation and the Community of Faith," in Baldovin, *Bread Not Stone: The Challenge of Feminist Biblical Interpretation* (Boston: Beacon, 1974), 23–42; Sandra Schneiders, *The Revelatory Text: Interpreting the New Testament as Sacred Scripture*, 2nd ed. (Collegeville, MN: Liturgical Press, 1999); Gerard Sloyan, "Some Thoughts on Liturgical Preaching," *Worship* 71 (1997): 386–99; Luke Timothy Johnson, "What's Catholic About Catholic Biblical Scholarship?," in Sloyan and William Kurz, *The Future of Catholic Biblical Scholarship: A Constructive Conversation* (Grand Rapids, MI: Eerdmans, 2002), 3–34.

exposition of the Scriptural texts but my accent is deliberately on the word *primarily*.

To give a current example, preachers who do not regularly work to incorporate concern with the coronavirus as well as concern for racial justice and healing into their sermons are being irresponsible. I would add that issues like care for the planet, gender equality, and social justice in general ought regularly to be themes of preaching. To give these matters attention is not to betray the Bible but on the contrary, to do (as we have said above) exactly what the Bible itself does: interpret how God is speaking today.

What I am proposing is obviously a difficult and challenging task, all the more so for occasional events like funerals. It presupposes preachers who are trained in biblical studies, communications, and current affairs. On the issue of current affairs I would differ somewhat from Pope Francis's otherwise splendid section on preaching in his programmatic exhortation *Evangelii Gaudium* (The Joy of the Gospel). There, Francis reminds preachers that it is not "fitting to talk about the latest news in order to awaken people's interest; we have television programmes for that."[34] One can sense what Francis is getting at, but all the same preachers have a duty to their listeners to hear the gospel preached *today*. In that vein Francis is clearly on the mark when he insists that the homily is not a lecture but in a real sense a dialogue and requires an intense effort at inculturation. If the people are to be truly listened to, then the priest must listen to them in their present circumstances.

Conclusion

In terms of bringing the Scriptures alive we cannot neglect the affective dimension. One of the most prominent spokespersons for renewed attention to affectivity in our educational, liturgical, and cultural life in general is James K. A. Smith, who has entitled his project "Cultural Liturgy." He puts it thus:

> I have emphasised that we are fundamentally noncognitive, affective creatures. The telos to which our love is aimed is not a list of ideas or propositions or doctrines; it is not a list of abstract, disembodied concepts or values. Rather, the reason that this vision of the

[34] Pope Francis, *Evangelii Gaudium* 155. The whole section covers pars. 135–59.

> good life moves us is because it is a more affective, sensible, even aesthetic picture of what the good life looks like. A vision of the good life captures our hearts and imaginations not by providing a set of rules or ideas, but by painting a picture of what it looks like for us to flourish and live well.[35]

Smith is right, since preaching without imagination and creativity would lead one to question why one would be interested in biblical literacy in the first place. Attentiveness to this reality brings us full circle to the need for imaginative use of media and communications outside of the liturgy. The content of the liturgy, preaching, and external means of evangelization need to complement one another.

We have come some distance from the initial lament about widespread biblical (and cultural) illiteracy. There can be little doubt that one of the challenges we face is recognising that illiteracy honestly, and attempting to respond to it by general extra-liturgical means like mass media and social media as a contemporary means of catechesis. But the kerygmatic challenge also needs to be faced by how well we appreciate the biblical nature of the liturgy—not only in the content of the liturgy but also in how the liturgy recapitulates the scriptural message today. Obviously, this cannot be achieved without biblically well-informed, socially alert, and imaginative preaching. I doubt that anyone reading this book would deny the relevance of the Bible. But the Bible's innate relevance means very little if we do not learn how to communicate it better. The title of this chapter says it all: "How Are They to Hear Without Someone to Proclaim Him?"

[35] James K. A. Smith, *Desiring the Kingdom* (Grand Rapids, MI: Baker Academic, 2009), 53. (As quoted in David Morlan, "A Review of J. K. A. Smith's *Cultural Liturgy* Series," *Bulletin of Ecclesial Theology* 3 [2016]: 3–4.)

Chapter 3

The Bible in the Context of the Eucharist

Thomas O'Loughlin

The Bible has, it appears, an integral and significant place in the eucharistic liturgy of Christians; and so, conversely, celebrations of the Eucharist—an activity with many names—have an important place in the interface between Christians and the Bible. We might seek to establish this with these four observations. First, for many Christians eucharistic celebrations are not only the most common, indeed the only, form of worship they regularly encounter, but are seen by those Christians as providing the paradigm for liturgical activity. As such, these gatherings are for those Christians the principal occasion when they come into contact with the Bible. Even for many who meet the Scriptures elsewhere—such as in private reading or study—the Eucharist may be the only event when they hear them within a group setting, or in which they meet the Bible's narratives as a performance of any sort, or where hearing these texts could be described as a community event. This fact alone makes the links between the Bible and the eucharistic liturgy an important area for study.

Second, while the Eucharist is one of the most contested areas of dispute among Christians, to those very disputants the place of the Scriptures within it seems unproblematic. The lectionaries of many of the churches of the Reformation for use at the Eucharist (where there was such a lectionary—and other Reformed churches eschewed the notion) were, until very recently, more or less identical with the lectionary of medieval origin that was used within the Roman Catholic Church.[1] This continuity seems to have been the result of few having given the matter of lectionaries any focused thought, so that it was continuity and commonality by default. While the performance language of the lections was a contentious issue (Latin as a liturgical language or the living language of the assembly), the fact and content of the lections was not. Likewise, today there has been a degree of convergence on the lectionary for the Sunday Eucharist that is far deeper than either agreement on liturgical forms or the interpretation of those forms.[2] In the fraught world of the theological discussion of the Eucharist, the significance of biblical reading escaped, and continues to escape, the attention of the warring parties.

Third, as a component of what is for many the central liturgical event, this context has a wider significance in that it provides them with a paradigm for their interaction with the Bible. It is the way that the readings are presented and experienced at the Eucharist that determines their view of the Bible, provides a hermeneutic for it (e.g., the unique status of the gospel reading at the Eucharist in many churches conveys an equivalent status and centrality to the four Gospels), and occasions whatever exegesis they engage with. Moreover, in many ministry training environments, it is with an eye towards this liturgical setting of the Scriptures that training in biblical studies is organised. Indeed, in some churches, were it not for the needs arising out of the presence of the Bible at the Eucharist, there would be even less attention paid to its study.[3] There is in many ministerial training programmes a direct, if unacknowledged, link between biblical studies and training for preaching at the Eucharist. By

[1] An example of this is the lectionary found in the *Book of Common Prayer* of the Church of England which is virtually identical with that of the 1570 *Missale Romanum* (see Thomas O'Loughlin, *Making the Most of the Lectionary: A User's Guide* [London: SPCK, 2012], 144–48, where the two lectionaries are compared); a similar reliance on an older lectionary can be found in other Reformed liturgies.

[2] See English Language Liturgical Conversation, *The Reims Statement: Praying with One Voice* (16 August 2011), https://www.englishtexts.org/the-reims-statement. The statement is published in *Studia Liturgica* 43 no. 1 (2013): 189–92.

[3] One of the arguments made against a reform of the lectionary, and in particular the introduction of lections from the Old Testament, was that Catholic clerical training did not equip priests for such a level of biblical engagement. See Annibale Bugnini, *The Reform of the Liturgy: 1948–1975* (Collegeville, MN: Liturgical Press, 1990), 415.

contrast, the eucharistic focus of biblical studies is not widely shared between Christian churches, hence some of the dissonance between them on the status of the Scriptures, and their basic hermeneutic is often a function (though rarely acknowledged) of whether the Scriptures are pastorally an adjunct of the Eucharist or a "stand-alone" liturgical reality.

Fourth, one of the outcomes of the liturgical movement has been a far greater emphasis on the role of the Scriptures within Christian liturgy, as can be seen in, for instance, the Roman Catholic Church where, for those following liturgical books, no celebration is to take place without a Liturgy of the Word.[4] Given the emphasis on the Eucharist in this movement, there has been a corresponding interest in the use of the Bible in its celebration. This has not only resulted in new, deliberately designed lectionaries—arguably the first such creations in Christian history—but also in attempts to justify theologically the combination, in the actual practice of the churches, of the celebration of a liturgy focused on the Scriptures (designated with names such as "the Liturgy of the Word" or "the Ministry of the Word") and that focused around the Christian table (termed "the Liturgy of the Eucharist" or "the Ministry of the Sacrament"). This discourse, which usually takes the form of an attempt to show an intrinsic link between "word" and "sacrament" and is often argued for by some quasi-causal connection (e.g., having *received* God's word in the readings, the community *responds* with the eucharistic celebration), is an important element in contemporary discussions of the link between the Bible and the liturgy. Moreover, it is probably the most pastorally significant aspect of this issue.

Sed Contra

Any discussion of this topic, however, must also begin with some serious notes of hesitation. While there have been biblical readings at eucharistic celebrations since at least the mid-second century, when we look back at the record of interest in the Eucharist we find that

[4] Across the reformed rites of the Catholic Church there is, theoretically, a common form for a Liturgy of the Word (one or more readings, a psalm, a gospel pericope, possibly a homily, and intercessions), but this pattern is rarely followed in practice at any celebration apart from the Eucharist.

the place of the Scriptures is a topic that attracts almost no attention. While there are many exhortations about the importance, spiritual benefits, and even the dangers of participation in the Eucharist, we find virtually no mention of the biblical component of eucharistic celebrations in this large corpus of theology and preaching.[5] The Eucharist is more a "theological event," rather than an actual experience, in the thinking and discussion of most churches most of the time; and "the Bible" falls within one world of discourse, and "the Eucharist" into another, with little overlap except the apologetic appeal to the Bible to somehow underpin the necessity of practice or defend a particular view of the Eucharist being advanced.

This neglect of the Bible in a eucharistic context can also be seen in the history of Christian law. While there are the most minute declarations on what is to be done/not done/not omitted from activities relating to the eucharistic elements and to the status of people involved, the regulations regarding the use of the Bible are minimal—usually no more than rubrics in liturgical books which echo practice and custom. A sixteenth-century example of the lack of concern can be seen in The [Thirty-nine] Articles of Religion of the Church of England. Five articles deal with the Eucharist, two explicitly with the Bible, but, apart from the statement that "transubstantiation . . . cannot be proved by holy Writ, but is repugnant to the plain words of Scripture," there is no linking of Bible and "Eucharist."[6] Turning to the twentieth century we find a similar disjunction in the Roman Catholic *Code of Canon Law* from 1983. It has sixty-one canons explic-

[5] A good example would be Gregory of Nyssa's *Oratio catechetica magna*, ed. John H. Srawley, *The Catechetical Oration of Gregory of Nyssa* (Cambridge: Cambridge University Press, 1903), which has been very influential in the development of eucharistic theology. It is chosen here as an example because it was also influential in the West in Latin translation. Gregory devotes three chapters (37–39) to the Eucharist, and, while he is happy to call it a "gospel mystery" (chap. 38), he never mentions that hearing the Gospels, or any other part of the Bible, was part of the actual liturgical encounter.

[6] Articles 6 and 7 deal with the Bible; articles 25, 28, 29, 30, and 31 deal with, or mention, the Eucharist. The comment on the notion of transubstantiation is found in article 28. It might be argued that the article 35—on the Book of Homilies—has a link to the eucharistic Liturgy of the Word but there is nothing in its wording to suggest such a link; moreover, classic commentators do not make any connection: cf. E. Harold Browne, *An Exposition of the Thirty-Nine Articles* 14e (London: Longmans, 1894), 776–79.

itly legislating for the practice of the Eucharist, which range from legal generalisations to technical details, but there is not one mention of the place of the Scriptures in its celebration.[7] Using the rule of thumb that that which is not legally prominent is not accorded value or importance, this would suggest that few made any serious connection between the Bible and the Eucharist.

While it is possible to justify prayer in a language other than that of everyday life, indeed in a language only known to a few ritual specialists, for there have been many such situations in our liturgical history, it is ridiculous to read narratives, where that narration has an educational or edificatory function, in a language not understood by the intended audience.[8] Such a performance contradicts its own rationale. However, by the fifth century the Western church—in contrast to others—no longer translated the readings in the liturgy for those peoples whose own language was not Latin. From the ninth century this situation—lections in Latin rather than a vernacular—became the norm for the Western church, and this would remain the situation for the Roman Catholic Church until the 1960s. This linguistic curtain between the reading and the listeners made the activity futile, but the fact that almost no attention was paid to this suggests that the lections were themselves seen as little more than a token, ritual act without importance.[9] Moreover, while the non-Western churches were usually more amenable to using local languages, often the original translation gained a permanence such that it was still used when no longer widely understood. While the sixteenth-century reformers of the Latin church stressed both a vernacular liturgy and the importance of the Scriptures in translation, these interests do not

[7] Canons 897–958; c. 897 is an example of a generalisation: the Eucharist is to be central to the Church's life; while c. 926 is an example of detail: only unleavened bread is to be used.

[8] A typical example of the often-felt need to give voice to a language unknown to the hearers in a liturgical setting is found in the story of Ezra proclaiming the Law (Neh 8:1-8), but in this case there was also a translation "so that the people understood the reading" (8:8). On the significance of giving veneration to Scriptures ("the law of Moses") in a liturgical context, see J. Blenkinsopp, *Ezra-Nehemiah: A Commentary* (Philadelphia: Westminster Press, 1988), 287–88.

[9] It could be argued that there were translations available for Roman Catholics in "people's missals" but these were a twentieth-century phenomenon among the devout, and themselves part of the liturgical revival that led to the abandonment of the practice.

come together in an explicit focus on hearing the Bible at a eucharistic celebration.

This impression that the readings were simply there because they were there—rather than seen as having any specific religious purpose or being the basis of community engagement—is supported by other evidence. The actual selection of pericopes found in medieval Latin missals, and which continued in use across many Western churches until the mid-twentieth century—and which is still in use in Anglican churches adhering to the *Book of Common Prayer*—was a narrow collection of snippets rarely more than a few verses in length, often with no respect for the internal coherence of the narratives, and with no overall coherence. They seem to be there because there was need to have some verses from "the apostle," from "a gospel" and—a legacy of a larger liturgy than "the private Mass" of a priest, which formed the basis of those missals—a few verses from a psalm.[10] That this selection was not taken seriously as of catechetical value can be seen in that the preaching patterns of the various churches took virtually no notice of the lectionary,[11] which itself had no physical existence as a liturgical book.[12] This lack of concern was echoed in the language used by several churches. Catholics, for example, used terms like "Mass of the Catechumens" or "Fore-Mass" for the liturgy of readings, and offered little training in their rubrics regarding it, while speaking of "the Mass of the Faithful" or "the Mass proper" for the remainder of the liturgy. From this perspective, the fact that the new

[10] The length of the readings was determined by the need to have a complete Mass text which could be performed in around twenty minutes, and it was expected that even a public "Low Mass" would not take more than thirty minutes; for one of the last discussions of this topic—and it is typical of a long tradition—see John O'Connell, *The Celebration of Mass: A Study of the Rubrics of the Roman Missal* (London: Burns, Oates and Washbourne, 1940), 139–41.

[11] I owe this observation to my colleague Professor Frances Knight who is engaged in an ongoing study of nineteenth- and twentieth-century preaching. See her "Parish Preaching in the Victorian Era: The Village Sermon," in K. A Francis and W. Gibson, eds., *Oxford Handbook of the British Sermon: 1689–1901* (Oxford: Oxford University Press, 2012), 63–78, at 75–76.

[12] Historically, by the term "lectionary" is meant the actual arrangement of biblical passages (which sometimes took on physical shape as codices that contained selections of readings—and these are also referred to as "lectionaries"). With the arrival of print, lectionaries became just parts of the standard books (e.g., the *Missale Romanum* or the *Book of Common Prayer*), and, arguably, with the arrival in 1969 of a distinct printed book for the Catholic liturgy, *The Lectionary*, the Liturgy of the Word attained a distinct visibility within the overall eucharistic liturgy it did not have previously.

Lectionary has not attracted the attention of reactionary culture-warriors is not a tribute to some latent ecumenism or biblical sophistication on their part, but simply that they care so little about the Liturgy of the Word that it does not register on the target radars. While one word's alteration in a eucharistic prayer can provoke torrents of protest, changes, curtailments, or omissions in the prescribed lections go unnoticed.

Hence, we are left with a conundrum. In Christian worship, biblical readings have been as ubiquitous as the celebrations of the Eucharist of which they are a mandated part, but in that context they have been so unheard and ignored as to have made no impact as Scripture.

Origins

One way to address this curious engagement–with–unengagement is to look at our early evidence for the combination of the liturgy of readings with the community meal of thanksgiving. Writing in the early 150s, Justin provides our first detailed evidence about the use of the Scriptures—though what he meant by this term would be radically different within a generation[13]—at the weekly gathering of the Christians:[14]

> Now on the day called "the day of the sun" all who live in cities or in the country assemble in one place, and the memoirs of the apostles (*apomnémoneumata*) or the writings (*suggrammata*) of the prophets are read for as long as time allows. When the lector (*anaginóskontos*) has stopped, the one presiding (*ho proestós*) encourages us with words to imitate these good things. Then as a group we all stand up and offer our prayers.[15]

[13] See Thomas O'Loughlin, "The *Protevangelium Iacobi* and the Status of the Canonical Gospels in the Mid-Second Century," in G. Guldentops, C. Laes, and G. Partoens, eds., *Felici Curiositate: Studies in Latin Literature and Textual Criticism from Antiquity to the Twentieth Century: In Honour of Rita Beyers* (Turnhout, BE: Brepols Publishers, 2017), 3–21.

[14] For the situation and dating of Justin's work, see Denis Minns and Paul Parvis, *Justin, Philosopher and Martyr: Apologies* (Oxford: Oxford University Press, 2009).

[15] *Apologia* 1.67.3–5; the translation is from Thomas O'Loughlin, "Reading, and Re-reading Justin's Account of 'the Eucharist,'" *Anaphora* 12, no. 2 (2018): 67–110, at 101.

This assumes that the principal Christian gathering is for the community's thanksgiving meal, of its nature a domestic event, but during this meal—possibly reflecting the familiar practice of having some sort of performance (e.g., recitation of poetry) at a *symposion*—there is this engagement with the communities' inherited writings, once again given voice by a lector. While one might speculate that this has certain similarities to the synagogue liturgy (recalled in Luke 4:16-30) or "the recitation" that was part of the [later] normative Passover meal, these are not helpful lines of enquiry. The synagogue liturgy was not simply transposed into a domestic setting, nor was the Passover meal the actual pattern for this weekly Christian meal, but rather it was probably the convenience of this weekly gathering—famously referred to by Luke as "the breaking of the loaf" (Acts 2:42)—for other community events that led to the custom described by Justin. We know that Paul spoke at gatherings and expected his letters to be read at gatherings—and that these were the same gatherings at which the community meal was eaten seems fairly certain. Paul seems to envisage the meal gathering of the Corinthians in 1 Corinthians 10–11 as *the* gathering of the community, while Luke, imagining a gathering with Paul present, envisages it as a eucharistic meal (Acts 20:7). Thus, it would be natural that visiting performers of "the good news"—those called "evangelists"—would give their performance in such a setting, and it would equally be the convenient setting for other visitors (e.g., "apostles") and so also for teachers.[16] We can imagine a network of churches and travelling evangelists who were made welcome in each location and gave their performance, a gospel, at the regular meal while leaving "recordings," books, which could be shared with other groups and then used when no travelling evangelist was present. Thus the first texts of the followers of Jesus were, when sounded by the lector, the virtual presence of their eminent visitors—and, as Papias noted in the second century,[17] many preferred

[16] See Michael B. Thompson, "The Holy Internet: Communication between Churches in the First Christian Century," in Richard Bauckham, ed., *The Gospel for All Christians* (Edinburgh: T&T Clark, 1998), 49–70.

[17] Fragment 7, Michael W. Holmes ed., *The Apostolic Fathers: Greek Texts and English Translations* (Grand Rapids, MI: Baker Books, 1992), 574–75. The detailed instructions on the treatment of visitors that we find in the Didache seem to envisage just such a situation of teachers who arrive, stay a few days, and then move on; cf. Thomas O'Loughlin, *The Didache: A Window on the Earliest Churches* (London: SPCK, 2010), 105–28.

the living voice of an evangelist or apostle to words read from a book.[18] As with any practice that becomes habitual within a group, it would not have been long before this matter of convenience—listening to visitors or their own teachers on the same occasion as they assembled for their community meal—became their customary practice, then their expected practice, and then remained there as somehow mandatory: because this was what we do (and have always done)! Familiarity and group repetition elides silently into the normative, which is then rationalised and defended as coming from the will of Christ.[19]

From this perspective we can read Justin again. He first mentions "the memoirs of the apostles," which is usually seen to equate with the later reading from an epistle ("The Epistle" of the later liturgies) and then from a gospel ("The Gospel"), and his unusual term *apomnémoneumata* is seen as Justin avoiding internal Christian terminology in favour of more widely comprehensible descriptive words in a book dedicated to the emperor. However, such an interpretation is built on two assumptions: first, that there was a recognisable entity, "the New Testament," in Justin's church. While a collection of writings was taking shape, Justin being a key piece of evidence for this, we cannot grant it the status nor the theological significance as a collection that the canonical collection would later acquire. Second, while Justin relates his select group of texts "to the apostles," we cannot assume this was identical in content with the later collection of texts (all attributed to authors of "apostolic" status) which we still use. While it probably included letters by Paul—though quotations or clear allusions to Paul are absent from Justin's work[20]—and other, now canonical, letters,[21] and our Gospels,[22] it may have included

[18] See Thomas O'Loughlin, "Υπηρέται τοῦ λόγου: Does Luke 1:2 Throw Light onto the Book Practices of the Late First-Century Churches?," in H. A. G. Houghton, ed., *Early Readers, Scholars and Editors of the New Testament* (Piscataway, NJ: Gorgias Press, 2014), 1–15.

[19] See Paul Connerton, *How Societies Remember* (Cambridge: Cambridge University Press, 1989), 41–71.

[20] In the biblical index to Minns and Parvis, *Justin, Philosopher and Martyr*, 340, there are three references to Paul's letters but these are cases where the editors see a similarity of teaching between Paul and Justin rather than citations or clear allusions.

[21] At *Apology* 1.16.5 there is a citation of "teaching" which is a variant of Matthew 5:34 and 7 or James 5:12, but the *dictum* now has the status of a living text rather than being evidence we could use to determine that Justin knew the letter of James.

[22] Whether or not our four Gospels were already circulating as a collection of four Gospels is too large an issue to enter in here. The case in favour was made most

much we no longer read in the eucharistic liturgy. For example, the materials that lie behind our gospels, such as Q, or parallel developments, such as the *Gospel of Thomas*, and other gospel-genre texts, such as the *Protevangelium Iacobi*,[23] may have been included. Equally "apostolic" were such texts as the *Didache* or the *Letter of the Romans to the Corinthians*, which fall under the general heading of "instructional texts" and would fit with his claimed purpose for such reading: that they provided instruction on how to act as a Christian. The second item mentioned is "the writings of the prophets," and clearly he is thinking here of a collection that has specific status as such. The term, the "writings of the prophets," probably embraced for him the whole of "the Scriptures" as these were taken over from Greek-speaking Jews (i.e., the Septuagint). We tend to see collective references to "the prophets" as a part of "the Scriptures" as in the phrase "the law and the prophets,"[24] but following from his own use of the Scriptures it probably stands for the whole of "prophecy" (i.e., what Christians later referred to as "the Old Testament"),[25] taken as what had been revealed before the time of Jesus and which was read as pointing towards, and finding fulfilment in, Jesus. However, the exact extent of the Septuagint in a particular place in the mid-second century is impossible to determine.[26] What is significant is that these two

---

elegantly by Graham N. Stanton, *Jesus and Gospel* (Cambridge: Cambridge University Press, 2004), where pp. 92–109 have a special focus on Justin, and the question had been examined in detail earlier by Arthur J. Bellinzoni, *The Sayings of Jesus in the Writings of Justin Martyr* (Leiden: Brill, 1967). However, the confidence of Stanton needs to be set against the re-examination of the evidence by Brent Nongbri, *God's Library: The Archaeology of the Earliest Christian Manuscripts* (New Haven, CT: Yale University Press, 2018), 247–68, where we see a convincing case for the weakness of any assertion about the existence of four-gospel codices in the second century.

[23] On Justin's awareness of this text we have his assumption that Jesus' birth took place in a cave in *Dialogue* 78,5; cf. George T. Zervos, "Dating the Protevangelium of James: The Justin Martyr Connection," in E. Lovering, ed., *Society of Biblical Literature 1994 Seminar Papers* (Atlanta, GA: Scholars Press, 1994), 415–34; and Thomas O'Loughlin, "The *Protevangelium Jacobi* and the Emergence of the Notion of Consistency as a 'Principle' within Christian Theology," in Jan N. Bremmer, J. Andrew Doole, Thomas R. Karmann, Tobias Nicklas, and Boris Repschinski, eds., *The Protevangelium of James* (Leuven: Peeters, 2020), 206–16.

[24] See, for example, Matthew 7:12.

[25] Moses, author of "the law" was *the* prophet.

[26] It would have been almost certainly much larger than the later Hebrew canon, but not yet include works such as the final, Greek form of IV Esdras; see Thomas O'Loughlin, "Esdras, Books of: II. Christianity," in H. J. Klauck, V. Leppin, B. McGinn

collections of potential readings are being given parity: the group's own memories replace, or are being replaced by, "the [inherited] Scriptures." However, while the hermeneutic of prophecy/fulfilment may have been a key theological theme of the period and of Justin's own writings, the formal rationale (at least for the putative non-Christian audience of the apology) of the activity of reading at the Eucharist is given in moral terms: they provide models for imitation and so promote righteous living.

The overall impression given by Justin, despite the fact that it has been appealed to any number of times in the process of liturgical renewal as setting out an architecture for the Liturgy of the Word, is one of informal fluidity. They read from either the Scriptures *or* their own collection of texts: these are equally useful for their purposes and seemingly interchangeable. They do not appear to make the selection of these readings because of their inherent status—be they considered canonical, or inspired, or related to a specific person, or because they belong to a specific category of writings—but because they are considered useful as suitably inspiring for their lives. Similarly, there is no hint of any order of readings—a lectionary—but of choices made in a somewhat random fashion, and the whole process being subject to the proviso that it has to be carried out in the available time. Indeed, it could be that the group's sense of the time at their disposal is the deciding factor in choosing what they read on a particular Sunday. Likewise, the need of the presider—who will "encourage" [them] with words "to imitate these good things"—who has already chosen his topic may have played a crucial role in the choice of the text read.[27] Indeed, this whole aspect of the assembly seems to hinge on it being a convenient preliminary to the meal gathering. The later developments can now all be seen in relationship to this informal, almost accidental, conjunction of meal and readings we see in Justin.

The Shifting Status of the Bible and the Eucharist

Just as the early repetitive choices of the churches for what they would read when they gathered was influential in determining which

et al., eds., *The Encyclopedia of the Bible and its Reception* (Berlin and Boston: De Gruyter, 2013), 7:1202–4.

[27] Justin Martyr, *First Apology* 1.67.

texts would be diffused, copied, retained, recopied and survive—their functional canon contributing to the formation of the notion of a prescriptive canon within the churches—so later, the development of more elaborate notions of the status of "Scripture" within the churches had a crucial influence on what was read liturgically. Principally, this meant that there were writings from their own movement that were on a par with "the law and the prophets" in terms of inspiration (a development that is linked to the last decades of the second century[28]) and then, later, that there was a prescriptive canon of these writings. As the notion that there was a collection of special writings took hold, so too did the notion that other writings were not to be accorded the same status, and so this canon became normative for use at formal gatherings. We should not imagine this process as either clear-cut—as the number of now non-canonical texts found in the great uncial codices witness—or arising out of formal decisions: but as one collection grew in status, that status determined what was available and considered suitable and safe for use. And so, probably by the fourth century we arrive at a position that the range of what was available to be read at a eucharistic gathering was co-extensive with the lists of books considered to be "Scripture."

It would be a small move, such as we can see supported by influential writers, notably Jerome,[29] with a "high" view of the value of reading biblical texts, for this to become necessary and mandatory: one must read these texts, and only these texts, at the liturgy. This is the position that still holds the field for virtually every church. The status of the collection, and what is extrinsically claimed as its qualities, such as inspiration, inerrancy, or sufficiency, justifies the liturgical use; the liturgical use reinforces the high view of the possible benefits of the event of reading these particular texts—though where one lays the stress in these two sequences will vary from church to church and theologian to theologian. To assess the range of attitudes, we could

[28] See n. 13, above.

[29] The classic statement is in his *Commentarium in Isaiam* where he states: "If, as the apostle Paul said, the Christ is the power of God and wisdom of God; then, whoever does not know the scriptures does not know either the power of God nor the wisdom of God: ignorance of the scriptures is ignorance of the Christ" (Prologus PL 24,17). The last phrase is frequently quoted, but is usually taken as referring to the Gospels—but, as is clear from the context, Jerome is referring to "the Scriptures" of the first Christians (not to the whole canon, much less to the New Testament) and his concern is with ignorance of what we refer to as the Old Testament.

use, as a rough guide, this principle: the more an individual or group identify with the claims for the Bible made by the sixteenth-century reformers, the more likely it is that they will favour moving from the status of the Bible to its presence at the Eucharist; while the more that one focuses on the tradition of the churches' use, and the Eucharist as an event, the more one justifies the presence of these readings by appealing to their scriptural status. From one perspective the arguments run something like this: the Bible is unique, so we must have readings from it at a Christian gathering. From the other perspective we hear: we have biblical readings at our Eucharists—and we must value these because they are from the Bible. Sometimes this tension is explicit and aggressive, sometimes it is just a subtle shift in emphasis, but it is present to some extent in most pastoral situations and is a shadowy presence in every pastoral publication that addresses the question of lections at the eucharistic celebrations.

However, at the same time—the third and fourth centuries—that the boundaries of what could and could not be read in eucharistic gatherings were shifting, that event was undergoing radical transformation in practice, in its social ecology, and in its formal significance within preaching. From being a real meal celebrated by a community with the blessing of the Father being performed in the fashion of Jesus over the loaf and cup, it moved to being a formalised event at which the blessings of the loaf and cup became not only the religious focus, but the rationale for the gathering, and ritually its core. While this disappearance of the meal is sometimes given a positive interpretation by modern theological apologists as if it was this "kernel"—the "actual" Eucharist—that had broken free from its ephemeral packaging, this does not take account of the facts. The transformation meant that a meal shared by all, a dinner that Paul insisted should break down the social stratification of the larger society, which was imagined as modelling the new community, and which was located in the secular domestic space, became the Christian variant of the temple tributes of the larger society.[30] It was now linked to a breakfast with only a token amount of food/drink, with ever more complex restrictions regarding who could enjoy this ritual food. Its table was now so identified with a Greco-Roman altar that it came to adopt its name and attributes, and it was located in a sacral

[30] Cf. Clemens Leonhardt, "Morning Salutations and the Decline of Sympotic Eucharists in the Third Century," *Zeitschrift für antikes Christentum* 18 (2014): 420–42.

area which reflected the sacral values of Roman temples—such as the desire for orientation[31]—and presided over by a specialist cadre who understood themselves in terms of those temples' *sacerdotia*.[32] The effect was to produce a sacralised ritual which, although ever more detached from the experience of most Christians, was rationalised as ever more central to their salvation.[33]

In this reduction of the eucharistic dimension of Christianity to a token sacral affair, which for most people was more a spectacle at which they were present than a celebration in which they were performers, there was a parallel tokenisation of the place of the Scriptures in the ritual. The continuity of ritual ensured that the biblical reading would not disappear, but the need to have a short, formalised service that could be performed daily, if desired, with a minimum of specially trained performers meant that the readings now evolved to be no more than snippets. A few verses from Paul, a couple of verses from a psalm, and then a few verses from a gospel—usually Matthew and often badly "cut" so that the pericope did not match a textual sense unit—became the token, but somehow essential, biblical presence. Ritually, the gospel lection became the focus of attention—standing, light, incense, and signs of reverence such as "signing" the book and then kissing it—but, for most of the time, this was not related to the rest of the liturgy. The epistle—snippets from Paul or occasionally Acts—became the only other reading, and it was signaled as having lesser status, while the Old Testament—apart from a handful of passages linked to the great feasts—simply disappeared. In coming to see these readings as no more than a prelude to the real business of the gathering for the Eucharist, Christians were no more than describing their experience.

The historical messiness of our liturgical inheritance, and the fact that the eucharistic liturgy is "as much the product of fallible human

[31] Orientation was a phenomenon of Greco-Roman temples which brought the sacrifices in alignment with the sacred geometry of the city; see Vitruvius, *De Architectura* 4,3 and 4,9. See Thomas O'Loughlin, "Orientation in the Eucharistic Liturgy: A Note on Its Sources," *Anaphora* 14, no. 2 (2020): 21–30.

[32] In early fourth-century Spain, ca. 306, at the Synod of Elvira, the *presbyteri* identified themselves functionally with the then dominant Greco-Roman priesthoods such as the *flamines* and the *pontifices*; see Samuel Laeuchli, *Power and Sexuality: The Emergence of Canon Law at the Synod of Elvira* (Philadelphia: Temple University Press, 1972).

[33] Gregory of Nyssa's comments, cf. n. 5 above, are a good example of this phenomenon.

minds as of the divine initiative"[34] and the work of the Spirit in guiding the churches, is something that many who set a high value on the tradition of "the liturgy" find hard to come to terms with. Likewise, the confused nature of our reception of the Jewish Scriptures of the second temple period combined with the messiness of what survived from the writings of first- and second-century Christians as "the New Testament," mean that the collection of texts now held in unique reverence is also "as much the product of fallible human minds as of the divine initiative" and the work of the Spirit in guiding the churches. And from these facts flow two corollaries: first, one cannot argue from the nature of the Bible to justify its necessary presence at a eucharistic gathering nor that only the Scriptures should supply the readings. Second, one cannot argue that there is an essential *ordo* within the eucharistic liturgy which demands the presence of the Scripture or only the Scriptures.

Rather, we must take our inheritance—and it is broadly the inheritance of all the churches who make any provision for eucharistic celebrations—as simply what is there because it is there. Then, we must seek those ways of performance, arrangement, and explanation that are most suited to the situation in which that church finds itself, how it relates to its cultural environment, and how it conceives of itself as fulfilling the Christian mission.

Interlocking Challenges and Tensions

How should the churches value and celebrate both the gathering around the common book and the gathering around the common table when both activities take place coupled together in one event? Since the 1950s when the first plans for a reform of the lectionary for use at the Eucharist were suggested, there have been many attempts to provide an internal logic for this combination, and then to provide homiletic and catechetical materials that support this logic. However, rather than seeking to discover some deep unifying principle—which will always be little more than a rationalisation after the fact—it might be more effective to take an alternative approach. We might begin by acknowledging the "shoved together" nature of our ritual of two parts that are found in every celebration of this Christian ritual,

[34] Paul F. Bradshaw, "Difficulties in Doing Liturgical Theology," *Pacifica* 11 (1998): 181–94, at 184.

whether it is called Eucharist, the Lord's Supper, Divine Liturgy, Holy Communion, or the Mass. Then, rather than seeking to justify this, we might approach the event with a series of overlapping tensions as our guide to effective celebration.

Tension 1: Why Are We Doing This?

In every celebration there is tension, whether it is expressed or not, between those who are concentrating on the biblical readings—hearing these is seen as the most important reason for the gathering—and those who are there for "the sacrament." In caricature, for the first group, the Holy Communion is an "add on" that might be justified occasionally (and I have been at celebrations where there was a formal gap to let people leave who did not wish to stay for this extra to the norm of their regular liturgy); for the second group, the Liturgy of the Word is just the bit to be "whizzed through" before "the real business" (and I have seen places where it was accepted that only "the devout" arrived before the end of the sermon). While only a minority opt for one or other of the extremes, not only every church, but each Christian at each celebration is located somewhere along this continuum.

Confronting this tension can allow us to see that not only can we not identify our practice with the Christian totality, but also to come to an understanding of how our different histories have shaped us. Christians *both* eat together *and* recount their common memory together—which we acknowledge by not making any "discovered" rationale for the combination of "word" and "sacrament" normative, much less the *voluntas Dei*; every tendency on the Christian continuum can learn from others.

Tension 2: The Challenge of Anamnesis

In recent years, many liturgists have taken to rendering anamnesis as "experiencing anew"[35]—and have been right to do so in the face of a propensity in modern Western culture to identify remembering

[35] This translation originated with Fred D. Gealy of the Perkins School of Theology in the early 1970s; cf. James F. White, "United Methodist Eucharistic Prayers: 1965–1985," in Frank C. Senn, ed., *New Eucharistic Prayers: An Ecumenical Study of Their Development and Structure* (New York: Paulist Press, 1987), 80–95, at 82.

with an individual noetic act focused on the past. However, it is often useful to envisage anamnesis as a continuum between the two poles of *remembering*—focused on the present recalling the past—and *encounter*—focused on the present moving into the future. Sometimes when this tension is ignored, the Liturgy of the Word becomes linked to the past and an educational exercise (caricatured by viewing the reading of the Old Testament as cold information—the past is past—about the Ancient Near East (which usually means that it is seen as existentially irrelevant) prior to encounter in the eucharistic liturgy (caricature: now we meet the warm living Jesus among us). But both word and sacrament involve both remembering and encounter. The ancient texts performed today are potentially an encounter with the living God and reading them can be a transformational event now for both the individuals and the community.[36] And this is an experience that is common across the spectrum of Christianity, though some churches place greater emphasis on the performance of the Scriptures in proclamation and preaching than others. In a parallel fashion, the experience of eating together must not degenerate into individualist sacral consumerism but must be a collective act of remembering—as characterised by the tradition cited in 1 Corinthians 11:24-25—but also holding out the potential of an encounter within the community today with the divine, while being expressive of its hope.

The tension of remembering and encounter is intrinsic to each part of eucharistic events and noting this common tension can contribute to more balanced appreciation of the parts irrespective of whether a church tends to begin at the biblical or "sacramental" pole. Every assembly is a community of memory, while every assembly seeks for its gathering that it be a moment of encounter.

Tension 3: Catechesis and Celebration

In a similar way to the previous tension, we can sometimes divide the two parts into a neat couplet of "word" = teaching/ "sacrament" = prayer, ignoring the fuzzy interconnection, running through every Christian gathering, between information and celebration, invitation and response. We are not conducting a Bible study class when we engage in the Ministry of the Word, and equally, we have a variety of

[36] See Walter Brueggemann, *Texts That Linger, Words That Explode* (Minneapolis: Fortress Press, 1999).

eucharistic prayers because they are not merely ritual formularies but convey to the assembly an understanding of itself and its activity.[37] Throughout our liturgy we have to balance and re-balance ourselves on the spectrum between imparting information at one end and becoming a ritualistic performance that borders on theurgy at the other. One can caricature these two positions by looking at the architectural setting of the liturgy. On one extreme we have the raked lecture hall as "the worship space" equipped with the technology of a classroom, but it is not a place one would like to meet friends, have coffee, or toast someone on their birthday. On the other hand, one could have a baroque chapel whose front, "the sanctuary," is a visual spectacle for observers, whose acoustic is designed for a choir concert, and which has only a mock pulpit, but the ensemble is also so separated from ordinary experience that one could never relax in such an unworldly place.

Between these extremes of auditorium and shrine lie most Christian gatherings, but the challenge is to recall that we are performing our memory in common with its didactic impact on our lives when we read the Scriptures, while our eating together is a wholistic experience that can perform our vision of our lives. The challenge to maintain this tension in a culture of constant complete information ("it's all there now on my smartphone") is perhaps the most difficult facing pastors: the Scriptures play a more complex role in Christianity than being "its Bible," while the liturgy's human value in forming communities with a Christian identity is more than being a provider for individual "spiritual" needs. We must now turn to a particular expression of this tension.

Tension 4: Liturgy and Scholarship

Whether it is the ritual of flanking the ambo with lights and then incensing the gospel book or that moment of intense focus when opening a Bible as the divinely revealed book, liturgy accords a status to the Scriptures—and their contents—against which we set major question marks in our scholarship. In all churches on a Sunday morning, Paul is still the author of Ephesians; in most he is still the author

[37] See Thomas O'Loughlin, "*Gratias Agamus Deo*: A Reflection on Specificity in Our Eucharistic Prayers," *Australian Journal of Liturgy* 15, no. 4 (2017): 254–65.

of the pastoral epistles; and in some he is even still given the credit for Hebrews. While there are many Christians who would defend these positions, there are many pastors who would not do so in a classroom setting but are happy to accept this at the liturgy. Does this mean that our liturgy should be a zone free of critical thinking, or should we recognise that we engage with the Scriptures, along with all of our liturgy, in a different manner to the ways we engage with the factuality of the world? The engagement in both parts of a eucharistic gathering belongs to a world of myth, where our basic currency is metaphor, in which we find meaning and which hovers between the factual world of rationality and the divine which is ineffable. While this can easily be set out as the ontology of the worlds of reading the Scriptures and celebrating liturgy, it does involve the difficulty that at any time it can degenerate into rationalist agnosticism at one extreme, and fundamentalist fideism at the other.

This tension also affects the content of what we read. How, for example, can we engage with the great myth of Genesis 1 in a society in need of great common stories for the value of the creation? How can we sing the Song of Moses (Exod 15:1-18)—a core mythic text for both Jews and Christians—and yet distance ourselves from the warlord imagery applied to God as both inappropriate and dangerous? This is a tension that has to be negotiated every time we read aloud a biblical text and conclude it with liturgical phrases such as "This is the word of the Lord," or "This is the gospel of the Lord." But this tension between factual description and metaphorical exploration of our Christian myth applies just as much to the Liturgy of the Eucharist. How does one proclaim the presence of the Christ in the assembly and in the meal while avoiding the physicalism that dominates so much popular Roman Catholic piety? How does one use images derived from the temple imagery of the Levitical priesthood of the actions of the presider at a Christian liturgy while (1) avoiding replacing the Christian vision of a priestly people and the Christ as the unique priest, or (2) without falling into a *fanum*-focused sacerdotalism? The tension of living within a liturgical myth, whether it is obviously "ritual" or book-based, exists between the parts of the gathering and within both parts of the gathering.

This tension has a corresponding implication for ministry training. Modules in biblical studies often do not take account of how these texts will be perceived when heard in combination with other texts in a liturgical setting, while liturgy modules often do not acknowledge the complexity of the biblical texts heard in the setting they study. This tension can also be a source of friction between the churches: those with a high view of the liturgy will often not invest the time needed to appreciate the complexity of biblical criticism, while those who do make that commitment forget that the minister will meet the texts in a ritual environment. Taking this tension seriously as a challenge for training and formation programmes is a weakness across the churches, and this becomes visible in the connection between the parts at eucharistic gatherings.

Tension 5: Spontaneity and Lectionary

The long debate over having a lectionary—a "system" of readings—over a spontaneous choice on the day—an "openness" to the Spirit—is quite arid for both extremes for it is little more than a particular instance of a deeper tension in human community between *chronos* (we live in temporal cycles and must plan our lives within them) and *kairos* (we recognise unique moments that demand specific responses). The first reality means that without a thought-out and well-planned lectionary—and we might note that this is a phenomenon of the twentieth century within Christianity—we will probably produce an idiosyncratic canon within a canon. The second reality means that if we do not have the freedom and sensitivity to respond to the moment and the situation, then readings become just more background noise, irrelevant to the community, and falsify its gathering as liturgy.[38]

In practice this means that while a lectionary offers the possibility of systematic exploration of our stories, we may need to drop or change them to fit the makeup of a gathering or the situation on the day. Likewise, while we may have the inherited canons as our normal

[38] The extreme situation is narrated in Hugh Brody's *Maps and Dreams: Indians and the British Columbia Frontier* (Vancouver: Douglas and McIntyre, 1981) of the First Nations funeral where there was no connection between the Catholic eucharistic service presided over by a priest who was an outsider to the community with the biblical readings performed by the school teacher—also an outsider—should be seen as warning by all who imagine that liturgy as a datum: "The service just carried on, the priest and teachers doing it their way, while the Indians did it theirs" (72–84, at 79).

content for Liturgies of the Word, we may need to adopt other readings that bring out particular needs. Just as the medieval Latin church developed a rich set of sequences and biblical dramas for the great feasts, we may need to use other materials to make the word of God—which is always more than any set of texts, however venerable as a canon—heard in our assemblies.

Tension 6: Local and Global

The networking that generated the collection of texts that stand behind the Christian canon highlights another fundamental tension within Christianity and which becomes manifest: the matter of lectionaries. Each assembly was a community in itself, but it shared and exchanged people, apostles and evangelists, narratives and codices, with the other churches. Some scholarship and some ecclesiologies emphasise the particularities of individual communities, while others stress the ecumenical nature of the Christian movement, but the reality can only be grasped when we deliberately acknowledge a fuzzy logic of borrowings.[39] As in the previous tension, this means that there are advantages in having ecumenical lectionaries which allow for widespread sharing and the formation of a common identity through that sharing of common texts, but having mechanisms which allow for local and particular identities to be expressed. The rather fuzzy situation with regard to the modern Sunday eucharistic liturgy among many western churches is a model of what can be achieved. All have compromised to an extent in producing a three-year gospel cycle, while for the other lections many churches have opted for arrangements that fit their needs, while the tweaking one finds in the gospel lectionary itself reveals their particular theological pressure points.[40]

Anyone who has ever given input on an in-service training day for preachers will know that one stock element of discussion will be proposals for the reform of the lectionary for Sundays. These proposals range from abandoning the Old Testament altogether (a favourite

[39] See Thomas O'Loughlin, "The Origins of an Ecumenical Church: Links, Borrowings, and Inter-Dependencies," *Analogia: The Pemptousia Journal for Theological Studies* 9 (2020): 39–60.

[40] See Fritz West, *Scripture and Memory: The Ecumenical Hermeneutic of the Three-Year Lectionaries* (Collegeville, MN: Liturgical Press, 1997).

Catholic proposal)[41] to a desire that whole biblical narratives be read as found in the biblical text, such as Matthew 5:1–7:28, as lections (a favourite Evangelical proposal), and from tweaking to make a theological point to having a four-year lectionary plan. This approach ignores the messiness of the human and Christian situation: compromises between needs are the foundation of all our lives, and this involves the negotiation of the tensions rather than their resolution. Compromises between conflicting needs will always be needed in the Church's ongoing practice of using the Bible when celebrating eucharistically.

Conclusion

The communal treasuring of their memories through writing, together with their regular performance—which eventually survived as our Bible—and loyalty to the regular celebration of the community thanksgiving meal—which survives in the ritual forms as our Eucharist—are two survivors from the early churches that have become central institutions of Christianity. In practice, these activities, or reading and re-reading and celebrating and re-celebrating,[42] have never been separate but have shared the same space and occasion within communities. Exploring these distinct but continually overlapping activities together can open up new possibilities for understanding each of them.

[41] See Thomas O'Loughlin, "'Old Testament, Old Hat': Should We Read the Old Testament at the Eucharist," *Anaphora* 13, no. 2 (2019): 65–73.

[42] Liturgists often note that at the heart of ritual is evolving repetition (and cite Jonathan Z. Smith, "A Twice-Told Tale: The History of the History of Religion's History," *Numen* 48 [2001]: 134–46), but this repetitive aspect is also fundamental to any text cited as "Scripture"—and establishes a basic ontological similarity between the liturgy and the Bible—because as Gerhard Ebeling noted: "The same word can be said to another time only by being said differently" (cited in Stanton, *Jesus and Gospel* [2004], 62).

Chapter 4

Living Lent and Engaging Easter: Scripture's Potential and Liturgy's Limits

Anne McGowan

Easter anchors the Christian liturgical year as its great Sunday, presenting the paschal mystery to the faithful for their anamnetic contemplation and appropriation in Scripture and sacraments. Opportunities to connect Bible and liturgy abound between Lent's launch and the Easter season's annual end at Pentecost. These weeks are privileged times for reviewing the grand sweep of salvation history featuring creation, redemption, and a future whose final fullness is still unfolding. They are also suitable for retelling very specific stories of how the self-emptying embodied entry into history of God's eternal Son culminated in Jesus Christ's death and resurrection "in accordance with the [Hebrew] scriptures" (1 Cor 15:3-4) that inaugurated his ongoing exaltation (Phil 2:6-11).

Reading the Bible with the church through the liturgies of Lent, Holy Week, and Easter, however, reveals ongoing tensions between salvation through Christ already accomplished for us but yet to be realised fully in us that impact how contemporary Christians live out the forty days of Lent and engage (or fail to engage) the fifty days of Easter. Certainly, this realised-future eschatological tension has existed since the earliest Christians sought to appropriate as mystery what happened in history, embracing the paradox of the cross and rejoicing in God's vindication of the Suffering Servant-Son who became the sacrificed Passover lamb whose blood spares people from death. The Lent-Easter cycle immerses liturgical participants in the paschal mystery, giving them opportunities to hear the foundational kerygma of the Scriptures and receive it through symbol and ritual. Lenten and Holy Week liturgies may deeply *affect* individuals and move them to accompany Christ through death to resurrection accomplished for him on Easter Sunday. But unless people let Christ *effect* them into Christ's risen, ecclesial, and eucharistic body, the liturgies of the Easter season will remain more difficult to engage.

Paschal Piety and Its Myriad Manifestations

If liturgy is first and foremost God's work on behalf of people, then it is no surprise that people and their pious proclivities get involved in the process of recognising and responding to God's saving activity. Liturgy is the common activity of all the baptized, not the preserve of liturgists-by-profession (i.e., ordained clergy and others with specialised training). A potent mix of embodied sacramentals and great Gospel themes draws droves of so-called "CAPE" Christians for ashes, palms, and Easter Sunday, even though they may not darken a church door again until Christmas.[1] Besides the "professionals" who prepare and lead liturgies and "regulars" who always participate year-round, liturgical celebrations during Lent and Holy Week especially attract and serve "movers" who are exploring, renewing, or intensifying their commitment to Christian worshipping communities (including people preparing for baptism and modern-day penitents) while accommodating "watchers" drawn into the orbit of the liturgical action through cultural habit or social obligation.[2] Given their numbers, movers and watchers influence the atmosphere of these significant liturgies as they are impressed (or not) by what happens within them and may over time even contribute to shaping them.

To that end, Kenneth Stevenson identified three pieties or sensibilities manifest in the liturgical meaning of Holy Week—and, by extension, the Lenten liturgies leading up to it and the Easter celebrations

[1] For one exploration of the acronym, see Fritz Bauerschmidt, "M.T.D. and C.A.P.E. Catholics," *Pray Tell* (blog), January 13, 2015, https://www.praytellblog.com/index.php/2015/01/13/m-t-d-and-c-a-p-e-catholics/.

[2] These categories representing ritual "hierarchy" within a worshipping community are described in Lawrence A. Hoffman, *The Art of Public Prayer: Not for Clergy Only*, 2nd ed. (Woodstock, VT: SkyLight Paths, 1999), 99–107.

extending from it.[3] Unitive piety insists on Christ's death and resurrection as *one* mystery and can manage celebrating Christ's death and resurrection together at one liturgy. Early Christians did this with a nightlong vigil either aligning with the Jewish Passover or transferred to the subsequent Sunday that served as their singular annual commemoration of Christ's death *and* resurrection.[4] Although he may not have known an Easter feast, Paul preaches this piety: "For our paschal lamb, Christ, has been sacrificed. Therefore, let us celebrate the festival" (1 Cor 5:7-8; cf. John 1:36; 19:14ff.; 19:32-36). Furthermore, early Christian preachers like Melito of Sardis situated this sacrifice of Christ the paschal lamb within the total context of redemption: "This is the one made flesh in a virgin, who was hanged on a tree, who was buried in the earth, who was raised from the dead, who was exalted to the heights of heaven" (*Peri Pascha* 70).[5] Unitive piety gives rise to religious experiences that are "stark and austere" yet saturated with liturgical symbolism. This piety persists most strongly today in liturgies like the Easter Vigil. There assemblies "pass from death to life with Christ" in light, words, water, and meal.[6] Such liturgies appeal most to the professionals and a self-selected subset of the regulars and can actually *incorporate* some of the movers by baptizing them and welcoming them into the fellowship of the body of Christ, ecclesial and eucharistic.

Rememorative piety stakes salvation history in human history. In its liturgical expression, "certain 'events' are celebrated in a vaguely historical fashion, with symbolism attached to each," in a matrix wherein "liturgy is allowed to find its own ambiance through context

[3] See Kenneth Stevenson, *Jerusalem Revisited: The Liturgical Meaning of Holy Week* (Washington, DC: The Pastoral Press, 1988), 9–12; Michael Perham and Kenneth Stevenson, *Waiting for the Risen Christ: A Commentary on Lent, Holy Week, Easter; Services and Prayers* (London: SPCK, 1986), 3–8.

[4] See Paul F. Bradshaw and Lawrence A. Hoffman, eds., *Passover and Easter: Origin and History to Modern Times* (Notre Dame, IN: University of Notre Dame Press, 1999), and the shorter summary of Easter's origins in Paul F. Bradshaw and Maxwell E. Johnson, *The Origins of Feasts, Fasts, and Seasons in Early Christianity*, Alcuin Club Collections (London/Collegeville, MN: SPCK/Liturgical Press, 2011), 39–59.

[5] ET from Melito of Sardis, *On Pascha*, translated, introduced, and annotated by Alistair C. Stewart (Yonkers, NY: St. Vladimir's Seminary Press, 2016), 71. This homily dates to ca. 165.

[6] Stevenson, *Jerusalem Revisited*, 9.

of scripture reading, geographical association, and continuity."[7] This sort of piety blossomed during the fourth and fifth centuries, the first great era of liturgical consolidation and renewal, and it influenced recent Western liturgical reforms that looked to this perceived "golden age" for inspiration. As the ranks of the post-Nicene church swelled with new members who either accepted the plunge of baptism or lingered long in the catechumenate, the liturgy developed a stronger interest in history and chronology giving us, among other things, the basic shape of the liturgical year as we know it today. The practice of venerating the cross on Good Friday exemplifies rememorative piety. The fourth-century Jerusalem pilgrim Egeria provides the oldest extant documentation; a relic of the wood of the true cross and its inscription are presented to the people who, "bowing at the table, kiss the holy wood and pass through" (*Itinerarium Egeriae* 37.2).[8] While this practice connects Christians with the historical and salvific event of Christ's crucifixion on the day of the church year that commemorates it, there is no attempt toward "re-enactment" of the first-century Roman execution of Jesus of Nazareth. Rememorative piety pairs well with "classical" or "traditional" liturgies. It gives their symbols and rituals a comfortable familiarity inviting engagement on multiple levels (sensory, intellectual, and spiritual) that can be effective at drawing the professionals, regulars, movers, and watchers to worship together, suffusing and sometimes surprising them with the depths of the Mystery of God.

Finally, representational piety revels in dramatic elaboration ostensibly aimed at helping those less mature in their faith find meaning and relevance through what they can see, hear, and sometimes touch. It is "the culmination of the pictorial mind [and] the result of popular piety."[9] This pious impulse flourished in the Middle Ages, inspiring passion plays and Easter pageants and the "burial" of consecrated hosts in temporary tombs on Good Friday.[10] It survives today in

[7] Stevenson, *Jerusalem Revisited*, 9.

[8] Anne McGowan and Paul F. Bradshaw, *The Pilgrimage of Egeria: A New Translation of the Itinerarium Egeriae with Introduction and Commentary*, Alcuin Club Collections 93 (Collegeville, MN: Liturgical Press Academic, 2018), 176.

[9] Stevenson, *Jerusalem Revisited*, 11.

[10] James Monti, *The Week of Salvation: History and Traditions of Holy Week* (Huntington, IN: Our Sunday Visitor, 1993), 26; Rózsa Juhos, "The Sepulchre of Christ in Arts and Liturgy of the Late Middle Ages," *Journal of Historical Archaeology & Anthropological Sciences* 3, no. 3 (2018): 349–57.

devotions like the Stations of the Cross. It persists too in elements absorbed into official liturgies, such as Holy Thursday foot washing (especially when understood and practised as the minister's modelling of Jesus washing the feet of exactly twelve male disciples) and in the "burial" of an image or object representing Christ on Good Friday. Examples of the latter include the *epitaphios* (an ornate cloth icon of Christ's burial venerated in the Byzantine Rite) and a cross wrapped and entombed within the altar (Syriac Orthodox Rite).

Stevenson credits extreme instantiations of representational piety with precipitating the sixteenth-century Reformations of the Western church and ironically persisting despite them. Although ceremonies and rituals that stretched symbol into superstition were eliminated in churches arising from the era of Reformations (sometimes along with most or all of the liturgical year), representative piety transposed itself into other modes beyond liturgical symbolism—such as hymnody—and thus continued to form and inform the experience of worship.[11] Stevenson's assessment aligns with Frank Senn's diagnosis of a prevalent issue in the post-medieval Western Christian tradition: "an affective rather than an effective understanding of memorial." Instead of letting God's word and the dynamism of the rite unite the present liturgical celebration with foundational saving events, Christians often perceive that "making the participant one with the saving event requires a dramatic re-enactment of the original event which elicits a subjective response from the participant."[12]

Elements of all three pieties certainly contribute to the way that individuals and praying communities experience Lent, Holy Week, and Easter. Since the boundaries between liturgy, piety, and life are porous, however, sorting out the predominant piety can be challenging, especially when pressed to distinguish rememorative and representational pieties. A liturgical rite that appears rememorative might be "read" by participants as representational. For example, those who venerate the cross on Good Friday might approach to imagine themselves, for a moment, in the presence of their crucified

[11] See Stevenson, *Jerusalem Revisited*, 11; Perham and Stevenson, *Waiting for the Risen Christ*, 6–7.

[12] Frank C. Senn, "Should Christians Celebrate the Passover?," in *Passover and Easter: The Symbolic Structuring of Sacred Seasons*, ed. Paul F. Bradshaw and Lawrence A. Hoffman, Two Liturgical Traditions, vol. 6 (Notre Dame, IN: University of Notre Dame Press, 1999), 197.

Saviour rather than stretching to touch the instrument of cosmic redemption, a seat of divine enthronement, and/or a sign of Christ's eschatological presence.[13] Similarly, the solemn reading of the passion in multiple voices can tip over into representational theatre, particularly when the assembly assumes the role of the crowd as the drama unfolds, shouting "Crucify him!" on cue.

Coordinating paschal pieties and their myriad meanings is beyond the scope of individual assembly members and liturgical ministers. The ways people prepare and celebrate liturgies may exacerbate potential problems, however, especially between Palm/Passion Sunday and the Ascension. During this period representational piety is most likely to run rampant since the Bible provides such abundant material for stimulating the pious imagination.[14] This becomes a problem for the liturgy and ultimately for the church because the celebration of the liturgy should move people beyond affective connection with the suffering and/or risen Christ to effective engagement as missionary members of Christ's body in the world.

People doing liturgy during Lent, Holy Week, and Easter meet the Bible through selected Scripture readings, preaching that interprets these readings for the contemporary context in which the worshipping community finds itself, and the interplay between Scripture's images, metaphors, and worldview on the one hand and the liturgy's symbols and rituals on the other. The summary explanation that follows will begin with the Triduum liturgies at the heart of Holy Week. Then it will move backwards to consider how Lenten liturgies prepare people for them and finally forwards to explore how the liturgies of the Easter season aim to extend the celebration for a full fifty days and beyond. Examples of liturgy's use of the Bible are drawn from two lectionaries with broad influence directly or indirectly in many Western churches—the Roman Catholic Church's *Lectionary for Mass* and the ecumenical *Revised Common Lectionary*. Members of other churches will nonetheless find some points of continuity since tradi-

[13] Patrick Regan, "Veneration of the Cross," in *Between Memory and Hope: Readings on the Liturgical Year*, ed. Maxwell E. Johnson (Collegeville, MN: Liturgical Press, 2000), 150–52.

[14] Of the 89 chapters in the four Gospels, 29.5 recount events from Jesus' irony-laden triumphal entry into Jerusalem five days before his death until the day when his "disappearance" into heaven culminated a series of post-resurrection appearances.

tion and biblical chronology inform the passages selected from the Bible to be read in the liturgy around Easter.

The Triduum: Three Days of Intense Anamnesis

By the late fourth century, the singular liturgical commemoration of Christ's death *and* resurrection at Easter was starting to stretch over several days in some places. Friday focused on Christ's death, Saturday on his burial and Sabbath "rest," and Sunday on the resurrection.[15] Approaching these three days as a cohesive liturgical-ritual unity, however, may result more from contemporary Western liturgical renewal of the Triduum than a revival of its pervasive perception as such in late antiquity.[16] Even in contemporary practice, the only worshippers who truly experience the Triduum as a unity are the minority who participate in all its major liturgies.

The Easter Vigil

Of the Triduum liturgies, the Vigil above all incarnates unitive piety. "In the Easter Vigil Christ applies the saving power of his death and resurrection to the Church in a privileged way, and the means by which he does this is the very celebration of that death and resurrection by the Church."[17] The extended series of readings from Scripture connects a contemporary Easter vigil to its ancient predecessors and upholds its essential character as a vigil. God's word proclaimed anew leads the Christian assembly to baptism and Eucharist through which they do what Christ commanded and unite themselves more closely to him. The number and content of biblical texts used at the Easter Vigil has varied widely with time and place. Ever since the tradition

[15] Today the Triduum officially extends from Thursday evening to Sunday evening—still covering these same "three days" according to calculations that begin a new day with sunset.

[16] Patrick Regan, *Advent to Pentecost: Comparing the Seasons in the Ordinary and Extraordinary Forms of the Roman Rite* (Collegeville, MN: Liturgical Press, 2012), 78–79; Harald Buchinger, "Was There Ever a Liturgical Triduum in Antiquity? Theological Idea and Liturgical Reality," *Ecclesia Orans* 27, no. 3 (2010): 257–70.

[17] Pierre Jounel, "The Easter Cycle," in *The Church at Prayer: An Introduction to the Liturgy*, ed. Aimé Georges Martimort, new ed., vol. IV (Collegeville, MN: Liturgical Press, 1986), 38–39.

linking baptism and Easter was strongly established in the fourth century, however, the Vigil readings have helped assemblies see and hear God's plan for salvation in Christ unfolding from the beginning, as selections of the Old Testament are read this night through paschal-tinted lenses. At least in late antiquity, the length and number of readings also helped the already-initiated pass the time while baptisms were happening, usually in a separate space nearby.

Current Western lectionaries present a relatively modest number of Old Testament readings, likely a pastoral decision growing out of twentieth-century renewal efforts to promote active participation of the people. There are seven in the *Lectionary for Mass* and nine in the *Revised Common Lectionary*. Readings common to both sets include the first story of creation (Gen 1-2), the near-sacrifice of Isaac (Gen 22), and the crossing of the sea (Exod 14–15), contributing to a typology of the Easter Vigil as the Christian parallel to the Jewish Passover. Exodus 14 especially illuminates a rememorative spark within this unitive liturgy. In the Western tradition, the Vigil readings are read by the light of the paschal candle, lit from the new Easter fire and acclaimed liturgically as "the light of Christ." Not just any utilitarian light source, this tall "column of wax provided a much more vivid and realistic symbol of the pillar of fire that featured prominently at the paschal vigil."[18] This connection finds other echoes in the Easter proclamation (*Exultet*), where it is used, and in the blessing prayer of the baptismal font (which might involve the candle itself passing through the waters).

The Vigil's gospel is the resurrection account proper to the current year's lectionary cycle (Matthew in Year A, Mark in Year B, and Luke in Year C). The epistle (Rom 6:3-11) develops the theme of divine deliverance introduced in the selections from the prophetic books and inundates listeners with a theological interpretation of baptism as a sharing in Christ's death and resurrection that is eminently appropriate for this paschal context, as some are about to be immersed in the waters of chaos, slavery, and death so they might emerge as new creations in Christ.[19] Insofar as the Vigil both recapitulates Lent

[18] A. J. MacGregor, *Fire and Light in the Western Triduum: Their Use at Tenebrae and at the Paschal Vigil*, Alcuin Club Collection 71 (Collegeville, MN: Liturgical Press, 1992), 303.

[19] Normand Bonneau, *The Sunday Lectionary: Ritual Word, Paschal Shape* (Collegeville, MN: Liturgical Press, 1998), 67.

and announces Easter,[20] its internal and symbolic logic—carried mostly through unitive piety—will make most sense to the professionals, the regulars, and those who have been moving intensively toward baptism. Watchers with low levels of biblical and symbolic literacy might find much of the Vigil bewildering or interminable unless well-prepared rites let the liturgy's symbols speak for themselves and preachers connect nature, culture, and the church's tradition in ways that evocatively explore Scripture and symbol without reducing them through formulaic explanations.

Holy Thursday

A Johannine trajectory connects the gospel passages appointed for reading on Holy Thursday (John 13) and Good Friday (John 18–19) with one another and with the Lent and Easter seasons, where John's Gospel predominates. "Having loved his own who were in the world . . . to the end" (John 13:1), Jesus gathers his disciples for a final meal; the next day he dies after declaring from the cross, "It is finished" (John 19:30). Within the contexts of biblical narrative and liturgical celebration, foot washing thus becomes an enacted parable proleptically interpreting the passion; both are acts of self-offering love.[21] In the Last Supper context, Jesus elevates this impetus to "love one another" to the status of a new commandment (*mandatum* in Latin, John 13:34). This verse is included in the gospel lection from the *Revised Common Lectionary*, is featured in the Roman Rite's gospel acclamation and may be the source of the day's designation as Maundy Thursday.[22]

The first reading from Exodus 12 details preparation of the Passover lamb and introduces the image of blood-smeared wood. The second reading proclaims the oldest biblical account of Jesus' words associating bread and his body, cup and his blood (1 Cor 11:23-26). Both these readings, therefore, connect eucharistic imagery with

[20] Laurence Hull Stookey, *Calendar: Christ's Time for the Church* (Nashville: Abingdon Press, 1996), 77.

[21] Barbara E. Reid, "Preaching the Cross of Christ," in *We Preach Christ Crucified*, ed. Michael E. Connors (Collegeville, MN: Liturgical Press, 2014), 106.

[22] An alternative etymology derives "maundy" not from *mandatum* but from *mendicare* (to beg). On various liturgical and extra-liturgical practices of foot washing and/or service to the poor associated with Holy Thursday, see Monti, *Week of Salvation*, 108–17.

Christ's sacrifice on the cross. Thus, the supper "ritually anticipates" Christ's passion, which in turn "fully authenticates" what was said and done at the supper, highlighting the unity of the paschal mystery.[23]

Foot washing done at this liturgy could be framed as either rememorative-anamnetic, (when it leads the washers, the washed, and the witnesses to contemplate their own call to voluntary self-sacrificing love in light of their share in baptismal washing [cf. John 13:8]) or representational-dramatic.[24] Similarly, Christians might engage eucharistic celebration this night as communion in the supper of the crucified and risen Lord or a semi-historicised memorial meal among friends. Those who have recently shared in a Christianised seder meal may go beyond the biblical text and Johannine chronology in viewing the Last Supper as a Passover meal.[25]

Good Friday

The solemn Liturgy of the Word and its proclamation of John's passion ground Good Friday. From John's perspective, Jesus freely lays down his life in love, revealing divine redemption and exaltation all through his arrest, trial, crucifixion, and death. The lengthy solemn intercessions of Good Friday draw the church into prayer for the redemption of the whole world, for which Christ suffered and died. People are emboldened to approach God with confidence since they have a high priest in heaven who intercedes on their behalf (as recounted in the reading from Hebrews 4–5). The fourth song of the Suffering Servant (Isa 52:13–53:12) similarly assures the assembly gathered on Good Friday that the paschal mystery draws in all of creation and that God will meet suffering and death endured in hope with nothing less than unfailing love that redeems. Both the venera-

[23] Bonneau, *Sunday Lectionary*, 72.

[24] On the background of the Western footwashing rite, see Paul Turner, *Glory in the Cross: Holy Week in the Third Edition of the Roman Missal* (Collegeville, MN: Liturgical Press, 2011), 63–65.

[25] On the historical, theological, and interreligious issues involved, see Marianne Moyaert, "Christianizing Judaism?: On the Problem of Christian Seder Meals," in *Is There a Judeo-Christian Tradition? A European Perspective*, ed. Emmanuel Nathan and Anya Topolski, 137–64 (Berlin/Boston: De Gruyter, 2016), and Senn, "Should Christians Celebrate the Passover?"

tion of the cross mentioned earlier and distribution of communion were added to the Roman Rite in the early medieval period.[26] Eastern churches generally did not include communion from presanctified gifts on Good Friday but did develop liturgies honouring Christ's burial.[27] In some Latin American traditions, *El Pésame* (condolences) honours the Blessed Mother bereft of her only son, providing a representational outlet for expressions of grief through popular piety.

Easter Sunday

The celebration of Easter, once concluding with the end of the Vigil, expanded into Sunday at least by the fourth century, acquiring a separate daytime eucharistic liturgy and a solemn form of Vespers. The principle of progressive solemnity dictates that Easter is celebrated as a *big* Sunday. Aside from festivity in music, adornment of the worship space, eucharistic celebration, and so on, however, the liturgy is much like any other Sunday. Some churches might add a ritual renewal of baptism (or actual baptism), and the Roman Rite includes a sequence sung between the second reading and gospel, which is John's resurrection account. (The *Revised Common Lectionary* presents the current year's synoptic gospel resurrection account as an alternative.) Easter Sunday morning also inaugurates the Easter season tradition of hearing a selection from the Acts of the Apostles as the liturgy's first reading. On this day so focused on Jesus' resurrection and so filled with CAPE Christians, preachers might make a special effort to emphasise that what is already accomplished in Christ is still unfolding in us and the church so that Easter will emerge as a beginning as well as an ending.

Easter liturgies, however, were not always such straightforward celebrations. The Gospels recount Easter Sunday events from dawn to dusk: women prepared to anoint a dead body at first light are derailed from their task by an empty tomb and a surprising message; Jesus meets women disciples and discouraged disciples and terrified disciples; Jesus breaks bread with them and shares his Spirit. Supplied

[26] Jounel, "Easter Cycle," 49–51.

[27] Elena Velkova Velkovska, "The Liturgical Year in the East," in *Handbook for Liturgical Studies: Liturgical Time and Space*, vol. V, ed. Anscar J. Chupungco (Collegeville, MN: Liturgical Press, 2000), 168–72.

with such evocative material, medieval Christian liturgies dramatised various aspects of the resurrection appearances.[28] Cathedrals and monasteries staged the *visitatio sepulchri* or *officium sepulchri* (office of the tomb) often featuring multiple Marys encountering an empty tomb, angel(s), and eventually the risen Jesus. (Jesus' mother Mary gets a part in these plays not documented in any gospel account!) One core component, the *Quem quaeritis* dialogue, may have emerged as a ceremony attached to the beginning or end of a pre-Mass procession that migrated into Mass itself in some places.[29] It springs from the question, "For whom are you looking?" that the risen Jesus asks Mary Magdalene alone in John 20:15. The *officium peregrinorum* portrayed the Emmaus encounter and was often placed within or at the end of Vespers on Easter evening.

This representational piety is nonetheless decidedly *liturgical* drama. It engages biblical-liturgical content; note, for example the resonance between *Quem quaeritis* and the Easter sequence of the Roman Rite. Originally, liturgical ministers were the "actors," and the set and costumes incorporated elements from liturgical use (e.g., altar, vestments, the Easter sepulchre. Anscar Chupungco observes, "Their place in the framework of the liturgy can be compared to the so-called explanatory rites of the celebration of the sacraments and sacramentals, except that they are in the form of drama."[30]

This comparison begs a question that Chupungco also asks: Among the Triduum liturgies, might the Easter Sunday liturgy especially make a little *more* room for forms of representational mimesis in drama, art, or symbol appropriate for our own times? If these forms emerged from local churches and cultures and resonated with a broad group of actual and potential liturgical participants, they would serve the original purpose of representational piety and perhaps encourage at least some occasional worshippers seeking a singular encounter

[28] Some thorough studies in English include Karl Young, *The Drama of the Medieval Church*, 2 vols. (Oxford: Clarendon Press, 1962); O. B. Hardison, *Christian Rite and Christian Drama in the Middle Ages: Essays in the Origin and Early History of Modern Drama* (Baltimore: Johns Hopkins Press, 1965); and Dunbar H. Ogden, *The Staging of Drama in the Medieval Church* (Newark, DE: University of Delaware Press, 2003).

[29] Timothy J. McGee, "The Liturgical Placements of the 'Quem Quaeritis' Dialogue," *Journal of the American Musicological Society* 29, no. 1 (1976): 1–29.

[30] Anscar J. Chupungco, *Liturgies of the Future: The Process and Methods of Inculturation* (New York: Paulist Press, 1989), 180.

with the risen Christ on Easter Sunday to return throughout the Easter season to encounter this same Christ again in the church. Dialogue and discernment could ensure that mimetic practices served the liturgy without getting "out of hand" as Stevenson fears they might.[31] Some practices sprung first from popular piety already touch the liturgy tangentially or actually. One example is the *procesión de encuentro*, which supplements the scriptural resurrection appearances with a meeting between the risen Jesus and his mourning mother. In the Philippines, this holy encounter (*salubong*) now serves as the official entrance rite of Easter Sunday Mass.[32]

Lent: A Season of Repentance and Redemption

The significance attached to Lent's "forty days" is scriptural, resonating with many references to God accomplishing something significant over forty days or years—in a flood (Gen 7:12, 17; 8:6), with Moses on Mount Sinai (Exod 24:18), with Israel in the desert (Num 14:33-34; 32:13; Ps 95:10), with Elijah's journey (1 Kgs 19:8); with Nineveh's timeframe for repentance (Jonah 3:4); and with Jesus' post-baptismal period of prayer, fasting, and temptation (Mark 1:13; Matt 4:2; Luke 4:2). Historically, Lent was also a sufficient time for final baptismal preparation, and thus it still functions today with the restoration of the catechumenate for adults.[33] Modern Western liturgical reforms have sought to recover the dual focus of Lent on baptism and penitence. Until the final days of Lent, the liturgy and the lectionary do not focus extensively on Christ's suffering and death. Fundamentally, "this season engages us in the process of confronting who we are by nature, who we are by God's purpose and redeeming action, and what we can become by divine grace."[34] Meanwhile, Lenten devotions emphasising passion piety, like the Stations of the Cross, may heighten penitents' affective attraction to redemption in Christ who stands in solidarity with their own suffering, thus intersecting

[31] Perham and Stevenson, *Waiting for the Risen Christ*, 8.

[32] Chupungco, *Liturgies of the Future*, 181.

[33] For a concise historical overview, see Bradshaw and Johnson, *Origins*, 89–108; Martin Connell, *Eternity Today: On the Liturgical Year*, vol. 2 (New York: Continuum, 2006), 60–75.

[34] Stookey, *Calendar*, 88.

with some (but not all) of Lent's primary concerns. Without accompanying conversion to deeper engagement in communities of faith where they can experience the ongoing dying and rising of Christ, devotions by themselves probably will not carry people far beyond Lent's perceived finish line.

Ash Wednesday

Many Western Christians are marked with ashes as they mark the beginning of Lent. The origins of this practice lie in a stational procession with a sung antiphon "Let us change our garments to sackcloth and ashes" (cf. Joel 2:17, Esth 4:1-3). Later this concept was enacted by penitents who were "cast out" of churches after donning sackcloth and receiving ashes, involved in "a liturgical drama, the enactment of the expulsion from Paradise and the first steps of the long journey of reconciliation with God."[35] Ashes have been imposed on the heads of anyone wishing to receive them since the twelfth century, often with the formula, "Remember that you are dust, and to dust you shall return," which draws on God's address to Adam in Genesis 3:19. Having confronted mortality, people are primed to participate in the Lenten disciplines of prayer, fasting, and almsgiving—even if they might absent themselves from most or all of its other liturgies (perhaps because they have heeded the call to repentance individually but not yet collectively).[36] Current readings for Ash Wednesday are from Joel 2, 2 Corinthians 5–6, and Matthew 6:1-6, 16-18.

Sundays of Lent

In the West, the beginning of Lent alludes obliquely to Jesus' death and resurrection by sharing stories of his temptation and transfiguration. Roman Catholics hear these gospel accounts according to Matthew, Mark, and Luke (in Years A, B, and C, respectively) on Lent's first two Sundays. The *Revised Common Lectionary* presents transfiguration accounts as alternative passages for the Second Sunday of Lent since many churches that use it have just celebrated Transfiguration

[35] Regan, *Advent to Pentecost*, 80–81.

[36] Bruce T. Morrill, "Faith's Unfinished Business: Can the Easter Season's Mysticism Empower Ethical Praxis?," *Proceedings of the North American Academy of Liturgy*, 2019, 13–14.

Sunday on the last Sunday *before* Lent. The third, fourth, and fifth Sundays of Lent also form a gospel grouping with a different orientation each year but dominated by readings from the Fourth Gospel. Year A features three Johannine readings traditionally used during the course of baptismal preparation in the Roman West: the Samaritan woman at the well (John 4), the healing of the man born blind (John 9), and the raising of Lazarus (John 11). Year B includes three other Johannine passages pointing to Christ's paschal mystery through kenosis and exaltation, and Year C emphasises the general Lenten themes of penance and conversion with two more excerpts from John's Gospel and one selection from Luke 15 (the Prodigal Son on the fourth Sunday).

The Old Testament readings for the first five Sundays of Lent follow a sequence of their own, emphasising key events in salvation history: (1) God in relationship with primeval people; (2) God's covenant with Abraham; (3) God's interactions with Moses; (4) Israel's history between Exodus and Exile; and (5) hope-filled prophetic words to exiled Israelites about God's eschatological plans. Only the fourth step in this sequence is without parallel at the Easter Vigil.[37] The apostolic writings (primarily from the Pauline epistles) function during Lent as they do throughout the year. They give glimpses of early Christian grappling with the paschal mystery and inspire ongoing engagement in faith. Taken together, the Lenten Sunday Scripture readings offer the already-baptized and the not-yet-baptized an extended meditation on what it means individually and collectively to die and rise with Christ.

Palm/Passion Sunday

The Sixth Sunday of Lent in the West inherits two traditions, palms and passion; individual churches and denominations might focus on one or both of these themes. As the Methodist liturgical scholar Lawrence Hull Stookey noted, however, churches that celebrate Jesus' palm-paved entry into Jerusalem with unrelenting triumph do their congregations a disservice insofar as they allow worshippers who might not participate in any intervening services, especially those of Good Friday, to skip straight from "Hosanna!" to "He is risen!" In

[37] Bonneau, *Sunday Lectionary*, 104.

keeping with biblical integrity, "[t]he church is constrained to insist that there is no route to an empty tomb except by way of the cross."[38]

Connecting history and biblical chronology, a procession with palms originated in Jerusalem, spread throughout the Christian East, and was eventually adopted in the West in the Middle Ages. A preliminary rite proclaiming Jesus' triumphant entry into Jerusalem was fused to the beginning of the liturgy, where the primary [Roman] gospel reading was the passion. This introductory rite was ritualised representationally into a procession with palms, sometimes including an object of devotional focus such as a representation of Christ on a donkey (*Palmesel* or *Palmchristus*), a cross or crucifix, the gospel book, the Blessed Sacrament, or even saints' relics.[39]

Current Western lectionaries pair the gospel of the liturgy's preliminary palm rite (retelling Jesus' entry into Jerusalem) with the passion narrative, hearing the perspectives of Matthew, Mark, and Luke in a three-year rotation. The other two readings are fixed. The Old Testament reading from the third song of the Suffering Servant (Isa 50) complements the first reading from Isaiah 52–53 on Good Friday. The second reading is the great christological hymn from Philippians 2, which explicitly encourages assemblies to identify Jesus with the Suffering Servant at the outset of Holy Week. Around this time, the attention of those who have been participating in Lent wholeheartedly, half-heartedly, or hardly at all intensifies as Lent becomes in its final days the journey of a repenting church on its way to dying and rising (again) with Christ during three days.

Easter: A Season of Encountering Christ in the Church

Easter Sunday is the last day of the Triduum and the first of the great fifty-day season of Easter. If church attendance is any indication, the forty-nine days after Easter Sunday are far less enticing. This is ironic because New Testament texts proclaiming the early church's understanding of Christ as the crucified and risen One provide a foundation for the central activities Christians have been doing ever since: baptizing and teaching (Matt 28:19), breaking open the Scriptures in the context of meals (e.g., Luke 24:30-32), calling on Christ

[38] Stookey, *Calendar*, 89.

[39] Monti, *Week of Salvation*, 44; Jounel, "Easter Cycle," 71.

in prayer with faith and confidence, and preaching Christ crucified and risen.[40] For those still regularly engaged in the church's liturgy, Easter is a season to incorporate the newly-baptized and the time when the whole church can aspire to live into the fullness of their Christian initiation. Having completed forty days of preparation, they are primed for fifty days of participation.[41]

The Sunday lectionary in the Easter season juxtaposes not just individual pericopes but entire biblical books. John's sweeping theological understanding of salvation history unfolding from "the beginning" (John 1:1) suffuses the season's gospel selections. The concern of the author of Luke-Acts for an "orderly account" of events (Luke 1:1) guides the ecclesiological focus presented in passages from the Acts of the Apostles.[42] The liturgy's first readings from the first half of Acts help the listening church understand how the church came to be. Meanwhile, the New Testament epistles help believers understand how they are to be the church with one another and in the world; these readings are primarily from 1 Peter (Year A), 1 John (Year B), and Revelation (Year C). The gospel readings (mostly from John, as in Lent) shed light on the glory of the risen Christ always shining within history and still supporting the church.

Like Lent, the Easter gospels group according to "themes." The second and third Sundays present additional appearances of the risen Christ. Assemblies invariably find Jesus meeting Thomas's doubts (John 20:24-29) on the second Sunday and sharing a meal with his followers on the third Sunday. The Paschal Lamb declares himself the Good Shepherd on the fourth Sunday, with John 10 read in three parts over the three-year lectionary cycle. The fifth through to the seventh Sundays of Easter feature excerpts from Jesus' farewell discourses at the Last Supper (John 14–17). As time passes linearly between Easter and Pentecost, the chronology of the gospel readings does not; nonetheless, the Sunday assembly appropriates its identity as the body of the risen Lord when gathered for word and sacrament in time with implications beyond time.[43]

[40] Gordon W. Lathrop, *Central Things: Worship in Word and Sacrament*, Worship Matters (Minneapolis: Augsburg Fortress, 2005), 29.

[41] Fritz West, *Scripture and Memory: The Ecumenical Hermeneutic of the Three-Year Lectionaries* (Collegeville, MN: Liturgical Press, 1997), 90.

[42] West, *Scripture and Memory*, 107.

[43] See Bonneau, *Sunday Lectionary*, 83–85.

With its rich feast of striking stories and exhortations to live more deeply into the mystery of Christ, why is Easter overall *not* more appealing? Bruce Morrill posits that "the fifty days of Easter flags in its long run because, unlike its shorter partner, the forty days of Lent, its terminus, its ending, is actually, paradoxically, an eschatological opening."[44] Jesus is risen indeed and the Spirit has come, but all of creation is not yet redeemed. The church's members are called to continue the mission of proclaiming Christ's resurrection from the dead as the foundation of their faith and hope in God's will to redeem all that is.

The Spirit began its work after the first Easter by remaking the community of Jesus' followers (John 20:19-23). The Spirit continues this work by effectively remaking Christians into Christ's Body, the church. The many Sundays of the Easter season provide opportunities to let God *effect* this work through engaging more deeply and intentionally with some of the season's central symbols that speak to ongoing incorporation of believers into the dying and rising of Christ. This would require little beyond deliberate, embodied attention to what is inherently available already in Easter liturgies. Touch or sprinkle the baptismal water that births and washes Christians into Christ's new life. Renew baptismal promises with boldness. Celebrate richly the Eucharist that initiates Christians again and again into the Body of Christ and is in every season a foretaste of the wedding feast of the Paschal Lamb. Reverence the people who are the local church's newest sacraments *this* Easter season, God's holy word written now in the lives of faithful people patterning their lives after the paschal mystery. Adapt the ancient tradition of mystagogical preaching, inviting people to consider their faith anew and discover new depths in it.

Ascension and Pentecost

Ascension and Pentecost were celebrated together until the late fourth or early fifth century, an arrangement which makes logical sense with Jesus' ascent as the prelude for the Spirit's descent. The singular feast split to honour the chronology of Acts: Ascension on the fortieth day post-resurrection (1:3) and Pentecost on the fiftieth

[44] Morrill, "Faith's Unfinished Business," 10.

(2:1). Unfortunately, finer focus hampered the feasts' accessibility. As Martin Connell cautions, "concentration on historical chronology resulting in a diminution of the community's recognition of the life of God in its own life is always a problem, and to that extent the historicisation would eventually become an impediment to faith." Once it became more difficult to see Ascension and Pentecost as integral parts of the resurrection, "narratives linked in a larger season of paschal joy for the church's renewal," the temptation to diminish the festivity of the days between them began almost immediately.[45] Fasting broke up the fifty days of feasting. By the later Middle Ages, it became customary to extinguish the Easter candle after the gospel of the Ascension had been read, representing the "departure" of Christ's visible presence on earth.[46] In more recent times, "Ascension Thursday" has become a movable feast. Some churches that celebrate it choose to transfer its observance to the following Sunday for pastoral reasons, displacing the Seventh Sunday of Easter. Ascension Thursday's Easter season call to collective conversion in Christ with its cosmic implications is clearly not as captivating as Ash Wednesday's invitation to confront death.[47] The current Roman Rite includes a seldom-used extended Pentecost Vigil with four Old Testament readings modelled after the Easter Vigil.

The readings for both Ascension and Pentecost are logical choices. For the Ascension, Acts 1 is always read alongside a shorter farewell or ascension account from Matthew, Mark, or Luke. On Pentecost, Acts 2, about the coming of the Spirit on what was *already* Pentecost for the Jewish people, is accompanied by John's account of a new community created on Easter evening through the inbreathing of the Spirit (John 20:19-23) in Year A. (The *Revised Common Lectionary* also suggests John 7:37-39, which the Roman Catholic *Lectionary for Mass* appoints for reading at the Vigil Mass or the Extended Vigil.) Years B and C admit other selections from John about the promised Paraclete. Pentecost sums up the Easter season as the church's living into the newness of the resurrection that created it as a community, a task it is called to continue until the Eschaton.

[45] Connell, *Eternity Today*, vol. 2, 178. For an extended reflection on Ascension's theological importance, see Stookey, *Calendar*, 67–72.

[46] MacGregor, *Fire and Light*, 396–400.

[47] Morrill, "Faith's Unfinished Business," 11.

For the vast majority of Christians through the ages who were *not* there when the Lord was crucified and who believe without having touched or seen the risen Christ with their bodily eyes, their primary mode of access to the fundamental saving mysteries must be non-historical. Relying on the pentecostal gift of the Paraclete whose passion for unity is undeterred by spatial or temporal separation of entities that belong in relationship, the ecclesial Body of Christ conforms itself to the paschal pattern of suffering, death, and eventually resurrection. Nonetheless, certain developments in liturgical history at the intersection of Scripture, liturgy, and popular piety have conspired to make it easier for most Christians to keep faith by fighting and finishing during the "acceptable time" of Lent's limited length (cf. 2 Tim 4:7; 2 Cor 6:2) than to embrace the Easter season's expansive mission of what the church and Christians within it are called to be, in Christ, forever.

Chapter 5

Light in the Darkness: Advent to Candlemas

David Kennedy

Introduction

The incarnational period of the church year, beginning in Advent, extending through the Christmas and Epiphany seasons, and concluding with Candlemas, provides a rich quarry of biblical material for reflection and proclamation through liturgical celebration. As well as the centrality of the infancy narratives of Matthew and Luke and the theological reflection of the Johannine prologue, during this period the reading of the Hebrew Scriptures and particularly the prophetic tradition has come to the fore. This presents hermeneutical challenges and issues. The infancy narratives themselves are complex, with diverse scholarly opinions of the relationship between history and myth or parable, between fact and theological interpretation.[1] The use of the Hebrew Scriptures varies even in the two New Testament infancy accounts. Biblical scholars recognize that Matthew's narrative employs "prediction-fulfilment'" formulae. In the words of Borg and Crossan, "Matthew's testimony to Jesus as the fulfilment

[1] See, for example, the comment of Davies and Alison on Matthew's narrative in Dale C. Allison Jr., ed., *Matthew: A Shorter Commentary; Based on the Three-Volume International Commentary W. D. Davies and Dale C. Allison* (London: T&T Clark, 2004), 19.

of prophecy treats specific texts from the Old Testament as if they were predictions of Jesus."[2] This itself is a recognition that Matthew was writing for his own community, "for Jews who already believed that Jesus was the Messiah."[3] Luke, by contrast, cites no explicit Old Testament passage in his account. Luke's methodology is to cast in narrative form "the continuity of Jesus with Israel and his fulfilment to God's promises to Israel,"[4] especially in his use of three "hymns," the *Benedictus*, *Magnificat*, and *Nunc Dimittis*. These contrasting methodologies testify to ancient Christian conviction that Jesus is "the embodiment of Israel's history;"[5] that Christianity arose in the context of the unfolding story and hope of Israel, bound up with the promise of the coming of Messiah and the in-breaking of God's kingdom in judgment and salvation. The coming of Christ, therefore, resonates with many of the salvific themes of the Hebrew Bible. This New Testament legacy of fulfilment and theological association has continued down the ages as the church has sought to "see Jesus in relationship to the ancient Scriptures of the Jewish tradition."[6] This is well expressed by John Baldovin, who insists that:

> the Bible is always interpretation, not the mere recounting of facts. It is always in some sense theology . . ., the Bible is the product of the primitive church's experience of what it means to live with the risen Jesus of Nazareth as the focus of human existence.[7]

It is this association of such themes and resonances that gives the worship of this period of the year its particular character, bound up with great images of light shining out of darkness, of the birth of a

[2] Marcus J. Borg and John Dominic Crossan, *The First Christmas: What the Gospels Really Teach about Jesus' Birth* (London: SPCK, 2008), 200.

[3] Borg and Crossan, *First Christmas*, 210, 211.

[4] Borg and Crossan, *First Christmas*, 212.

[5] Raymond E. Brown, *A Coming Christ in Advent: Essays on the Gospel Narratives Preparing for the Birth of Jesus (Matthew 1 and Luke 1)* (Collegeville, MN: Liturgical Press, 1988), 12. See also Brown's *The Birth of the Messiah: A Commentary on the Infancy Narratives in Matthew and Luke* (London: Geoffrey Chapman, 1977), 96–104, and J. Neil Alexander, *Waiting for the Coming: The Liturgical Meaning of Advent, Christmas, Epiphany* (Washington, DC: The Pastoral Press, 1993), 33–36.

[6] Borg and Crossan, *First Christmas*, 211.

[7] John F. Baldovin, SJ, *Worship, City, Church and Renewal* (Washington DC: The Pastoral Press, 1991), 213.

child of promise, a new king of righteousness and peace as "great David's greater Son,"[8] and so of a new dawn for the human race in the coming of Christ, the "sun of righteousness" (Mal 4:2).

Advent

The Western season of Advent is complex. In current church observance it embraces both strong eschatological themes around the *parousia* or "appearance," commonly referred to as the "second coming" of Christ, as well as preparation for the festival of Christmas.

In the *Revised Common Lectionary*, this is borne out by the sequence of readings for the principal Sunday service. Advent 1 is overtly eschatological with gospel readings drawn from the apocalyptic passages of the coming of the Son of Man (Matt 24:36-44; Mark 13:24-37; Luke 21:25-36).[9] Advent 2 and 3 focus on John the Baptist: Advent 2 on the Baptist as forerunner with the call to "prepare the way of the Lord," and Advent 3 on the ministry of John anticipating the revealing of Jesus as the Christ. The former theme of "preparing the way" is often linked with the contemporary call to the church to prepare the way for the *parousia*. Advent 4 is directly related to the proximity of Christmas with the annunciation narratives in Luke and Matthew. The other readings for these weeks straddle this double focus, with Old Testament prophetic oracles which could be interpreted both in relation to Christmas *and* the coming of the "Day of the Lord," while the predominantly Pauline New Testament lections relate to anticipation of Christ's expected imminent return in judgment and salvation in the earliest Christian communities.

This tension between these two polarities of the Lord's "coming" runs through the history of this season. Contemporary scholarship suggests that the origins of Advent in Rome were strongly eschatological, and that in a linear sense, Advent marked the end of the civil

[8] James Montgomery, "Hail to the Lord's Anointed" (1821), *Ancient and Modern: Hymns and Songs for Refreshing Worship* (London: Hymns Ancient and Modern, 2013), no. 99.

[9] This concludes eschatological lectionary themes in the Sundays immediately before Advent. See Kenneth W. Stevenson, *Watching and Waiting: A Guide to the Celebration of Advent* (Norwich: The Canterbury Press, 2007), 3–8, for a brief historical summary.

year by contemplating the end of all things.[10] So, the proximity to Christmas is "more accidental than deliberate."[11] However, the establishment of the Festival of Christmas on 25 December in the West inevitably affected the nature and understanding of Advent over time. Another important factor, also of ancient pedigree, was the establishment in the East, but also in some parts of the West, of a period of fasting and preparation before the celebration of baptisms at Epiphany. Martin J. Connell separates out three basic yet interrelated traditions from this complexity—the first scripturally based on the Gospel infancy narratives; second, ascetic, associated with baptismal preparation and penitence; and third, eschatological.[12] From the complexities of Western liturgical history and the development of the medieval liturgy "rich in antiphons, versicles, responsories, graduals, sequences, tracts, alleluias and tropes,"[13] Martin Dudley identifies five Advent "voices": *In illa dies*, the eschatological voice; *vox clamantis*, the penitential voice; *O Adonai*, the expectant voice; *Ave gratia plena*, the angelic voice , and *Veni, Domine*, the imploring voice.[14] These voices draw on the biblical lections, but also the many allusions to diverse biblical texts that appear in the various devotional enrichments. While Dudley seeks to show how first the Reformation and then modern liturgical reform have either silenced or diminished the clarity of these voices,[15] it can be observed that they are reflected in the Advent section of hymnals, and in many forms of contemporary Advent intercessions and prayers.

Hence, we find in contemporary liturgical celebration, including hymnody, strands that have been woven together—including salvation, judgment, penitence, joyful anticipation, and expectant wait-

[10] Paul F. Bradshaw and Maxwell E. Johnson, *The Origin of Feasts, Fasts and Seasons in Early Christianity*, Alcuin Club Collections 86 (London: SPCK, 2011), 165, 166.

[11] Bradshaw and Johnson, *Origin of Feasts*, 168.

[12] Martin J. Connell, "The Origins and Evolution of Advent in the West," in *Between Memory and Hope: Readings on the Liturgical Year*, ed. Maxwell E. Johnson, 351 (Collegeville, MN: Liturgical Press, 2000). See also Martin Connell, *Eternity Today: On the Liturgical Year, Volume 1* (New York/London: Continuum, 2006), 57–67.

[13] Martin Dudley, "Vox clara: The Liturgical Voice in Advent and Christmas," in *Like a Two-Edged Sword: The Word of God in Liturgy and History; Essays in Honour of Canon Donald Gray*, ed. Martin Dudley, 74 (Norwich: Canterbury Press, 1995).

[14] Dudley, "Vox clara," 75–80.

[15] Dudley, "Vox clara," 75, 82–87.

ing—centred around a unitive understanding of three comings: the Christ who came at the incarnation, who comes to his church in word and sacrament, and who will come as universal Lord when the kingdom of God is revealed in fullness.[16] The inculturation of the season in Europe with its position at the end of the civil year, yet marking the beginning of the church year, brings into the spirituality of Advent in the northern hemisphere the themes of the onset of winter and the shortening of the days with the dominance of darkness over light, with the anticipation of the winter solstice and the solar associations with christological themes, as Christ is acclaimed as the light that banishes darkness.

All of these themes and resonances offer considerable scope for the use of the Bible in Advent liturgy. The Church of England directory on the liturgical year, *Common Worship: Times and Seasons*, includes various patterns of readings for carol services in Advent and Christmas, (first published in an earlier directory of resources *The Promise of his Glory*).[17] So, for Advent, four specimen patterns of readings are given. They all adopt the pattern of five Old Testament readings with accompanying psalmody, a New Testament reading followed by a canticle, and a concluding gospel. The compilers of these sequences sought to move away from eclectic choices of lections to a thematically based compilation that has a higher degree of theological cohesion and integrity. One aim of the compilers was to seek to "restore the distinctive eschatological thrust of Advent,"[18] and to challenge the approach to special Advent services that have had "too much of the feel of a first Christmas carol Service about them."[19]

[16] For an exposition of the themes of "three comings" in the teaching of St. Bernard of Clairvaux (1090–1153), see Connell, *Eternity Today 1*, 53–57.

[17] Archbishops' Council of the Church of England, *Common Worship: Times and Seasons* (London: Church House Publishing, 2006), 46, 47. A rubric states that these "sequences may be shortened or varied according to local circumstances and a sermon may be preached" (46). See also *The Promise of His Glory: Services and Prayers for the Season from All Saints to Candlemas* (London: Mowbray/Church House Publishing, 1991), 22–26. These patterns of readings are envisaged as part of a vigil or carol service. However, they are easily adapted for other forms of non-sacramental worship.

[18] Michael Perham and Kenneth Stevenson, *Welcoming the Light of Christ: A Commentary on The Promise of His Glory; Services and Prayers for the Season from All Saints to Candlemas* (London: SPCK, 1991), 91.

[19] Perham and Stevenson, *Welcoming the Light*, 93.

Two examples will illustrate this attempt to be more theologically cohesive. The first is related to the theology of Matthew's Gospel. Helpfully, the compilers provide alternative gospels, one eschatologically orientated and one Christmas orientated depending on when in Advent the liturgy is celebrated.

The King and His Kingdom[20]

Zechariah 9:9-10	Psalm 72:1-8	*Rejoice greatly, your king comes to you*
Jeremiah 23:5-6	Psalm 21:1-7	*I will raise up for David a righteous branch*
Psalm 118:19-29	Psalm 24	*Open to me the gates of righteousness*
Isaiah 9:2, 6, 7	Psalm 28:7-10	*The people that walked in darkness have seen a great light*
Isaiah 7:10-15	Psalm 132:10-16	*Behold a virgin shall conceive and bear a son*
Romans 12:1-2; 13:(8), 11-14	*Te Deum*	*Salvation is nearer to us now than when we first believed*
Gospel in Advent	Matthew 25:1-13	*Keep awake for you know neither the day nor the hour*
Gospel at Christmas	Matthew 1:18-25	*An angel tells Joseph of the coming birth of Jesus*

Here, specific Matthean themes such as the kingship of Christ, his Davidic lineage and the title Emmanuel are reflected, all of which are cited in the gospel narrative. Romans 13 picks up the darkness/light imagery of Isaiah 9, and the gospel reading for Advent is the parable of the wise and foolish bridesmaids.

[20] *Times and Seasons*, 46.

The second example is an extended biblical meditation on the theme of light:

Looking for the Light[21]

Genesis 1:1-5	Psalm 136:1-9	*And God said: Let there be light*
Psalm 13	Psalm 43	*Give light to my eyes, lest I sleep in death*
Isaiah 45:2-8	Psalm 97	*I form light and create darkness*
Baruch 4:36–5:9 *or* Isaiah 60:1-5a	Psalm 84:8-12	*Look to the east*
Isaiah 9:2-3, 6, 7	Psalm 36:5-10	*The people that walked in darkness have seen a great light*
1 Thessalonians 5:1-11, 23-24	Song of the New Jerusalem (from Isa 60)	*You are not in darkness, for you are children of light*
Gospel	Luke 12:35-40	*Let your loins be girded and your lamps burning*
or	John 3:16-21	*I am the light of the world*

This selection of readings is well suited to an Advent "darkness to light" stational or processional liturgy. The Isaiah 9 passage resonates with the incarnation, while the gospel looks to the eschaton.

The tension between eschatological and incarnational focus is surely reduced if at least the first half of Advent, preceding *O Sapientia*, keeps the eschatological and ascetic emphases outlined by Connell. In one English cathedral, the Advent procession held at the *beginning* of Advent focused on the prayer "Thy Kingdom come." As such, it

[21] *Times and Seasons*, 47. Other patterns are "The forerunner," 46, and "A vigil for prisoners and those who sit in darkness," 47. *The Promise of His Glory* also gives expression to the ascetic/eschatological emphases including a rite exploring the "Last Four Things," death, judgment, heaven, and hell; the Advent antiphons, "The Great Os"; and other penitential resources, 102–27.

reflected the strongly eschatological nature of Advent 1. The experiential context was high, with the congregation sitting in a pitch-black church in stillness, experiencing darkness and disorientation and the themes of watching and waiting. Like many such services, it is a dramatic movement from west to east and from darkness to light. The lections sought to express the juxtaposition of realism and hope. After the familiar Matin Responsory and Bidding Prayer, the first reading from Amos 5:18-21, 23-24 warns of the Day of the Lord being darkness, not light and of God's rejection of external religion. This is followed by Micah 6:6-8 and the divine requirement for justice. Thus the service has a strong penitential tone while "darkness" still dominates. Only as light begins to spread are prophetic oracles from Isaiah 35 and 40 then read, introducing the hope of redemption and renewal. As the action moves further east and light increases, the eschatological emphasis is heightened as the challenging parable of the sheep and the goats is read. Finally, at the east and as the church is flooded with light, is the hope of the new Jerusalem proclaimed from Revelation 21:22-24; 22:1-5. Here, the incarnation is given only tangential reference, through Advent hymnody (which itself often holds together the two "comings" of Christ in poetic tension) and anthems, one or two of which were chosen from the reflective Christmas corpus as the procession reached the east of the cathedral, but this was done subtly. The liturgy is thus a stark mix of comfort and challenge. In past years, after rejoicing in the light of the promised New Jerusalem, the lights were again dimmed to half-light, to express the truth that as yet, God's ultimate purposes in Christ are not yet fulfiled. We still need to pray "Thy Kingdom come" in a world of light and shade and where in places darkness is dark indeed.

By contrast, the Advent carol liturgy from the United Methodist Church of the US focusses on the prophets with an incarnational rather than eschatological climax.[22] Here Advent is viewed as a period of preparation for Christmas and the temporal in-breaking of the kingdom of God in Jesus' public ministry:

[22] *The United Methodist Book of Worship* (Nashville: The United Methodist Publishing House, 1992), 263–65.

Isaiah 40:1-8	*To God's people in a faraway land, the prophet Isaiah announces good news: God is coming back, and bringing the exiles home!*
Jeremiah 23:5-6	*The prophet Jeremiah offers hope for a righteous branch, a just king who is yet to come*
Zechariah 9:9-10	*To a nation weary of war and weapons, God promises a king who will establish a reign of peace*
Haggai 2:6-9	*The prophet Haggai promises to God's people a temple even more glorious than the temple of old*
Isaiah 35:1-6	*The prophet Isaiah announces the renewal both of the land and of God's people on the coming day of redemption*
Luke 1:26-35, 38	*The angel Gabriel announces to the virgin Mary that she will give Birth to a ruler whose reign shall never end*
Mark 1:1-15	*Jesus proclaims the coming of the Kingdom of God*

Perhaps Advent 3 or 4 would be the fitting time for this incarnation-focussed rite. The order could easily be adapted by using final lections from Matthew's Gospel that quote the prophetic tradition; for example, Matthew 1:18-25, citing Isaiah 7:14, could replace the annunciation reading, or Matthew 4:12-17, citing Isaiah 8:23-9:2,[23] could replace Mark 1.

Similarly, the Episcopal Church provides a Festival of Lessons and Music for Advent and Christmas, both adapted from the King's College, Cambridge pattern. A recension of the Bidding Prayer composed by Eric Milner-White is given for both, signifying that the Advent order also has preparation for Christmas as its object.[24] The Advent pattern of readings (from which a selection is taken) begins with two readings from Genesis (creation and fall), with ten prophetic lections (and a reading from Baruch). Significantly, a rubric states that a gospel reading is optional, suggesting either the annunciation to Zechariah

[23] Isaiah 8:23 in the Hebrew Bible is 9:1 in English translations. Matthew renders the Hebrew with some vocabulary similarities to the LXX equivalent (numbered 9:1-2), see David Hill, ed., *The Gospel of Matthew*, New Century Bible (London: Oliphants, 1972), 104.

[24] See below (p. 85) for a fuller discussion of the design of the King's College Carol Service.

or the annunciation to Mary. So, unusually, this service could be drawn entirely from the Hebrew Scriptures and Apocrypha, giving it a very different grammar, almost as if a liturgical adjournment is made, having explored promise, and anticipating the Christmas carol service to come with its fulfilment in the incarnation. The Christmas order also has the same Genesis readings, three prophetic readings, six readings drawn from Luke, Hebrews 1, and the Johannine prologue (extended to verse 18).[25]

Christmas

The use of the Bible in liturgy at Christmas is challenging. Many Christmas services attract people from far beyond the regular congregation, and there are often strong expectations about what will be sung and read. There is often an instinct to keep such services popular and accessible. Here, the Lukan and Matthean narratives are likely to be central, including the visit of the Magi, on the basis that no distinction is made in popular culture between Christmas and Epiphany as witnessed by countless children's nativities, Christmas cards, and Christmas decorations with kings and stars. The challenge is how to enable exploration of the theological and radical aspects of Luke and Matthew's narratives, as well as the *magnum mysterium* of the Incarnation.

For eucharistic worship, the *Revised Common Lectionary* provides three sets of readings. On Christmas Eve, for celebrations at night, Isaiah 9:2-7, Psalm 96, Titus 2:11-14, and Luke 2:1-14 (15-20) are given. The second set is similar in scope: Isaiah 62:6-12, Psalm 97, Titus 3:4-7, Luke 2:(1-7), 8-20. The third set comes from the medieval lectionaries, Isaiah 52:7-10, Psalm 98, Hebrews 1:1-4, (5-12), John 1:1-14.

The first set with Isaiah 9 and the visit of the shepherds perfectly complements what the Roman Lectionary calls "Mass at night" (whether midnight or before), where darkness and light imagery through nighttime celebration and light-focussed hymnody and symbol all come together in this holy night. The second set also complements the Lukan gospel, whereas set three, while of ancient pedigree, is more theologically challenging. While the Johannine prologue is

[25] *The Book of Occasional Services 2003: Conforming to General Convention 2003* (New York: Church Publishing, 2004), 31–34, 38–41.

unsurpassed, it means that no narrative of the birth of Christ is read. This can be remedied if the tradition of a "last" or "dismissal" gospel is utilised. If John 1 is read as the first gospel, Luke 2:16-20 could be effectively read as a dismissal gospel, not least because it cites the mission of the shepherds in "making known what had been told them about this child" (2:17) and the shepherds' joy (2:20), but also the contemplative response of Mary which we are called to imitate (2:19). If the Lukan narrative is read first, John 1 is, of course, the "Last Gospel" of the medieval Mass.

There is also, however, the great popularity of carol services held usually from Advent 4 through to the Sunday after Christmas, which enable an extended reflection on the biblical readings. Many of these follow a pattern of lessons, either following or adapting the pattern adopted by Eric Milner-White in the world-famous annual Festival of Nine Lessons and Carols from King's College, Cambridge.[26]

The time-honoured pattern of nine lessons from King's employs a traditional "salvation history" approach, beginning with the Fall ("the first days of our disobedience"). The promise to Abraham that in his seed all the nations of the world will be blessed then follows (although this rather presupposes some knowledge of Paul's rabbinic gloss on "seed" as a singular in Galatians 3:16). The principal prophetic "messianic" passages of Isaiah 9 and 11 (or Micah 5) follow before excerpts from the Lukan and Matthean infancy narratives, including the story of the Magi from Matthew and finally the Johannine prologue. This approach, while greatly loved, is open to the criticism that it involves "mixing gospel accounts."[27]

There have been many adaptations of this pattern. In the 1980s, Durham Cathedral adopted a "Wisdom Christology" approach. The service introduction quotes Luke 11:31, "[they] came from the ends of the earth to listen to the wisdom of Solomon, and see, something greater than Solomon is here," and Colossians 1:17, "He himself is before all things, and in him all things hold together." With some variations over the years, the sequence of readings is:

[26] The service was introduced in 1918 and broadcast for the first time in 1928.

[27] Perham and Stevenson, *Welcoming the Light*, 61, 62. On the other hand, Borg and Crossan state that there is "nothing intrinsically wrong with harmonizing" the gospel narratives, but rather, "great value in recognizing their differences," *First Christmas*, 23.

- Proverbs 8:22-30 ("Wisdom proclaims her presence with God in creation from the beginning," a passage appropriately read by a representative of the local university);
- Wisdom of Solomon 9:1-4, 10, 13-14a, 16-17 ("King Solomon prays for the gift of wisdom," or 1 Kings 8:22-30 ("Solomon's prayer of Dedication of the Temple");
- Isaiah 10:33-11:6 ("The prophet foretells the coming of a king on whom rests the spirit of wisdom and understanding"); followed by readings from Luke's infancy narrative;
- Colossians 1:15-20 ("St Paul sets out the significance of Christ in creation and redemption") before the Johannine prologue.

While it could be argued that the wisdom theme is theologically complex, it roots the incarnation in the context of both creation and redemption; the Colossians passage also including an explicit reference to the cross.

Of course, there is nothing sacred about the number nine. Many churches will value a sequence of readings interspersed with well-loved congregational carols and Christmas anthems by choirs. However, some communities will also wish to include a homily or present the Christmas story through drama or visual engagement.

Common Worship: Times and Seasons provides two alternatives to the King's pattern. The first is a series of readings from the Lukan narrative. Luke, in contrast to Matthew, cites no Old Testament passage in the whole of his infancy narrative. The Lukan narrative is rich and links Advent and Christmas through the annunciations and births of both the Forerunner and Messiah. The rubric states, "There is virtue in reading the whole infancy narrative with hymns, songs and canticles interspersed." The virtue is that rather than simply hearing the narratives of the Annunciation to Mary and the narrative of the birth and the shepherds from Luke 2, the whole sweep of Luke's magnificent narrative is heard.[28] The suggested pattern is:

[28] *Times and Seasons*, 90, 91. This omits the brief reference to Christ's circumcision (Luke 2:21) and the visit of Jesus to the Temple at the age of twelve, the final section of Luke's narrative (2:41–52).

Luke 1:5-25	*The annunciation to Zechariah*
Luke 1:26-38	*The annunciation to Mary*
Luke 1:39-56 *or* Luke 1:39-49 if the *Magnificat* is used as a canticle	*The visit of Mary to Elizabeth*
Luke 1:57-80 *or* Luke 1:57-67 if the *Benedictus* is used as a canticle	*The birth of John*
Luke 2:1-7	*The birth of Jesus*
Luke 2:8-20	*The shepherds*
Luke 2:22-40 or Luke 2:22-28 if the *Nunc Dimittis* is used as a canticle	*The Presentation in the Temple*
Canticle	*Benedictus, Magnificat, Nunc Dimittis*
Titus 2:11-14; 3:3-7	*The grace of God has appeared for the salvation of all*

A second pattern, "Good news for the poor,"[29] is thematically based:

Micah 5:2-4	Psalm 89:1-4	*Bethlehem, from you shall come forth a ruler*
Isaiah 35	Psalm 126	*The wilderness and the dry land shall be glad*
Haggai 2:5b-9 *or* Jeremiah 22:13-16; 23:5-6	Psalm 97:7-12	*I will fill this house with splendour* *Your Father judged the cause of the poor*
Isaiah 11:1-9	Psalm 132:10-16	*There shall come forth a shoot from the stump of Jesse*
Isaiah 52:7-10 *or* Isaiah 40:1-11	Psalm 85:8-13	*How beautiful on the mountains* *A voice cries in the wilderness: Prepare the way of the Lord*
Philippians 2:5-11	*Magnificat*	*He took the form of a servant*

[29] *Times and Seasons*, 90. Both sequences first appeared in Church of England, *The Promise of His Glory* (London: Church House Publishing, 1990), 26, 27.

Gospel: in Advent	Luke 1:26-38	*The annunciation*
Gospel: at Christmas	Luke 2:1-20	*The birth of Jesus*

This sequence may not be deemed suitable for more "popular" carol services. However, it is worth noting that in many churches, almost all Christmas worship is popular in tone. This begs the question of how the Christian community itself can be encouraged to reflect more insightfully on the great mystery of the incarnation and in greater depth. For some, this will mean that, as well as mission-related services (perhaps before and at Christmas to catch the popular tide), there is good reason for having a post-Christmas sequence of readings and music. *The Promise of his Glory* provides a Johannine sequence on the theme of the new creation with the following lections:

Proverbs 8:22-31 (Ps 33:1-11)
Genesis 1:1-5 (Ps 19:1-6)
Isaiah 55:6-11 (Ps 19:7-14)
Isaiah 65:17-25 (Ps 147:1-6)
Revelation 22:1-15 (Ps 148)
Hebrews 1:1-12 *or* 1 John 4:7-14 (Canticle: Col 1:13-20)
John 14:1-14.[30]

Another tradition that still has currency in some places is the "Watch-night" service for New Year's Eve. This gives a welcome opportunity to reflect on the passage of time. The Episcopal Church order gives the following scheme[31]:

The Hebrew Year	Exodus 23:9-16, 20-21	Psalm 111 *or* 119:1-8
The Promised Land	Deuteronomy 11:8-12, 26-28	Psalm 36:5-10 *or* 89 part 1 (89:1-18)
A Season for All Things	Ecclesiastes 3:1-15	Psalm 90
Remember Your Creator	Ecclesiastes 12:1-8	Psalm 130

[30] Church of England, *The Promise of His Glory*, 30, 31.

[31] *Book of Occasional Services*, 42–46. This can be compared with the sequence in *The Promise of His Glory*, 31–32.

Marking the Times, and Winter	Ecclesiasticus 43:1-22	Psalm 19 *or* 148 *or* 74:11-22
The Acceptable Time	2 Corinthians 5:17–6:2	Psalm 63:1-8 *or* *Nunc Dimittis*
While it Is Called Today	Hebrews 3:1-15 (16–4:13)	Psalm 95
New Heaven and New Earth	Revelation 21:1-14, 22-24	The Song of the Redeemed (Rev 15:3-4)

Epiphany and Candlemas

In the Western tradition, historically the feast of the Epiphany has centred on the narrative of the coming of the Magi in Matthew 2:1-11. This has been understood as a revealing or manifestation of Christ to the Gentiles. In the East, by contrast, the Epiphany, which historically predates Western Christmas, has focussed on the narratives of the baptism of the Lord (Matthew 3:13-17; Mark 1:9-11; Luke 3:21-22) and the miracle at Cana in Galilee (John 2:1-11) as theophanies of his divine nature and glory. However, even in the West, while the Magi narrative dominates, the other two narratives are not entirely absent.[32]

In contemporary church calendars, post-Christmas observance therefore focusses on two related festivals, the Epiphany on January 6 (although often celebrated on the Sunday between 2 and January 8) and the feast of the Baptism of the Lord (on the Sunday after the Epiphany). The Baptism of the Lord was adopted in the Roman calendar in 1960 and has spread to other Western churches. Hence, the first Sunday after the Epiphany in the *RCL* celebrates the Baptism of the Lord.

In the Roman calendar, the Baptism of the Lord marks the formal end of the incarnational cycle; the next day sees the beginning of Ordinary Time. Nevertheless, Epiphany-style lections continue on the following Sundays. So, for example, for the Second Sunday of the Year the revelatory passages from the beginning of the Fourth Gospel appear: John 1:29-34, John 1:35-42, John 2:1-11 (the wedding at Cana). For the Third Sunday, the call of the disciples (Matthew

[32] For the origins of Epiphany, see Bradshaw and Johnson, *Origins of Feasts*, 131–57; Connell, *Eternity Today 1*, 13, 17, 151–74.

4:12-23; Mark 1:14-20), and the Lukan prologue and sermon at Nazareth (Luke 1:1-4; 4:14-21) are set.

For this reason, the contemporary calendar of the Church of England keeps the Epiphany as both a festival and a season extending to the feast of Candlemas, with the liturgical colour white used throughout. This seeks to give a forty-day incarnational season, during which the meaning of the coming of God among us in Christ is explored.

Like Advent and Christmas, Epiphany carol services and processions are becoming more popular. The Church of England's "Three Wonders" service for the feast of the Baptism of the Lord (or any other suitable occasion) is based around the three great Gospel readings of the season, the visit of the Magi, the baptism of the Lord, and the first sign at the wedding in Cana.[33] The liturgy suggests three symbols—incense, the baptismal ewer, and a flagon of wine—and three processional foci—the crib, the holy table, and the font. The service can be eucharistic or non-eucharistic. If the former, the logical order is crib, font, and holy table continuing with the Liturgy of the Sacrament; if the latter, it is crib, holy table, and font, culminating in the renewal of baptismal promises, or the renewal of the covenant using material from the Methodist Covenant Service. The congregation is encouraged to move in turn to each of the three stations, placed at different points in the church. The gospel account of the Magi is proclaimed at the crib, with the offering of incense and response in worship through music and silence. A flagon of wine is then taken to the holy table where the Cana gospel is proclaimed, once more with response in silence and music. Finally, at the font, responding to the baptism of Christ, the renewal of baptism promises is undertaken with asperges or an invitation to make the sign of the cross with the water, or the water is poured over the threshold of the church as a *missio*.[34] The power of this liturgy is that the congregation worships *with* the Magi, beholds the transformative power of the new wine of the kingdom in association with the Eucharist, and renews

[33] *Times and Seasons*, 184–93. For a commentary on this service see Perham and Stevenson, *Welcoming the Light*, 79–83.

[34] In the Church of England Liturgical Commission's 2007 report, "Transforming Worship" (GS 1651), *missio* is defined as "a challenge to engage with God's transforming work in the world." (General Synod of the Church of England, 2007, paragraph 2.2.)

our sense of our incorporation into Christ's *baptisma*. In other words, through Scripture, symbol, movement, and music we enter more deeply into the mysteries we are celebrating. Here, Scripture is rooted in engaged celebration and proclamation.

However, there are other possibilities for Epiphany carol services. It has long been recognised by biblical scholars that Matthew's narrative of the Magi draws on a catena of Old Testament references and allusions. Christopher Evans distinguished six sections; namely, genealogy, angelic appearance to Joseph in a dream, the journey of the Magi, the command to take the child into Egypt, the slaughter of the children, and the return to Israel and finally to Nazareth, each episode "organized in relation to an OT text."[35] Behind the narrative is Matthew's conviction that Jesus is a new Moses who will achieve a greater exodus, that he is "great David's greater Son" who comes as Messiah, and that his mission is to make the promises given to Israel open to all the world. In the following liturgy, short readings, interspersed with verses from the hymn *Hail to the Lord's Anointed*, amplify these themes, with the Matthean account read twice:

Introduction and Bidding Prayer
Reading: Matthew 2:1-11

Jesus as the New David, Born of David's Line
Hymn: *Hail to the Lord's anointed*
1 Samuel 16:4, 11-13a; Jeremiah 23:5-6; Micah 5:2, 4
Collect

Jesus as the New Moses
Hymn: *He shall come down like showers*
Exodus 14:27-31; Deuteronomy 34:10-12
Collect

Jesus as Light to the Nations
Hymn: *He comes with succour speedy*
Numbers 24:15b-17a; Isaiah 60:1-3, 19-22
Collect

[35] Christopher F. Evans, *St Luke*, TTPI New Testament Commentaries (London/Philadelphia: SCM Press/Trinity Press International, 1990), 138.

Jesus as the One Worthy of Worship
Hymn: *Kings shall bow down before him*
Psalm 72:15-19; Psalm 45:6-9; Isaiah 60:4-6
Collect

Conclusion
Hymn: *O'er every foe victorious*
Reading: Matthew 2:1-11
Collect and Blessing

By using the gospel reading at beginning and end, the echoes of the various Old Testament allusions enable a deeper engagement with Matthew's theology.

Another possibility is to reflect biblically on baptism with an extended Ministry of the Word as part of a renewal of baptismal commitment at Epiphany-tide. Baptismal liturgies traditionally make use of salvation history water imagery (the flood, crossing of the Red Sea, the Jordan crossing into the Promised Land, the baptism of Christ), while prophetic oracles like Isaiah 42:1-9, Isaiah 43:15-19, and Ezekiel 36:24-28 provide imagery and theological resonances with the New Testament narratives. The Acts of the Apostles has a series of baptism narratives, while passages like Romans 6:1-4 or 1 Corinthians 12:12-13 illustrate developing New Testament baptismal theology.[36]

The Church of England in its liturgical provision for the season of Epiphany also emphasises two distinctive themes. One is the unity of the church, responding to the ecumenical Week of Prayer for Christian Unity commonly held from January 19 (The Confession of St. Peter) to January 25 (The Conversion of St. Paul).[37] The second is the theme of the mission of the church reflecting the themes of the Gentile mission and Paul's vocation to be the Apostle to the Gentiles.[38] Once again, a service based around selected readings from the Acts

[36] Suggestions for a Vigil Service for the Baptism of the Lord are provided in *The Promise of His Glory*, 33, 34, and the *Book of Occasional Services*, 51, 52. See also Michael Perham et al., *Enriching the Christian Year* (London SPCK/Alcuin Club, 1993), 194, 195, for a general pattern of baptismal readings.

[37] *See Times and Seasons*, 138–48, and *The Promise of His Glory*, 246–58. *The Promise of His Glory* provides a selection of readings on unity, see 402.

[38] See *Times and Seasons*, 149–58, and *The Promise of His Glory*, 241–45. See also sets of readings for Advent or St. Andrew's-tide, and for the Epiphany or the Conversion of St. Paul in *Patterns*, 34, 35.

of the Apostles would enable liturgical engagement with Luke's schema that the gospel would go from Jerusalem and Judea, to Samaria and to the end of the earth (Acts 1:8). A possible sequence is:

Acts 1:6-8	*Jerusalem, Judea, Samaria and the ends of the earth*
Acts 2:37-47	*The first converts in Jerusalem*
Acts 8:1-7	*The mission of Philip to Samaria*
Acts 8:26-39	*The baptism of the God-fearing Ethiopian*
Acts 10:34-48	*The baptism of the first Gentiles*
Acts 26:12-18	*Paul recalls his conversion and the commission as Apostle to the Gentiles*
Acts 28:11-16, 23-30	*Paul comes to Rome*

Finally, we come to the culminating incarnation festival, the Presentation of Christ in the Temple, or Candlemas, celebrated on February 2 (or the Sunday nearest), forty days after Christmas. Like Luke's entire infancy narrative, no Old Testament text is quoted explicitly, but the narrative is theologically rich in Old Testament imagery. Like the annunciation to Zechariah, the scene is the Jerusalem Temple and sacrifice is offered. Obedience to the law is cited four times (Luke 2:22, 23, 24, 27). The themes of purification and presentation of the firstborn are referenced (it is recognised by both biblical and liturgical scholars that Luke conflates purification and the redemption of the firstborn).[39] The word "purification" may recall Malachi 3:1-3, the Lord coming to his temple to purify the sons of Levi, with its associated theme of judgment. Simeon and Anna, representing the prophetic tradition, the former watching for the "consolation of Israel" and the latter speaking of "redemption," signify the expectant hope of the righteous.[40]

[39] See Evans, *St Luke*, 210–14; Kenneth Stevenson, *All the Company of Heaven: A Companion to the Principal Festivals of the Christian Year* (Norwich: Canterbury Press, 1998), 28, 29; Michael Perham, *Glory in Our Midst* (London: SPCK, 2005), 103, 104. The phrase "*their* purification" (2:22) is problematic historically unless Luke is making a broader theological point.

[40] For a contemporary exploration of the roles of Mary and Anna in this narrative, see Todd Klutz, "The Value of Being Virginal: Mary and Anna in Luke's Infancy Prologue," in *The Birth of Jesus, Biblical and Theological Reflections*, ed. George J. Brooke, 71–87 (Edinburgh: T&T Clark, 2000).

Simeon's *Nunc Dimittis* reveals Christ as both light to the nations and the glory of Israel, prominent themes in second and third Isaiah (salvation and *light* Isaiah 51:4f, salvation and *glory*, 40:5; *light* and *glory* 60:1, 19; 58:8).[41] To explore these themes, *The Promise of His Glory* provides this pattern of readings for a Vigil Service, or the pattern could be adapted for a meditative Service of the Word to conclude the incarnational cycle:

Exodus 12:51; 13:2, 11-16	*Consecrate to me all the first born*
Leviticus 12:6-8	*The Law of Purification*
Isaiah 6:1-8	*I saw the Lord, and his train filled the Temple*
Isaiah 19:1-4, 19-21	*In that day the Egyptians will worship*
Haggai 2:1-9	*I will fill this house with splendour*
Hebrews 10:1-10	*We have been sanctified by the offering of the body of Jesus*
Psalm 40:8-13	
Luke 2:22-40	*The Presentation in the Temple*

Malachi 3:1-3, read at the Candlemas Eucharist, could also easily be incorporated into this pattern.

Conclusion

Throughout this exploration of the liturgical use of the Bible from Advent to Candlemas, the christological focus of this major part of the liturgical year is writ large. It is a reminder that in liturgical celebration, the reading of Scripture testifies to Christ as the *living* Word of God. In a real sense, how the church hears Scripture today in Advent, Christmas, and Epiphany worship is consonant with the earliest Christian communities. The significance of Christ is set forth in relationship to both the Hebrew and Christian Scriptures to reflect *Christian* convictions of the coming of Christ as the fulfilment of all the longings of the covenant people of God. In this sense, the comments of Matias Augé are pertinent:

[41] Evans, *St Luke*, 217.

The liturgy confers a certain reality on the Word of God insofar as it announces that the Word is accomplished in our day: ". . . the Church, especially during Advent and Lent and above all at the Easter Vigil, re-reads and re-lives the great events of salvation history in the 'today' of her liturgy" [*Catechism of the Catholic Church* 1095].

In the celebration of the liturgy, Jesus' statement becomes true once again: "Today this scripture has been fulfilled in your hearing" (Luke 4:21, NRSV). We may affirm . . . a still greater actualization, in that Christ himself "is present in his word since it is he himself who speaks when the holy scriptures are read in the Church" (*SC [Sacrosanctum Concilium]* 7).[42]

[42] Matias Augé, CMF, "A Theology of the Liturgical Year," in *Handbook for Liturgical Studies: Liturgical Time and Space*, vol. V, ed. Anscar J. Chupungco (Collegeville, MN: Liturgical Press, 2000), 323.

Chapter 6

Sunday, the Week, and Ordinary Time: A Return *ad Fontes*

Normand Bonneau, OMI

I. Introduction: Sundays in Ordinary Time

Promulgated in 1969, decreed as mandatory for the universal church in 1971, the Roman Catholic *Ordo Lectionum Missae* (the Latin name for the *Lectionary for Mass*; henceforth *OLM*) has since been a standard feature in the church's worship. It also serves, with some adjustments and adaptations, as the basic template for the *Revised Common Lectionary* (*RCL*), the Sunday lectionary used by a broad swath of churches and denominations in the English-speaking world and beyond.[1]

The regular use of the *OLM* and of the *RCL* over these now many decades, however, does not preclude criticism and suggestions for improvement. Indeed, from the very outset, concerns have been raised regarding one or another feature of the *OLM*'s structural design

[1] For the *RCL*, see Consultation on Common Texts, *The Revised Common Lectionary: 20th Anniversary Annotated Edition* (Minneapolis: Fortress, 2012). For an extensive and current list of the churches using the *RCL*, see Regina A. Boisclair, *The Word of the Lord at Mass: Understanding the Lectionary* (Chicago: Liturgy Training Publications, 2015), 63–64. "The Reims Statement: Praying with One Voice of August 16, 2001," note 7, lists "churches in Scandinavia, Hispanic speaking areas, Korea, Japan, Netherlands, Venezuela, Polynesia, South Africa (including Afrikaans speaking churches)."

and its scriptural content.[2] Perhaps the greatest disquiet concerns the Sundays in Ordinary Time, the thirty-three or thirty-four "numbered" Sundays (hence the term "ordinary," from "ordinal") between Christmas and Lent, resumed between Pentecost through to the following Advent. That these Sundays should be the source of so much consternation is no small matter, for together they represent some two-thirds of the yearly liturgical cycle.

The issue, raised for the most part by preachers and homilists, pertains to the lack on these Sundays of a more thoroughgoing thematic link ("vertical correspondence") among the three readings assigned to a given eucharistic celebration. Why could there not be—why *should* there not be—correspondence among all three readings as found elsewhere in the lectionary's annual cycle?[3] This "disharmony" results from the principles of reading selection and reading distribution implemented for these Sundays. On the one hand, both the gospel passages and the second reading excerpts from the apostolic writings follow independent, semicontinuous tracks ("horizontal sequences") from Sunday to Sunday. Hence, the second and third readings rarely if ever show vertical (thematic) correspondence. On the other hand, the first readings from the Old Testament, unlike the second and third readings, do not display any sequential horizontal pattern. Rather, pericopes from the Old Testament are selected to correspond thematically with the gospel passage of the day.[4]

[2] On the first readings from the Old Testament, see, e.g., *Streit am Tisch des Wortes? Deutung und Bedeutung des Alten Testaments und seiner Verwendung in der Liturgie*, Pietas Liturgica, ed. Ansgar Franz (St. Ottilen: EOS Verlag, 1997), esp. the essays in Part III: "Liturgie: Über des Stellenwert des Alten Testamentes im Gottesdienst," 491–868. For difficulties regarding the second reading, see, e.g., Vincent Truijen, "Les lectures du Nouveau Testament dans la liturgie rénovée," *Questions Liturgiques/Studies in Liturgy* 67 (1986): 235–51, 244, 251; Adrien Nocent, "La parole de Dieu et Vatican II," in *Liturgia, opera divina e umani: Studi sulla riforma liturgica offerti a S. E. Annibale Bugnini in occasione del sue 70e compleanno*, ed. Pierre Jounel, Reiner Kaczynski, and Gottardo Pasqualetti, 133–49, 142–43 (Roma: CLV—Edizioni Liturgiche, 1982).

[3] See, e.g., Nocent, "La parole," 148; William Skudlarek, *The Word in Worship: Preaching in a Liturgical Context* (Nashville: Abingdon Press, 1981), 37–39. This concern goes as well for the *RCL* as expressed by the task force for the revision of the Common Lectionary (which led to the current *RCL*) and recorded by Fred Kimball Graham in his introduction to the CCT's *The Revised Common Lectionary*, ix–xxv, xxiii–xiv.

[4] For further details on the reading selection and reading distribution for the Sundays in Ordinary Time, see Normand Bonneau, *The Sunday Lectionary: Ritual Word, Paschal Shape* (Collegeville, MN: Liturgical Press, 1998), 141–62.

Attempted remedies to overcome or at least palliate the resultant "disharmony" are of two kinds. The simplest and most frequently adopted approach, sanctioned by the church's official documents and practised in a number of dioceses, is simply to omit either the first or the second reading.[5] The other more tentative and experimental approach, which has met neither with official nor with general approval, foregoes the semicontinuous pattern for the second reading, instead selecting passages from the apostolic writings that correspond thematically with the other two readings of the day.[6] As a result, in such proposals there is vertical correspondence among all three readings on any given Sunday, with a horizontal, semicontinuous sequence reserved for the gospel reading only.

What to make of this concern? What was, at least implicitly, the rationale informing the lectionary design for the Sundays in Ordinary Time? My reflections below on this issue were prompted by Pierre Jounel's succinct and intriguing assessment of these Sundays: "[t]he thirty-four Sundays *per annum* or of Ordinary Time represent *the ideal Christian Sunday*, without any further specification. That is, each of them is *the Lord's Day in its pure state as presented to us in the Church's*

[5] On the option to use either only the Old Testament readings or only the readings from the apostolic writings, see the Introduction to the *Lectionary for Mass* in *The Liturgy Documents: Essential Documents for Parish Worship* (Chicago: Liturgy Training Publications, 2014), 325–63, nos. 12, 78, 79, notes 106 and 107; however, the *General Instruction of the Roman Missal* in *The Liturgy Documents*, 95–177, nos. 60–61, seems to contradict this. See Nocent, *A Reading of the Renewed Liturgy*, trans. Mary M. Misrahi, 18 (Collegeville, MN: Liturgical Press, 1994), who mentions "France, Germany, and other countries." See also his article "Eine 'kleine Geschichte am Rande': Zum Lektionar für die Messfeier der 'gewöhnlichen' Sonntage," in *Streit am Tisch des Wortes*, ed. Franz, 649–57, 655–56. Interestingly, Martin Klöckener, "Présence et rôle de la Bible dans la liturgie: Résultats et perspectives," in *Présence et rôle de la Bible dans la liturgie*, ed. Martin Klöckener, Bruno Bürki and Arnaud Join-Lambert, 387–409, 398 (Fribourg: Academic Press, 2006), writes that the same structural difficulty has led to the omission of the first reading from the Old Testament.

[6] For an example of thematically selected second readings for the Sundays in Ordinary Time, see Nocent, *A Reading*, 9–17; for a proposal creating a semicontinuous horizontal track for the first reading from the Old Testament, with second and third readings selected to correspond thematically with the first reading of the day, see Hansjakob Becker, "Wortgottesdienst als Dialog der beiden Testamente: Der Stellenwert des Alten Testamentes bei einer Weiterführung der Reform des *Ordo Lectionum Missae*," in *Streit am Tisch des Wortes*, ed. Franz, 659–89, esp. 678–87.

tradition"[7] [emphasis added]. The Sundays in Ordinary Time, then, embody the most ancient tradition. They are Sundays celebrated very much the way each and every Sunday was celebrated in the earliest decades of the church before solemnities of the Lord and festal seasons developed. Why and in what sense does Jounel thus characterise these Sundays? And, as a result, why did the designers of the lectionary opt for the principles of reading selection and reading distribution mentioned above to express the foundational and originary significance of these Sundays?

In a first step, I scrutinise the assumption that there is (pervasive?) vertical correspondence elsewhere in the annual lectionary cycle (Part II). I then turn to official church documents to glean pertinent statements on Sunday and the week (Part III), showing how these descriptions impinge on the Sundays in Ordinary Time and on their current design in the lectionary (Part IV). Finally, I offer two concluding observations on the importance of assessing any individual part or sector of the Sunday lectionary in light of its overall design and architecture (Part V).

II. Horizontal and Vertical Patterns outside Ordinary Time

Despite having become a persistent *desideratum* for the Sundays in Ordinary Time, a more thoroughgoing vertical correspondence among all three readings remains a less pervasive pattern elsewhere in the lectionary than is oftentimes imagined:[8]

1. *Major Feasts.* The most obvious and thorough vertical correspondence among all three readings assigned to a celebration occurs, as can be expected, on major feasts such as Christmas, Epiphany, Easter, Ascension, and Pentecost. These and similar instances call for scriptural passages most apt to express the event being celebrated.

[7] Pierre Jounel, "Sunday and the Week," in *The Church at Prayer: An Introduction to the Liturgy*, vol. IV: The Liturgy and Time, new ed., ed. Iréné Henri Dalmais, Pierre Jounel, and Aimé Georges Martimort, trans. Matthew J. O'Connell, 11–29, 23 (Collegeville, MN: Liturgical Press, 1986).

[8] For a more detailed and extensive presentation of the principles of reading selection and reading distribution for the festal seasons, see Bonneau, *Sunday Lectionary*.

2. *Festal Seasons*. The situation is more complicated for the festal seasons. With the exception of Christmas, the liturgical seasons of Advent, Lent, and Easter all consist of extended sequences of Sundays, each employing varying combinations of the principles of reading selection and reading distribution. As will be seen, horizontal patterns take priority, with vertical correspondence as a secondary pattern implemented where possible.

a. *Lent*. For the first five Sundays of Lent, the gospels present two related horizontal patterns: Sundays 1 and 2 feature accounts of the Temptation and the Transfiguration drawn from each of the respective synoptic narratives (Matthew in Year A, Mark in Year B, Luke in Year C). The second horizontal pattern structures Sundays 3, 4, and 5: Year A presents texts oriented to baptism; Year B, Johannine images of the paschal mystery; Year C, aspects of repentance and conversion. The first readings from the Old Testament display their own horizontal pattern, with each Sunday highlighting a distinct theme in the history of salvation: Sunday 1, primeval history; Sunday 2, ancestral history; Sunday 3, Moses; Sunday 4, the Holy Land; Sunday 5, eschatological fulfilment. Unlike the first and third readings, the second readings exhibit no horizontal pattern, but are selected rather to correspond thematically with either of the other two readings or with both. While vertical correspondence, at least between two readings and often among all three, occurs on nearly every Sunday, the horizontal patterns are the primary structural design.

b. *Easter*. The Easter season, consisting of a sequence of seven consecutive Sundays (Easter Sunday to the Seventh Sunday), also contains salient horizontal patterns. Three related patterns structure the sequence of gospel readings for all three years of the cycle. After Easter Sunday, which presents accounts of the discovery of the empty tomb, Sundays 2 and 3 relate appearances of the risen Jesus; Sunday 4 features excerpts from the Good Shepherd parable in John 10; Sundays 5, 6, 7 assign passages from the farewell discourses (John 13–17). As for the first reading, the lectionary foregoes the Old Testament, instead reviving an ancient tradition of reading Acts of the Apostles between Easter and Pentecost. Passages are selected and distributed in a somewhat loosely conceived semicontinuous pattern, highlighting the key moments in the development and expansion of the primitive church. The second readings follow their own semicontinuous tracks: Year A, excerpts from 1 Peter; Year B, from 1 John; Year C, from Revelation. All three readings, therefore, have independent and distinct horizontal patterns, thus precluding in most instances any real possibility of vertical correspondence.

c. *Advent*. The four Sundays of Advent offer their own blend of horizontal patterns and vertical correspondence. The gospels are organised in a horizontal sequence of time in reverse: Sunday 1 focuses on eschatological fulfilment, Sundays 2 and 3 deal with the ministry of John the Baptist, Sunday 4 announces the Messiah's imminent birth. The Old Testament readings, all but one excerpt drawn from prophetic literature, mirror the sequence of gospel themes through prophecies of the end-time, of Israel's salvation, or of a coming messiah. Finally, the second readings are selected to correspond with either or with both of the other two readings. Vertical correspondence, while present in many instances, is not always particularly prominent.

d. *Christmas*. The Christmas season, since it is based on the two pillar feasts of the Nativity and the Epiphany rather than on a sequence of Sundays, manifests no horizontal patterns. Vertical correspondence on Sundays and the season's feasts, therefore, plays a more obvious and important role than in the other three festal seasons.

As this brief exposé shows, vertical correspondence, the thematic linkage of all three readings on any given feast or Sunday, is not a pervasive principle characterizing the annual Lectionary cycle of readings. More important and consequential are horizontal patterns, with vertical correspondence playing a secondary role. This is because the horizontal patterns are a primary means of articulating the main themes of a liturgical feast or season, themes set forth in the *Universal Norms on the Liturgical Year and the General Roman Calendar*. Seasonal themes, horizontal patterns, vertical correspondence, in that order, then, underlie the reading selection and distribution patterns structuring the lectionary.

III. Ordinary Time

If, as concluded above, the sequence seasonal theme(s) → horizontal patterns → vertical correspondence determines the reading selection and reading distribution patterns for feasts and festal seasons, is there something similar at work for the Sundays in Ordinary Time?[9] The following documents provide the necessary elements: (1) Constitution on the Sacred Liturgy (*Sacrosanctum Concilium*); (2) *Universal Norms on the Liturgical Year and the General Roman Calendar*; (3) *General Introduction to the Lectionary for Mass*.[10] The first identifies *Sunday* and the *week* as originary and foundational for, and in the history of, Christian liturgy. Next, the *Universal Norms* sets forth the themes of each liturgical season in turn, representing the first step toward implementing *Sacrosanctum Concilium*'s understanding of the annual liturgical cycle. Finally, the *General Introduction* elaborates the lectionary principles of reading selection and distribution (horizontal and vertical patterns) that flesh out, in the annual cycle of Sundays, feasts, and seasons, the theological and thematic criteria expressed in the first two documents.

A. Vatican II: Sunday and the Week

The Vatican II document Constitution on the Sacred Liturgy supplies the constituent elements of liturgy. Of paramount importance, because foundational and originary—and of particular pertinence for grasping the significance of the Sundays in Ordinary Time—are *Sunday* and the *week*. The key features of both, highlighted in italics, are contained in two paragraphs:

> The church believes that its nature requires it to celebrate the saving work of the divine Bridegroom by devoutly calling it to mind on certain days throughout the year. *Every week, on the day which it has called the Lord's Day*, it commemorates the Lord's resurrection. It also celebrates it *once every year*, together with his blessed passion, at *Easter*, that most solemn of all feasts. (102)

[9] Strictly speaking, Ordinary Time is not a "season" in the same sense as Advent, Christmas, Lent, and Easter (as implied in the use of prepositions: *of* for the Sundays *of* Advent, Christmas, Lent, and Easter, but *in* for the Sundays *in* Ordinary Time).

[10] The full texts of these documents can be found in *The Liturgy Documents, Volume One: Fifth Edition; Essential Documents for Parish Worship* (Chicago: Liturgy Training Publications, 2014).

By a tradition handed down *from the apostles*, which took its *origin from the very day of Christ's resurrection*, the church celebrates the paschal mystery *every eighth day*, which day is appropriately called *the Lord's day or Sunday*. For on this day Christ's faithful are bound to come together so that, *by hearing the word of God and taking part in the Eucharist*, they may commemorate the suffering, resurrection, and glory of the Lord Jesus, giving thanks to God who "has given us a new birth into a living hope through the resurrection of Jesus Christ from the dead" (1 Pet 1:3). *The Lord's Day is the original feast day*, and it should be presented to the faithful and taught to them so that it may become in fact a day of rejoicing and of freedom from work. Other celebrations, unless they be truly of the greatest importance, *shall not have precedence over Sunday, which is the foundation and kernel of the entire liturgical year*. (106)

1. *Sunday*[11]

- Sunday is the original Christian feast. It was on "the first day of the week" that Jesus was raised from the dead. Since the Jewish calendar at that time did not, with the exception of the Sabbath, provide names for the days of the week, the first day of the week was therefore the day after the Sabbath or, in our current

[11] Among the key sources consulted (and for further elaboration): Pope John Paul II, *The Lord's Day: Apostolic Letter* Dies Domini *of the Holy Father John Paul II to the Bishops, Clergy and Faithful of the Catholic Church on Keeping the Lord's Day Holy* (Sherbrooke, QC: Médiaspaul, 1998); Henri Dumaine, "Dimanche," in *Dictionnaire d'archéologie chrétienne et de liturgie* 4/1, ed. Fernand Cabrol and Henri Leclercq, cols. 858–994 (Paris: Letouzey et Ané, 1920); Pierre Jounel, *Le Dimanche*, Horizon du croyant (Paris/Ottawa: Desclée/Novalis, 1990); Jounel, "Sunday and the Week," in *The Church at Prayer*, ed. Martimort, 11–29; Oskar Mueller, "The Paschal Mystery and Its Celebration during the Liturgical Year and in the Sunday Mass," in *The Liturgy of Vatican II: A Symposium in Two Volumes*, vol. 2, ed. William Baraúna, English ed., ed. Jovian Lang, 209–29 (Chicago: Franciscan Herald Press, 1966); Willy Rordorf, "Origine et signification de la célébration de dimanche dans le christianisme primitif," *La Maison-Dieu* 148 (1981): 103–22; Rordorf, *Sunday: The History of the Day of Rest and Worship in the Earliest Centuries of the Christian Church*, trans. Andrew Alexander Kenny Graham (London: SCM Press, 1968); Philippe Rouillard, "Les Pères. Signification du dimanche," *Introduction, Assemblées du Seigneur, 1ère série* (Bruges: Biblica, 1962), 43–54; Bernard Botte et al., *Le Dimanche. 9e Semaine liturgique, Institut Saint-Serge, Paris, 1963, Lex Orandi* 39 (Paris: Cerf, 1965); Jean Daniélou, *Bible et liturgie, Lex Orandi* 11 (Paris: Cerf, 1958), 329–54; Jean Gaillard, "Où en est la théologie du dimanche?," *La Maison-Dieu* 83 (1965): 7–32; Hansjörg auf der Maur et al., *Feiern im Rhythmus der Zeit, Gottesdienst der Kirche: Handbuch der Liturgiewissenschaft Teil 5–6* (Regensburg: F. Pustet, 1983).

calendar and appellation, Sunday. Sunday as a Christian feast most probably arose at the outset, even before Paul's apostolic career.[12]

- From very early on, what became known as the *Day of the Lord* marked the occasion for the community of believers to gather for the celebration the Lord's Supper, the Eucharist, thus underlining the paschal mystery of Jesus' death and resurrection as the foundation not only of worship but of all of Christian life.[13] Its antiquity is further corroborated by the fact that already in the first century the day of assembly acquired the name "the Lord's day" (κυριακὴ ἡμέρα). By the second century, the name of the day and the tradition of assembly had become so engrained that the word Κυριακή alone became a sufficient designation for both.[14] Based on these and similar observations, scholars conclude that the Sunday observance, that is, as the regular time for Christians to assemble, is a totally Christian invention.
- The regular celebration of Sunday preceded the annual commemoration of the resurrection on Easter.[15]

[12] Dumaine, "Dimanche," col. 895; Jounel, *Le Dimanche*, 14–17; John Paul II, *Lord's Day*, nos. 21–22. Richard J. Bauckham, "The Lord's Day," in *From Sabbath to Lord's Day: A Biblical, Historical, and Theological Investigation*, ed. Donald Arthur Carson, 222–50, 230 (Grand Rapids, MI: Zondervan, 1982); Matias Augé, CMF, "A Theology of the Liturgical Year," in *Handbook for Liturgical Studies: Liturgical Time and Space*, vol. V, ed. Anscar J. Chupungco, 317–30, 320 (Collegeville, MN: Liturgical Press, 2000); Irmgard Pahl, "The Paschal Mystery in Its Central Meaning for the Shape of Christian Liturgy," *Studies in Liturgy* 26 (1996): 16–38, 34; Willy Rordorf, *Sunday*, 274–75.

[13] Bauckham, "Lord's Day," 238.

[14] Bauckham, "Lord's Day," 230; Augé, "Theology of the Liturgical Year," 320; Pahl, "Paschal Mystery," 34.

[15] Rouillard, "Les Pères," 45; Dumaine, "Dimanche," cols. 905–6; Cyrille Vogel, *Introduction aux sources de l'histoire du culte chrétien au Moyen Âge* (Spoleto: Centro Italiano di Studi sull'Alto Medioevo, 1964), 264. Rordorf, *Sunday*, 215, 237. To avoid ambiguity, it is helpful to distinguish between Easter as the once-and-for-all *event* of Jesus' resurrection, on the one hand, from Easter as the annual liturgical commemoration of that event that emerged only in the second century, on the other hand. Thus, every Sunday is a mini-Easter, here Easter referring to the unrepeatable and originary *event* of Jesus' resurrection; Easter Sunday as the annual, liturgical commemoration of Jesus' resurrection is Sunday writ large.

2. *The Week*

- The foundational and originary significance of the week arises from the gospels' indication that Jesus was raised "on the first day of *the week*."
- The week is a discrete and arbitrary measure of time, a cultural contrivance untethered to lunar or solar reckonings of time. The week goes on indefinitely and uninterruptedly in a recurrent and mathematically regular sequence, irrespective of calendar dates.[16] As well, and unlike cycles based on nature (which always have fractions), the week is based exclusively on whole numbers.[17]
- As a cultural and arbitrary measure of time, the week can comprise varying numbers of days.[18] The origin of the seven-day week is not altogether clear. Scholars generally point to two ancient traditions, the Jewish Sabbath tradition and the Greco-Roman planetary tradition, which eventually influenced each other in the early centuries of the first millennium CE.[19] Nevertheless, by the time the Scriptures were written, the seven-day week had become the accepted measure of time in Jewish life and tradition. Given the nature of the week, major feasts in the Jewish annual calendar did not interrupt the weekly procession of time. For example, Passover was (and is) celebrated on 14 Nisan, no matter on what day of the week it falls in any given year.
- The gospels do not refer to lunar or solar computations to mark Jesus' resurrection—they do not specify, for example, at what time of the month or phase of the moon or when in

[16] Eviatar Zerubavel, *The Seven Day Circle: The History and Meaning of the Week* (Chicago/London: University of Chicago Press, 1985), 4: "The week is the only major rhythm of human activity that is totally oblivious to nature, resting on mathematical regularity alone." Daniel J. Boorstin, *The Discoverers* (New York: Vintage Books, 1983), 12.

[17] According to Zerubavel, *Seven Day Circle*, 11 and 70, the lunar month is 29.5306 days, the solar year is 365.2422 days; also 60–61. Even the day, unlike the week, is not a whole number, requiring an occasional "leap second," https://en.wikipedia.org/wiki/Day.

[18] Zerubavel, *Seven Day Circle*, 4, 44–59, 139; Boorstin, *Discoverers*, 13.

[19] Rordorf, *Sunday*, 9–42; Boorstin, *Discoverers*, 13; Zerubavel, *Seven Day Circle*, 5–26.

the annual solar cycle his resurrection occurred. While lunar and solar computations are presupposed for determining each year the date of the Jewish Passover, and therefore of Jesus' Last Supper and crucifixion, only the week factors in reckoning his resurrection.

3. *Current Calendrical Traces of the Preeminence of Sunday and the Week*

Historically and liturgically, later developments in Christian worship constitute additional layers superimposed on and emerging out of the foundation of Sunday and the week.[20] The fundamental themes of Sunday enhance the themes of the festal season Sundays, while the festal season themes in turn never override or suppress the foundational realities of Sunday and week, as the following instances attest:

- *The Annual Celebration of Easter Sunday*. Since many eastern churches celebrated the crucifixion of Jesus on the Jewish calendar date 14 Nisan, which could fall on any day of the week and not necessarily on a Friday, Jesus' resurrection three days later would then also not necessarily fall on a Sunday. The issue was finally resolved at the Council of Nicea in 325, which determined that the annual commemoration of the Lord's resurrection always be celebrated on a Sunday (as had been the tradition in the West).[21]

[20] As Vogel, *Introduction*, 264, n. 77, opines: "Le problème n'est pas de savoir pourquoi le christianisme a développé une année liturgique à une époque relativement tardive, mais pourquoi une année liturgique comme telle a pu se constituer, avec un cycle de fêtes spécialisées, dont le christianisme n'avait nul besoin. En effet, chaque fois que l'Eucharistie est célébrée, la vie, la mort et la résurrection du Christ, donc le mystère du salut, sont célébrés. Chaque Eucharistie est une liturgie pascale; l'apparition de récurrence chronologiques spécialisées est un signe de l'historisation progressive du cérémonial et de la perspective événementielle introduite dans le culte."

[21] On the Quartodeciman controversy, see Adolf Adam, *The Liturgical Year: Its History and Its Meaning after the Reform of the Liturgy*, trans. Matthew O'Connell (New York: Pueblo, 1981), 58–59; Joseph A. Jungmann, *La liturgie des premiers siècles jusqu'à l'époque de Grégoire le Grand*, *Lex Orandi* 33, trans. Francis A. Brunner (Paris: Cerf, 1962), 46–48. The gravitational pull of Sunday is attested today as well where the Ascension is celebrated not on a Thursday, the fortieth day after Easter, but rather on the following Sunday.

- *The Eighth Day*: Although developed in the post-apostolic era, this tradition presupposes the biblical seven-day week, playing as it does on the symbolism of the seven days of creation recounted in Genesis. Jesus' resurrection on the first day of the week, therefore, represents the eighth day of creation as well as the first day of a new week, hence the beginning of a new creation.[22]
- *Octaves*: Related to the symbolic meaning of the eighth day, an octave extends a feast through the following week into its eighth day. For example, the (first and original) octave of Easter computes Easter Sunday as the first day and extends to include the following Sunday.[23]
- *Festal Seasons*: With the exception of the Christmas season, the Advent, Lenten, and Easter seasons are sequences of Sundays and their intervening weeks. These three festal seasons all begin on a Sunday, with the Sundays termed Sundays *of* their respective seasons.[24]

4. *Perennial Preeminence of Sunday and the Week*

Regarding the possibility of celebrating Easter every year on a fixed calendar date, the *Appendix to Sacrosanctum Concilium: A Declaration of the Second Vatican Ecumenical Council on Revision of the Calendar* comments:

> The sacred council likewise declares that it does not oppose efforts designed to introduce a perpetual calendar into civil society. But among the various systems which are being devised with a view

[22] On the topic of the Eighth Day, see Dumaine, "Dimanche," cols. 879–80; Rordorf, *Sunday*, 275–85; Daniélou, *Bible et liturgie*, 355–87; John Paul II, *Lord's Day*, no. 26; Jounel, *Le Dimanche*, 17.

[23] Jean Hild, "Les dimanches verts et Mystère Pascal," *La Maison-Dieu* 46 (1956): 7–34, 8–9: "D'une semaine à l'autre, le dimanche rappelle alors l'*octave* avec tout le réalisme chrétien qui s'y rattache, et, d'un dimanche à l'autre, le mystère pascal communique son rythme et sa lumière, sa grâce et son eucharistie à toute la structure de l'année liturgique"; also Zerubavel, *Seven Day Circle*, 96.

[24] Liturgical Lent begins on a Sunday, counting six consecutive Sundays and the intervening weeks to the threshold of Holy Week; penitential Lent begins on Ash Wednesday. True to the fundamental meaning of Sunday as the original Christian feast, there are no penitential observances on the Sundays of Lent.

> to establishing a perpetual calendar and introducing it into civil life, those and only those are unopposed by the church *which retain and safeguard a seven-day week, with Sunday, without the introduction of any days outside the week, so that the succession of weeks may be left intact*, unless in the judgment of the Apostolic See there are extremely weighty reasons to the contrary[25] [emphasis added].

The Vatican II reform of the liturgy, then, rightly insists, as the above church documents show, on the foundational and originary nature of Sunday and the week. How, then, is this preeminence of Sunday and the week borne out in the Sundays in Ordinary Time and their lectionary elaboration?

B. Universal Norms on the Liturgical Year and the General Roman Calendar

Regarding Sunday, the week, and Ordinary Time, the document states the following:

> On the first day of each week, which is known as the Day of the Lord or the Lord's Day, the Church, by an apostolic tradition that draws its origin from the very day of the Resurrection of Christ, celebrates the Paschal Mystery. Hence, Sunday must be considered the primordial feast day. (4; referring to *Sacrosanctum Concilium* 106)
>
> Besides the times of year that have their own distinctive character, there remain in the yearly cycle thirty-three or thirty-four weeks in which no particular aspect of the mystery of Christ is celebrated, but rather the mystery of Christ itself is honored in its fullness, especially on Sundays. This period is known as Ordinary Time. (43)[26]

Paragraph 4 reiterates the description of Sunday and the week found in Sacrosanctum Concilium. Paragraph 43, however, which comes after the document's treatment of the festal seasons, deals

[25] "Appendix: A Declaration of the Second Vatican Ecumenical Council on Revision of the Calendar," in Austin Flannery, ed., *Vatican Council II: Constitutions, Decrees, Declarations; The Basic Sixteen Documents* (Collegeville, MN: Liturgical Press, 2014), 159–61. For the underlying rationale, see Zerubavel, *Seven Day Circle*, 80–82.

[26] For a more detailed commentary on the significance of the paschal mystery in the liturgical year, see Mueller, "Paschal Mystery," 210.

specifically with Ordinary Time. Of signal importance is the distinction it posits between festal seasons, which celebrate a "particular aspect of the mystery of Christ," and the remaining weeks (especially Sundays), which celebrate "the mystery of Christ . . . in its fullness." How, in light of all this, does the lectionary go about articulating, appending scriptural flesh on the calendrical bones of, the Sundays in Ordinary Time?

C. General Introduction to the Lectionary for Mass

This document briefly explicates the principles of reading selection and the patterns of reading distribution implemented for the Sundays in Ordinary Time (see my Introduction above):

> In contrast, the Sundays in Ordinary Time do not have a distinctive character. Thus the texts of both the apostolic and Gospel readings are arranged in order of semicontinuous reading, whereas the Old Testament reading is harmonized with the Gospel. (67)

The next paragraph offers the rationale for its design choice:

> The decision was made not to extend to Sundays [in Ordinary Time] the arrangement suited to the liturgical seasons mentioned [festal seasons], that is, not to have an organic harmony of themes devised with a view to facilitating homiletic instruction. Such an arrangement *would be in conflict with the genuine conception of liturgical celebration*, which is always the celebration of the mystery of Christ and which by its own tradition makes use of the word of God not only at the prompting of logical or extrinsic concerns but spurred by the desire to proclaim the Gospel and to lead those who believe to the fullness of truth. (68; emphasis added)

Due to the foundational and originary nature of Sunday, particularly as this is manifested in the Sundays in Ordinary Time, other structural reading patterns would, the document seems to imply, vitiate the "genuine conception of liturgical celebration." The rationale underlying this statement appears in the rest of the sentence, which bears a measure of elaboration. First, as the Vatican II document *Sacrosanctum Concilium* underscores, all liturgy celebrates the paschal mystery of Christ (5–7). Second, the Sunday Eucharist, by dint of being both *Sunday* (the Lord's Day [see above]) and the celebration of the *Eucharist* (the great thanksgiving whose climax is the death and resurrection of Christ), constitutes the summit of the church's liturgical activity (*Presbyterorum Ordinis*, "Decree on the Ministry and Life of Priests," 5). This liturgical context, then, permeates and suffuses all aspects of the Sunday eucharistic celebration, including the Liturgy of the Word. Third, as a result, the Liturgy of the Word calls to mind the reason for gathering—and for gathering at the table—as the *General Introduction to the Lectionary* goes on to explain: "The Church is nourished spiritually at the twofold table of God's word and of the Eucharist: from the one it grows in wisdom and from the other in holiness. In the word of God the divine covenant is announced; in the Eucharist the new and everlasting covenant is renewed. On the one hand the history of salvation is brought to mind by means of human sounds; on the other it is made manifest in the sacramental signs of the Liturgy" (10).

In light of these contextual factors, the proclamation of the Scriptures at the Sunday Eucharist is, in Paul Bradshaw's historical review of the various ways that biblical readings have been (and are) used in worship, first and foremost kerygmatic or anamnetic rather than didactic (instructional or catechetical). That is, the Scriptures "provide the biblical warrant and foundation for the liturgical rite being celebrated" (. . .) and are "intimately related to the meaning of what is being celebrated, interpreting and stimulating the liturgical action itself."[27] This well articulates what the second part of *General Intro-*

[27] Paul F. Bradshaw, "The Use of the Bible in Liturgy: Some Historical Perspectives," in *Studia Liturgica* 22, no. 1 (1992): 35–52, 39, 41. He points out, however (36, 41, 43), that while the four different ways he identifies are not mutually exclusive, usually one predominates or is primary. Regarding the Roman Catholic Sunday Lectionary more specifically, see Reinhard Messner, "La liturgie de la Parole pendant la messe: L'anamnèse du Christ mise en scène," in *La Maison-Dieu* 243, no. 3 (2005): 43–60. William Skudlarek, *Word in Worship*, 33–34, captures well the blend of primary and secondary roles of the readings in the Roman Catholic Lectionary for Sundays and solemnities when he observes that the post-Vatican II commission charged with its revision ". . . rejected, at least implicitly, other ways of going about its task. The lectionary was not to be ordered around a 'history of salvation' motif (understood as a line running from the creation to the second coming), or around a systematic presentation of the theological teachings of the church, or according to a literary analysis of the parts of the Bible that were to be used. Nor were the readings to be chosen and ordered for the primary purpose of exhorting and encouraging people

duction 10 asserts: "It can never be forgotten, therefore, that the divine word read and proclaimed by the Church in the Liturgy has as its one purpose the sacrifice of the New Covenant and the banquet of grace, that is, the Eucharist. The celebration of Mass, in which the word is heard and the Eucharist is offered and received, forms but one single act of divine worship."

In this way the lectionary's selection and distribution of readings for the Sundays in Ordinary Time lends a sharper relief than elsewhere in the annual cycle to the "genuine conception of liturgical celebration."

IV. Implications for the Sundays in Ordinary Time in the *OLM*

Given the preeminence of Sunday and the unique character of the week, then, the *semicontinuous reading* arrangement of the second and third readings was deemed by the Lectionary's designers to be a fitting way to express the "theme(s)" of the weekly procession of Ordinary Time Sundays. Because they are "numbered," these Sundays are meant to evoke the ongoing, undetermined, and uninterrupted weekly succession of time. This becomes all the more evident when compared to the Sundays of Advent, Lent, and Easter. For these festal seasons, the sequence of Sundays suggests progress toward a major feast (Christmas, Easter, Pentecost, respectively); the Sundays in Ordinary Time, however, point to the whole mystery of Christ. The only implied movement is toward the eschatological fullness of the kingdom of God. Thus, if there is a "theme" for these Sundays, it is the continued, sustained, and uninterrupted fidelity of discipleship, of following in Jesus' footsteps throughout one's life and the life of the believing community. The *correspondence between the first and third reading*, for its part, is intended to evoke the overarching story of salvation of which Jesus is the climax and fulfilment. Together, these two interlocking patterns were reckoned by the designers of the Lectionary to be the most appropriate in structuring these Sundays

---

to lead more Christian lives. The lectionary was there to proclaim the passion, death, resurrection, and ascension of Christ, fully realised in him and being realised in us who, through faith and baptism, have been joined to him."

in the Lectionary.[28] The following excerpt from John Paul II's encyclical *Dies Domini*, while dealing with Sunday generally, summarises well what the arrangement of the Sundays in Ordinary Time in particular seeks to express:

> 75. Since Sunday is the weekly Easter, recalling and making present the day upon which Christ rose from the dead [here, Easter in the sense of the *event* of Christ's resurrection], it is also the day that reveals the meaning of time. It has nothing in common with the cosmic cycles according to which natural religion and human culture tend to impose a structure on time, succumbing perhaps to the myth of the eternal return. The Christian Sunday is wholly other! Springing from the resurrection, it cuts through human time, the months, the years, the centuries, like a directional arrow that points them toward their target: Christ's Second Coming. Sunday foreshadows the last day, the day of the *Parousia*, which in a way is already anticipated by Christ's glory in the event of the resurrection.[29]

V. Concluding Reflections

While the above discussion might not dissipate, let alone resolve, the discomfort arising from the lack of thoroughgoing vertical correspondence among the three readings on any given Sunday in Ordinary Time, it nonetheless seeks to set the matter in its broader liturgical, calendrical, and especially lectionary contexts. These reflections prompt two concluding observations:

First, it is important to assess any individual part or sector of the lectionary in light of the whole, of its intended overarching architecture—intended, because the designers of the *OLM* had inherited a one-year Lectionary, in use for more than a millennium, that had no obvious plan or design, particularly for what were then called the

[28] The *RCL*'s second option for the first reading, a broadly-conceived semicontinuous track for each lectionary year, results in three distinct horizontal patterns, one for each of the three readings. Vertical correspondence is therefore essentially precluded. For a fuller presentation, see Consultation on Common Texts, *The Revised Common Lectionary*, 3–4, 57–58, 113–14. The *RCL*'s second option for the Old Testament reading works best for narrative books, as Ansgar Franz, "Die Rolle des Alten Testamentes in Perikopenreformen des 20. Jahrhunderts," in *Streit am Tisch des Wortes?*, ed. Franz, points out: ". . . eine lectio continua / semicontinua sinnvoll nur bei stark narrativen Texten funktionieren kann" (641).

[29] *Liturgy Documents*, 43–83.

Green Sundays.[30] It is one of the main insufficiencies that the revisers of the lectionary sought to address, and they did so by devising an integral arrangement whose constitutive parts can best be understood in light of its entire architecture. That is why the *General Introduction* urges that those who espouse the revised Lectionary gain "a thorough knowledge of the structure of the Order of Readings, so that he [or she] will know how to work a fruitful effect in the hearts of the faithful. Through study and prayer he [or she] must also develop a full understanding of the coordination and connection of the various texts in the liturgy of the word, so that the Order of Readings will become the source of a sound understanding of the mystery of Christ and his saving work" (39).[31]

Second, because Sunday is foundational and originary, epitomizing the pristine experience of Christian worship, the *functions* of the three readings remain the same throughout. No matter where located in the annual cycle and irrespective of their specific content on any given Sunday or feast, the readings always relate to each other as follows: The first reading from the Old Testament evokes the wider story of salvation, of which Jesus, proclaimed in the gospel, is the climax and fulfilment, interpreted and appropriated for Christian life as modelled in the second reading from the apostolic writings. Just as it is helpful to consider the Lectionary as a whole rather than piecemeal, so is it important here as well to consider the readings in light of the unity of Scripture, centred on the paschal mystery of Christ, and not simply as individual, discrete entities.[32]

[30] The gospels among themselves had no obvious rationale or pattern; the epistles seem to have followed a sort of semicontinuous pattern in canonical order for the excerpts from the Pauline letters between Pentecost and the following Advent. However, there was no link between the epistles and gospels. Gaston Godu, "Épîtres," in *Dictionnaire d'archéologie* 5/1, ed. Cabrol and Leclercq, cols. 325, 331–32, 343; James Moudry, "Unfolding the Mystery of Christ: The Liturgy of the Word," *Catechumenate* 13, no. 5 (Sept. 1991): 2–12, 5; Thomas O'Loughlin, "Language, Music, Liturgy: Communicating the Word," *Music and Liturgy* 41, no. 3 (Feb. 2016): 27–38, 35.

[31] Helpful in this regard: *General Introduction to the Lectionary for Mass* (indispensable); Boisclair, *Word of the Lord at Mass;* Thomas O'Loughlin, *Making the Most of the Lectionary: A User's Guide* (London/Harrisburg, PA: SPCK/Morehouse, 2012); Bonneau, *Sunday Lectionary;* Consultation on Common Texts, *The Revised Common Lectionary.*

[32] See, for example, Congregation for Divine Worship and the Discipline of the Sacraments, *Homiletic Directory* (Ottawa: Canadian Conference of Catholic Bishops, 2015), nos. 17, 18, 19.

A return *ad fontes*, to the living waters of Christian worship, as I have tried to show here, might help foster a better appreciation of the Lectionary design for the Sundays in Ordinary Time.

Chapter 7

The Role of the Bible in Anglican Marriage Rites

Catherine Reid

A clear commitment to Scripture can be discerned in Anglican (Church of England) marriage rites. This is hardly surprising for a church whose identity is partly anchored in the Reformed tradition. It is also clear that the nature of its marriage rites is liturgical, and that they have a sacramental understanding of marriage rooted in biblical foundations at their core. In response to the reality of marriage commonly taking place outside of the Eucharist, the Church of England's successive revisions to its rites show an increasing priority given to Scripture as an integral part of the marriage service, with the newest rites (*Common Worship* 2000) placing at least one Bible reading before "The Marriage." The Bible features in the Church of England's marriage rites in more ways than simply Bible readings, as the present work will show. However, as we shall see, there are also several instances, in performance and practice, where there is a clear departure from Scripture in favour of prioritising a more pastoral ministry. The case of marriage after divorce is a clear example, as is the change in the use of "obey" as part of the bride's vows. At the time of writing, as will be considered below, the challenge of same-sex marriage is confronting Anglican churches.

When looking at the Church of England's successive marriage rites, although a commitment to Scripture can be discerned, its relationship seems increasingly nuanced and complex. In the current rites in *Common Worship*, clear pointers to the biblical foundations, which underpin the theology of marriage and inform the liturgical celebration, are removed in favour of the rite being "less obscure." This limits and narrows the liturgical celebration of marriage, as well as weakening how Christian marriage is understood in relation to the kingdom of God, particularly how, in marital union, man and woman are called to reflect the model of love given in the union of Christ and his church.

The particular marriage rites examined in this study are the successive Church of England revisions: *Book of Common Prayer* (*BCP*) 1549, 1552 and 1662; and the revisions in Series 1 in 1966 (which mainly authorised the marriage service in the proposed 1928 *BCP*); Series 3 in 1977, which was a first draft of the rite in the *Alternative Service Book* of 1980 (*ASB*); and finally, the Church of England's current marriage rites in *Common Worship* of 2000 (*CW*), which are discussed in more detail. The biblical foundations of the theology of marriage as presented in these rites are explored, and the ways in which the Bible features are identified. It is considered further how the function of Scripture is not limited to catechesis and teaching but goes beyond these in virtue of the fact that Scripture is embodied in a context of liturgical celebration.

Biblical Theology in the Marriage Rite

The Preface in the marriage rites of the Church of England is a good place to begin when wanting to know how the church understands marriage.[1] The Prefaces have a clear Anglican character, one aspect of this being a tension in how Christian marriage stands alongside an understanding of marriage functioning as a social and secular institution existing long before the church offered any liturgical celebration of marriage. Despite the Church of England Liturgical Commission noting only minor changes to the Prefaces of Anglican marriage rites since the *BCP* 1662 Preface they have, in fact, altered

[1] See Prefaces from marriage rites *BCP* 1662, Series 1 (same as 1928 "the deposited book"), *ASB* (same as Series 3), and *Common Worship*. Archbishops' Council of the Church of England, *Common Worship: Pastoral Services* (London: Church House Publishing, 2000, 2005).

considerably.[2] Given that the Preface, while being a part of the rite itself, also provides a hermeneutic for the marriage liturgy, it is worth reflecting on it briefly here.

The most significant change is evident in the *CW* Preface, revealing a diminished understanding of marriage as a sacrament rooted in biblical origins.[3] Even though the theology of Christian marriage as a sacrament has a complex history in the Church of England, prior to *CW* its marriage rites allowed in their prefaces for a clearly sacramental interpretation of marriage.[4] The *CW* Preface now makes no explicit biblical links or references in what it says about marriage. Marriage in the *BCP* 1662 and Series 1 was presented as "instituted of God," which is itself an interpretation of the Genesis narrative. In the *ASB* this changes to "the Scriptures teach us that marriage is a gift of God in creation." In *CW* this becomes "marriage is a gift of God in creation," giving no specific link to Genesis and allowing marriage to be seen simply as a gift like many other "gifts" in creation. *CW*'s removal of "a means of his grace, a holy mystery in which man and woman become one flesh" serves to weaken the theology of Christian marriage presented in the rite, and, even more so, its absence disassociates the specific purpose of the union of male and female in its unique role in the coming kingdom of God, which the Eastern Rites—particularly The Crowning—pick up so well.[5] A further problem with

[2] See "Marriage," in *General Synod 1298Y: The Pastoral Rites, Report of the Revision Committee* (London: General Synod of the Church of England, 1999), paragraphs 18–21, and Henry Everett, "Marriage," in *A Companion to Common Worship*, vol. 2, ed. Paul F. Bradshaw, 185 (London: SPCK, 2006).

[3] This refers to Genesis 2:23-24, that male and female are created for union with one another and that this is God's purpose for them.

[4] The Preface to the *BCP* 1662 states that holy matrimony is "instituted by God in the time of man's innocency, signifying unto us the mystical union that is betwixt Christ and his Church"; in *ASB*: "the scriptures teach us that marriage is a gift of God in creation and a means of his grace, a holy mystery in which man and woman become one flesh. It is God's purpose that, as husband and wife give themselves to one another in love throughout their lives, they shall be united in that love as Christ is united with his Church."

[5] John Meyendorff, *Marriage: An Orthodox Perspective* (New York: St. Vladimir's Seminary Press, 1975), 44: "The important point in the text of St Paul is that the union of Christ with the Church, His Body, is seen as the model—the absolute model—of the relationship between husband and wife, and even of the story of man's and woman's creation. It is not marriage which serves as a model for the understanding of Christ-Church relationships, but on the contrary this relationship is declared as

the removal of the Genesis reference, and the explicit theology of Christian marriage as the "holy mystery in which man and woman become one flesh," is that the subsequent biblical imagery drawn from Ephesians—itself rooted in the Genesis link of husband and wife becoming "one flesh"—now makes little sense.[6] Commentaries on the current *CW* rite seem to suggest the changes made are so that "its wording is judged more accessible to non-churchgoers,"[7] and it is suggested in *A Companion to Common Worship* that *CW* set out consciously to "avoid obscure phrases," with "one flesh" as an example.[8] Undoubtedly, there is a range of meanings of "flesh" in the Scriptures: the Genesis use also possibly referring to family/clan.[9] The use of "one flesh" in the *BCP* and *ASB* pointed to a sense of a permanent change (though this carries obvious pastoral implications and Christian teaching issues in the face of divorce and remarriage),[10] and the clear omission in the *CW* Preface can only be seen to weaken the theology of union in marriage as previously understood. Henry Everett points to this issue when he writes, "marriage is no longer said to have been created by God," noting this as "a major departure for the Church of England."[11]

Clearly there are issues with Ephesians 5:21-33 in connection with contemporary marriage liturgy, particularly in its presentation of how a wife is to relate to her husband, with a general rejection of the notion she should "obey".[12] Yet, given the significance this passage places

---

part of Christian experience which marriage is called to reflect. As we have seen above, marriage, as a sacrament, is the introduction and the transposition of man-woman relationships into the already given Kingdom of God, where Christ and the Church are one body." See also 45–46.

[6] Ephesians 5:21-32.

[7] *GS 1298Y*, par. 20.

[8] Everett, "Marriage," 185.

[9] Colin Hamer, *Marital Imagery in the Bible* (London: Apostolos, 2015), par. 1.4.3.

[10] It is also the case that divorce and remarriage took place in the Old Testament and that Old Testament marriage practice is not as in Genesis 2:23-24. See Hamer, *Marital Imagery*, par. 5.14.

[11] Everett, "Marriage," 186.

[12] In Series 1 the bride is no longer required to "obey" and the vows become identical, although there is still the option for the bride to say "obey" if she wishes. See Alternative Vows in *CW*. Note also here that Ronald Jasper and Paul F. Bradshaw, *A Companion to the Alternative Service Book* (London: SPCK, 1986), 384, make clear that "nowhere in Scripture, and in particular Eph 5:22, Col 3:18, and 1 Pet 3:1-5, is equality in marriage urged." This is a clear case where experience of human relationships

on marriage between a man and a woman, pointing to its origins in creation as well as looking to it as a way of life that is part of salvation, it seems integral to how we understand and celebrate marriage in the church. In the call for a mutual submission in marriage, Ephesians points back to Genesis: "'For this reason a man will leave his father and mother and be joined to his wife, and the two will become one flesh.' This is a great mystery, and I am applying it to Christ and the Church" (5:31-32). It is in the united desire to serve God through each other that the husband and wife grow more intensely united as one. Rather than speaking of domination of one over the other, each obeys and submits to the other as they learn to submit to and obey God. In marriage, we are to see a model of love that reflects the love Christ has for his church. The biblical theology of marriage provides a particular lens to draw out the richer and fuller meaning of the Ephesians passage, deepening our understanding of what marriage is and pointing to further possibility for liturgical celebration. A sacramental understanding of marriage is also linked to the Ephesians passage. Kenneth Stevenson was a strong advocate for marriage as the concern and interest of the whole church: more—not less—is to be made of marriage, and the role and place of the Ephesians passage in the church's biblical theology of marriage seems too important to lose or put aside. Instead, it is worth looking at how an exploration of this one-body theology, with an emphasis on how husband and wife are to relate to one another in their reverence to Christ, can form part of the marriage preparation of couples.

The *CW* Preface makes three concise statements on the nature of Christian marriage: that it is a gift of God in creation, that it is a way of life made holy by God, and that it is a sign of unity and loyalty. The first makes some, albeit now weakened, link to creation and marriage in Genesis, the second to the biblical account of Jesus attending a wedding at Cana of Galilee, and the third to marriage as enriching and strengthening community. The role of the witnesses (the priest and the people) in the marriage rite also gains in recognition, particularly the presence of family and friends, both acknowledged in the Preface and in the Declarations. They pray for God's blessing on the couple, share in their joy, and they celebrate their

---

has influenced our connection to Scripture on this point, and so also enlarged and extended the relationship between husband and wife.

love,[13] all firmly placing the marriage celebration in the context of a joyous and festive occasion. The biblical reference and account of Jesus at a wedding is part of this tone of celebration and joy, his presence being taken to show that the state (and "way of life") of marriage is blessed.[14] We notice that the *BCP* 1662 Preface also includes reference to "the first miracle that he wrought."

When we compare the significance of this biblical event in The Crowning of the Orthodox Rite to how it is employed in the Anglican context, as with the Genesis and Ephesians link to the coming kingdom of God, we again have a diminished and barely visible sign. Nothing is said about the significance of Jesus' changing water into wine in Cana, pointing to "a transfiguration of the old into the new, a passage from death to life," and the way this might characterise marriage as part of God's kingdom, where we see a "transforming of the natural order of things into a joyful celebration of God's presence among men."[15] Anglican theology does draw on biblical foundations in its understanding of marriage, evident in the Prefaces. Yet although biblical origins for marriage can be discerned in its approach and thinking, it does not employ the significance of this biblical witness to enrich its theology fully. A further consequence of this is that the scope of liturgical celebration becomes limited. We might ask, though, whether drawing on the riches of the Eastern tradition, with its crowns and canopies, is really an option for Western marriage liturgies and congregations. Certainly, as with any symbolism in any liturgy, we can question the level of meaning and significance that has actually been grasped. This, however, misses the point and sidesteps the invitation. The scope of the liturgical celebration of marriage is both wide and deep *because of* the richness of the biblical and sacramental theology underpinning marriage. Stevenson could see the possibilities that marriage liturgies offer to the whole church in her own celebration of the kingdom on earth as a foretaste of the kingdom to come. As marriage points to this kingdom theology, we should expect the liturgy celebrating it to embody something of its magnificence and richness.

[13] See beginning of Preface in *CW* marriage service.

[14] In the *ASB* Preface, "to share in their joy. Our Lord Jesus was himself a guest at a wedding in Cana of Galilee, and through his Spirit he is with us now."

[15] Meyendorff, *Marriage: An Orthodox Perspective*, 45.

Pastoral Role of Marriage: Rites of Passage

Stevenson says that Christian marriage is a combination of human resolve and divine blessing, and we can clearly discern this in the *CW* marriage rite.[16] Weddings can be seen as serving two purposes simultaneously, being both Christian liturgy and social rite of passage.[17] Anthropologist Arnold van Gennep argued in his classic work, *The Rites of Passage* (*Les Rites de Passage*, 1909), that all societies have three clear stages in changes in social status: separation, where a person leaves their old status; liminality, where the person is in between two social states of life; and incorporation, where the person re-enters society with a new status.[18] These three stages of "rites of passage" can be discerned in Christian pastoral rites, this perhaps being the reason for Van Gennep's influence in the revision of such rites.[19] Applying this to marriage, we can discern stages two and three: stage two in the period of engagement, and stage three when they are married. Stevenson, building on Van Gennep's model, writes that "rite is the primal means for the Christian to cope with reality."[20] He argues that liturgy should *ritualise* reality, good liturgy speaking to ordinary men and women where they are, into the deeper structures and phases of life.[21] This is surely a further rationale for the church's pastoral rites and we can see this intention in the rites themselves. The question becomes then, how Scripture functions in the liturgical celebration of marriage, where the rite is understood and partly conceived as (though not exclusively) a pastoral rite. Any thoughts here must recognise that Scripture is set in the context of *liturgical celebration*.

[16] Stevenson, *To Join Together: The Rite of Marriage* (New York: Pueblo, 1987), 171. It is of note also that earlier Anglican rites were unclear in when the couple were blessed, and only the Blessing in the *CW* marriage rite follows Stevenson's model of marriage blessing, drawing on the witness of tradition.

[17] Sarah Farrimond, "Weddings and Funerals," in *The Use of Symbols in Worship*, ed. Christopher Irvine (London: SPCK, 2007), 97.

[18] Stevenson, *To Join Together*, 190–92, and also Farrimond, "Weddings and Funerals," 94. See Arnold van Gennep, *The Rites of Passage*, trans. Monika B. Vizedom and Gabrielle L. Caffee (Chicago: University of Chicago Press, 1960). A revised edition published by Routledge appeared in 2004.

[19] Farrimond, "Weddings and Funerals," 94.

[20] Stevenson, *To Join Together*, 213.

[21] Stevenson, *To Join Together*, 191.

Marriage Rite and Eucharist

Traditionally, marriage would take place in the context of a eucharistic celebration, and certainly marriage rites in both East and West were developed with this setting in mind, even though the Eucharist may not, in practice, have actually been celebrated as part of the marriage service.[22] The *BCP* 1662 rite made a shift from its predecessors in recommending rather than requiring that the newly married receive communion immediately. This was apparently owing to "Presbyterian objections that some couples would be unfit or unprepared for communion, [and] that it should not be mandatory to communicate when coming to be wed."[23] Despite the practice of communicating at the time of marriage being laid aside and discontinued,[24] the couple would still, towards the closing part of the marriage rite, proceed to the Lord's table for prayers. This practice continues today in the present *CW* rite. That the *BCP* 1662 and Series 1 rites anticipated that marriage would be followed by the Eucharist is evidenced by the fact that no place for the Word is included in the liturgies themselves. In the event of the Eucharist not being celebrated, only a scriptural exhortation or a sermon on the duties of husband and wife would be given to conclude the rite. From 1928, when Communion did not follow the marriage and a sermon was not given, the rubrics state that the Exhortation from the 1662 service or a "portion of scripture" is to be read. A place for the reading of Scripture is finally included in the marriage rite, albeit only as an option.

The widespread practice of marriage taking place outside the celebration of the Eucharist comes increasingly to determine the place of readings in the structure of Church of England marriage rites. The *ASB* made proper provision for Scripture as part of the liturgy, where at least one lesson from the Bible is read during the marriage service. The *ASB* and *CW* also made provision for marriage to be celebrated within, rather than before, the Eucharist, and readings were an integral part of the rite.[25] As marriage has been acknowledged, in practice,

[22] This is across the churches both East and West, as Meyendorff, *Marriage: An Orthodox Perspective*, 47.

[23] Jasper and Bradshaw, *Companion to Alternative Service Book*, 381.

[24] Jasper and Bradshaw, *Companion to Alternative Service Book*, 381. See reference to Wheatly's 1710 commentary on the Prayer Book.

[25] Everett, "Marriage," 183.

to take place apart from the celebration of the Eucharist, revisers ensured the reading of Scripture become a central part of the marriage rite. Henry Everett writes that "CW certainly integrates Scripture into the rite better than its predecessors."[26] In a notable difference to *ASB* the Preface and declarations precede the readings.[27] This structure can also be seen to follow an overall eucharistic structure of word and sacrament, making the marriage service a clearly recognisable act of Christian worship as well as following the shape of the *CW* family of rites.

The prioritisation of Scripture through the placing of readings between the Declarations and the Vows in the *CW* marriage rite is clear, ensuring that if the marriage does not take place in the context of a celebration of the Eucharist, then Scripture is still an integral part of the rite. On the one hand this is to be commended, given that revisers faced the issue that marriage was generally being celebrated as a stand-alone rite. On the other hand, however, it is to be wondered why the important connection between marriage and Eucharist has been so readily abandoned in Anglican marriage.[28] Bryan Spinks rightly calls the "Western protestant satisfaction with an 'occasional office' alarming," observing the placing of the marriage rite firmly in the context of word and Eucharist, as done in the Catholic Church, as correct.[29] Although there are undoubtedly good reasons for the

[26] Everett, "Marriage," 186.

[27] This follows the Episcopal Church's 1979 *Book of Common Prayer*. For the Church of England, the placing of readings and sermon between the Declarations and Vows was not without issue in the Revision Committee of the Liturgical Committee and in discussions at General Synod. Although this is the "normative" position, allowance is still made for deferring both Readings and Sermon (or Sermon alone) to a position *after* the marriage. The change has been interpreted as restoring and reasserting the notion of betrothal, which in the Sarum rite took place at the church door. The consent (declarations, first part), therefore, is separated from the vows. See *GS 1298Y*, pars. 5–8. Unlike Western rites, consent was not considered the "content" of the sacrament in Eastern marriage rites until the seventeenth century. See Meyendorff, *Marriage: An Orthodox Perspective*, 38.

[28] The report of the Revision Committee in its work leading up to the present rite makes the intention clear from the outset that the outline and structure of the marriage service itself should not necessarily be tied to the form of the Eucharist. See *GS 1298Y*, par. 6.

[29] Bryan Spinks, "Symbolism and the Sacraments," in *Grove Liturgical Study No. 26*, ed. Kenneth Stevenson, ed., *Symbolism and the Liturgy*, Grove Liturgical Study 26 (Bramcote Notts: Grove Books, 1981), 24–33, 32–33. In the Roman Catholic marriage rites, provision is made for celebrating marriage outside of Mass for cases of a Catholic

Church of England's own path in this matter, not least in being the "established church" and so for those of faith and those of none, the consequence of its marriage rites being commonly celebrated apart from the Eucharist is that the significance of Christian marriage is not fully realised or expressed within its rites. Spinks recognises this when he writes, "the full significance of the celebration of marriage is only apparent in the context of the wedding feast of the kingdom."[30] While we can acknowledge this, it is likely that the majority of marriages will continue to be celebrated as a stand-alone rite. Given the link of Christian marriage to a rich kingdom theology, the present use of symbol in marriage liturgy could be extended to include crowns during the nuptial blessing. Friends and family could be a part of this, placing the crowns on their heads at the start of the blessing and removing them at the end.[31] The significance of this symbol could be explored with the couple during marriage preparation.

Roles of the Bible in the Marriage Rite

The Bible can be seen to have multiple roles, and is present in several ways, in Church of England marriage rites. Scripture is the foundation of some theological statements made about marriage, such as those made in the Prefaces; certain biblical teachings are highlighted in the rite itself and are ritually enacted within the service;[32] biblical witness is the authority for the use of particular words, such as "forsaking all others" (Gen 2:24) and the (now optional) use of "obey" (Eph 5:22-4; 1 Pet 3:1-6); biblical witness imparts the original meaning and context for some actions in the marriage rite, such as the "giving away;"[33] Scripture forms some of the liturgical text itself,

---

and a baptized person who is not a Catholic. A faith context, even if minimal, is assumed of the couple seeking marriage in the Catholic Church. *The Rites of the Catholic Church*, vol. 1 (Collegeville MN: Pueblo, 1990).

[30] Spinks, "Symbolism and the Sacraments," 32.

[31] Stevenson, *To Join Together*, 224, 225.

[32] Matthew 19:6 is said by the minister after joining their right hands together as part of the Proclamation. Jesus' teaching here is also the foundation of the church's teaching on marriage as lifelong.

[33] Jasper and Bradshaw, *Companion to Alternative Service Book*, 383, cite the York Manual: "'Who gives me this wife?,' indicating that the father was giving the woman to the priest, representing God, who then gave her to the man, as God gave Eve to

such as the Greeting and the Opening Sentence as part of the Welcome;[34] several prayers use biblical imagery and allusions and some include biblical characters.[35] Notably, the Blessing of the Marriage in the current *CW* rite, while following a Jewish *berakah* prayer form, also makes reference to Isaiah in its inclusion of "crown"[36] and to the Song of Solomon in its use of "love as a seal on their hearts."[37] The Blessing, as the rite generally, alludes to the Genesis narrative of God's blessing and fruitfulness.

Rationales for the Selection of Bible Readings

Perhaps the most obvious way the Bible features in the marriage service, particularly from the perspective of "non-churchgoers," is through readings. *CW* provides a selection of twenty-two readings, expanding the previous eleven offered (though only five printed) in the *ASB*. As a point of comparison, the current Catholic rite includes a selection of twenty-eight readings, giving more from the Old Testament than *CW*, fewer from Romans and more from 1 and 2 Corinthians, and also includes a reading from Revelation.

According to Paul Bradshaw's outline of the four liturgical functions of Scripture, the nature of Anglican marriage rites as pastoral rites means the primary function of Scripture is paracletic.[38] Weddings, along with funerals, are typically seen this way, Scripture being chosen for its capacity to strengthen and support, as well as its capacity to provide Christian teaching suitable to the context. As a pastoral

---

Adam." This has had a whole history in itself in the marriage rite, with the current *CW* marriage rite not including the words at all in the main text but making it an option, and the word is changed from "give" to "bring"—"Who brings this woman to be married to this man?" The notion of "escorting" is evident, and provision is made instead for both sets of parents of the couple to "entrust" their son and daughter to one another (see *CW Pastoral Services*, 133).

[34] A common Pauline greeting is given and 1 John 4:14 as the opening sentence follows: "God is love, and those who live in love live in God and God lives in them."

[35] See the Prayer following the giving of a ring in the 1662 marriage rite. Mention is made of the "holy marriage couple," Isaac and Rebecca. The first and fourth prayers also name specific biblical figures.

[36] Isaiah 61:10.

[37] Song of Solomon 8:7.

[38] Bradshaw, "The Use of the Bible in Liturgy: Some Historical Perspectives," *Studia Liturgica* 22, no. 1 (1992): 35–52.

rite, the marriage rite responds to a specific need of the couple, who experience a new stage of personal union in becoming husband and wife and seek their union to be blessed by God as they make a new lifelong commitment to one another. The pastoral nature of the marriage rite sets the rationale for the chosen lections. Yet although the primary liturgical function of Scripture in Anglican marriage rites is *paracletic*, the role and function of Scripture here goes beyond this one liturgical function. An *anamnetic* liturgical function of Scripture in the marriage rite can also be discerned.[39]

For Stevenson, the choice of Bible readings in a marriage service should give some insight into what the church understands marriage to be, so that the couple and all attending can reflect theologically on marriage.[40] The readings provided in the *CW* provision convey some aspect of the broader Christian faith and life that could easily be said to relate generally to marriage, and only two of these could be said to give *specific* teaching on marriage, namely Ephesians 5:21–end and Mark 10:6-9.[41] During the development of the Series 3 marriage rite, it is interesting to note the Liturgical Commission's suggestion to the Synod to omit the reading from Ephesians 5 from those available "as the Commission believes the complicated analogy of this lesson is difficult to understand."[42] This was not carried.

However, the diminished connection in the *CW* Preface between the Genesis reference and the Ephesians imagery reduces the impact of the readings in the context of a liturgical celebration that should look to celebrate marriage as part of the fullness of the kingdom. The Christ-church relationship is part of Christian experience which marriage is called to reflect.[43] The link to Genesis refers to the integral connection between creation, marriage, and God's purpose for humankind, which relates to the meaning of the Ephesians' imagery of Christ and his church. The union of Christ and church is seen to model the relationship between husband and wife because of the

[39] Bradshaw, "Use of the Bible," 35–52.

[40] Stevenson, *To Join Together*, 177.

[41] Jeremiah 31:31-34 gives the background to the idea of covenant and Romans 7:1, 2, 9-18 refers to marriage ending on a partner's death.

[42] See *General Synod GS 228 Alternative Services Series 3: The Wedding Service, A Report by the Liturgical Commission of the General Synod of the Church of England* (London: SPCK, 1975).

[43] Meyendorff, *Marriage: An Orthodox Perspective*, 44.

nature of their union in creation. The theology and teaching of the selected readings in the *CW* provision is extended and enriched when marriage is understood in connection to this Christ-Church relationship.

Given that the main *CW* marriage rite is set apart from the Eucharist, which is *the* sacrament of the kingdom, an anamnetic function of Scripture in the liturgical celebration is, of course, limited. It is also true that arguments for an anamnetic interpretation of how Scripture is functioning in the marriage rite are likely to link to how marriage is considered to work as a sacrament. Again, it is important to consider how marriage, as the transposition of a new man-woman relationship into the already given kingdom of God where Christ and the church are one body, relates to the Eucharist as a foretaste of the heavenly banquet. All of this takes place in a context of festal joy and celebration, often articulated through marriage imagery such as the Invitation to Communion: "Blessed are those who are called to his supper." This links to Revelation 19, which depicts Jesus the bridegroom uniting himself to his bride, the church. An angel announces this union by saying, "Blessed are those who are invited to the marriage supper of the lamb." At the Eucharist, we hear the angelic invitation to the heavenly wedding feast.

Bradshaw says the liturgical function of Scripture is anamnetic when it is "intimately related to the meaning of what is being celebrated, interpreting and stimulating the liturgical action itself."[44] This function of Scripture is easily discernible in the celebration of the Eucharist, especially in the eucharistic prayer, formed itself from Scripture and accompanied with a series of manual acts that further interpret and stimulate liturgical action. In the case of the marriage rite, and particularly in *CW*, a clear example of Scripture functioning in an anamnetic way is at the Proclamation, when the priest joins the right hands of the couple together and says the formula based on Matthew 19:6, "Those whom God has joined together let no one put asunder."[45] It is common for the priest to wrap his or her stole around

[44] Bradshaw, "Use of the Bible," 41.

[45] Despite there being issues around the translation of this, "asunder" as it is in the popular mind has been restored in the *CW* marriage rite, having been "let not man divide" in *ASB*. See Everett, "Marriage," 189, for further details on this point.

the couple's right hands before saying the gospel quotation.[46] According to Bradshaw's description of Scripture functioning in the liturgy anamnetically, The Blessing of the Marriage in *CW* can be considered a further example. Firstly, the position of the nuptial blessing straight after the vows and proclamation links it better to tradition, making it clear that Christian marriage is human resolve (consent and commitment) and divine blessing. Secondly, the nuptial blessing itself is cast in the Jewish *berakah* prayer form, and includes scriptural references to Isaiah and the Song of Solomon, following better the model of nuptial blessing witnessed by tradition.[47] The movement and celebration in the marriage rite from vows to blessing, and the function of Scripture in this, is surely at the heart of what is being celebrated, "interpreting and stimulating the liturgical action itself": the union of a man and a woman before God and the bestowal of his blessing on their union. This mirrors Genesis and places marriage in a context of blessing and fruitfulness, rooted in creation itself and God's purpose for humankind.

Marriage and Symbol

As Louis-Marie Chauvet highlights, "Christian liturgy, because it is exercised according to particular laws of *rituality*, functions in an eminently symbolic way."[48] The very way liturgy carries itself out is through symbol, linguistic and otherwise. Language is descriptive, but it is also evocative and effective, and is a matter of symbols as well as signs. All aspects here are active in the celebration of the marriage rite, functioning also with pastoral effect. There is significant symbolism in marriage taking place within an act of Christian worship and within a consecrated space.[49]

[46] Stevenson thinks this a confusing gesture which can be taken to imply the priest does the joining when it is the couple, as the ministers of the sacrament themselves, through their consent in the vows they make to one another. This was partly the rationale for changing the verb from "announce" to "proclaim," so that the minister was understood to be simply declaring (proclaiming) what had already been effected through the consent of the couple. See *To Join Together*, 222.

[47] No doubt the nuptial blessing in the *CW* marriage rite is Stevenson's composition.

[48] Louis-Marie Chauvet, "What Makes the Liturgy Biblical?—Texts," *Studia Liturgica* 22, no. 2 (1992): 130.

[49] Farrimond, "Weddings and Funerals," 96.

Symbols can have several meanings at the same time and, in the context of liturgical celebration especially, are evocative and powerful. Liturgical celebration is enriched when it does not seek to explain and describe its symbols too readily. The veil and its rich symbolism rooted in Scripture (ultimately going back to Genesis 24:65) and having a rich history in the Western tradition, will have a number of meanings for the bride, as for others, that are not limited to its biblical origin or practice in tradition. The exchange of rings is another example of rich symbolism in the marriage rite. Rings have been used as a symbol as long as there have been Christian weddings and, although the wedding ring was opposed by many in the Reformation,[50] the giving of the ring has persisted in Anglican marriage rites and is the only mandatory symbolic act in the whole rite. Indeed, in another aspect of the equality of the couple, it is now general for the groom as well as the bride. The priest prays over the rings, asking that God let, by his blessing, the ring(s) be "a symbol of unending love and faithfulness." This prayer makes a link between the couple's marriage union, described here as a "covenant," and the ring(s): they are to remind them of their "vow and covenant." This reference to "covenant" links back to the Lord's covenant with his people Israel, and forward to the new covenant with Christ and his church, of which marriage is a part. Although the origin of rings in Christian marriage is unclear, a link can be seen in the Jewish domestic marriage rites and the giving of jewellery, silver, and gold to the bride's family.[51] The giving of rings can be said to symbolise permanence (a ring is a neverending circle) and also a mutual sharing of wealth. The exchange of coins has been suggested to take place at this point in the rite, affirming further, like the vows, the sharing of all that each possesses together.[52] Stevenson comments on our tendency in the West to want to understand everything, and that instead, we "have to learn what it is to *relate* to symbolism."[53] He gives many suggestions that draw on the tradition of crowns, canopies, anointing, and others, to

[50] Farrimond, "Weddings and Funerals," 103.

[51] This is a custom embedded in early narrative strands of Hebrew Scripture. See Rebekah and Isaac as an example: Genesis 24:52-54. Stevenson describes ring blessings in marriage liturgies in the tenth and eleventh centuries and the connection between a ring and consent in *To Join Together*, 39.

[52] Farrimond, "Weddings and Funerals," 104.

[53] Stevenson, *To Join Together*, 199.

extend the symbolism of our marriage rites and so further enrich the liturgical celebration itself.[54] Certainly, there is potential in the liturgical celebration of marriage for more symbolism. Stevenson also sees opportunity for liturgical celebration at the stage of couples becoming engaged (betrothal). He suggests couples ritualise their intention to marry within a public betrothal liturgy which could take place during the Sunday service, starting after the sermon or the Creed. Such liturgy could include questions and answers between the priest and couple, and prayers by the community which are then brought to a climax in a prayer by the priest with the laying on of hands. The engagement ring could be given to the woman just before this prayer and the man could also receive a suitable symbol.[55]

Conclusion

The role of the Bible in marriage rites is perhaps inevitably multifarious, given the fact that it is acting in the context of liturgical celebration. Chauvet describes liturgy as shaped by the Bible, as being "profoundly biblical," and the Bible as "always the object of a reprocessing from the simple fact of its extraction from the book . . . and from the fact of its transposition into the liturgical action."[56] The Bible in liturgy is not only about teaching but is embodied celebration. The various ways the Bible features and acts in the *CW* marriage rites are most fully appreciated when viewed in the setting of liturgical celebration. The aim of this chapter has been to identify how the Bible interacts with the marriage rite. Church of England marriage rites show a clear desire to incorporate teaching on Christian marriage, notable especially in the place and inclusion of the Preface (which is itself a Reformed approach) and now in its inclusion of Bible readings before "the Marriage." The strong presence of the Bible is clear in the *CW* marriage rites: in the biblical roots of its theology of marriage; quotations from Scripture as liturgical text with an accompanying action; biblical allusions and imagery in the Blessing of Marriage, and also in its prayers generally. It is also the case, however, as has been highlighted, that the removal of explicit biblical references

[54] Stevenson, *To Join Together*, chap. 8.
[55] Stevenson, *To Join Together*, 212.
[56] Chauvet, "What Makes the Liturgy," 121–22.

(namely the link between Genesis and Ephesians) and the regular practice of marriage being celebrated outside the Eucharist mean the relationship of Christian marriage to the celebration of the fullness of God's kingdom is neither visible nor grasped. Consequently, the significance of Christian marriage (and depth of liturgical celebration) is diminished, and with it a sacramental interpretation of marriage. The restoration of the marriage blessing in the *CW* rite, its present form a better witness to tradition, and its position following the Vows and Proclamation, are certainly to be praised, now making clearer what that rite is doing. Stevenson clearly felt more could be done with marriage, and in his "hopes and fantasies"[57] set out a number of possibilities, drawing on the rich liturgical history around marriage and its rites across both East and West. This brief study also concludes that marriage has significant scope to be made a fuller rite, enriching the biblical and symbolic content of the celebration.

Further Developments?

At the time of writing, the Church of England has begun a period of discernment following the publication of the *Living in Love and Faith* material, which includes an invitation from the bishops to everyone in the Church of England to engage in a conversation about identity, sexuality, relationships, and marriage. The *LLF* material suggests a series of decisions are likely to follow this discernment period[58] and many believe this may involve same-sex (same-gender) unions being celebrated in the Church of England, bringing a change to the doctrine of marriage. Some provinces in the Anglican Communion already celebrate same-sex unions, including the Episcopal Church in the US, and Anglican churches in Canada, New Zealand, and Brazil. Given that the biblical theology which underpins the Church of England's marriage rites holds that marriage is between a man and a woman, which also informs the liturgical celebration of these rites and is connected to their sacramental picture of marital union, an adequate starting point for a same-sex marriage rite and its liturgical celebration is not immediately clear.

[57] Stevenson, *To Join Together*, chaps. 8 and 9.

[58] *Living in Love and Faith* (London: Church House Publishing, 2020), 420.

Chapter 8

Scripture Shaping Funerals or Cultural Funerals Shaping Scripture?

Lizette Larson-Miller

My child, let your tears fall for the dead, and as one in great pain begin the lament.
Lay out the body with due ceremony, and do not neglect the burial. . . .
make your mourning worthy of the departed.

Sirach 38:16-18

But Jesus said to him, "Let the dead bury their own dead; but as for you, go and proclaim the kingdom of God."

Luke 9:60

Bidding farewell to our dead, caring for their bodies in myriad ways, commending them to God and carrying them to the places of the dead, ritually assuring the living that the dead will rest in peace (neither suffering nor returning to haunt us), comforting and supporting those who depended on the dead members of the community, remembering the dead at regular intervals—these have all been fundamental to being human for as long as history (written records) and archeology (material remains and artifacts) have provided glimpses of our common human ancestry. This long view reminds us that rites with the dead—funerals—are not solely the domain of Christians but essentially human, and Christian beliefs and practices surrounding the dead reflect ancient human needs, particular cultural patterns, Christian traditions and beliefs, the written record of faith in Scripture, and what is ritually possible in given times and places.

The focus of this essay is on the use and influence of Scripture in the ritual patterns which accompany the death of a Christian. Even a cursory glance at the history of Christian funerals reveals both great variety in the shape of the rituals as well as unity in the narrative of faith shaping those practices. The plurality of what is known in early church adaptations to cultural burial practices gave way to greater uniformity in particular geographical churches, each locally united because of institutional leadership, culture, and language. As uniformity in funeral practice was arrived at in some places and times between the sixth and the sixteenth centuries, the differences between those constituted churches continued to grow. With the arrival of multiple ecclesial reformations starting in the fifteenth and sixteenth centuries, variety in funeral practice exploded exponentially, along with theological differences in the understanding of what happens to the Christian after death. Many scholars (this author included) would argue that with the arrival of the twentieth century (and well into the twenty-first century now), there has been another profound shift in the practices of accompanying the dead in Christian circles. Heavily influenced by culture, psychology, and secularism, this series of reformations in theology, ecclesiology, and formation by culture has led to changes in how Scripture influences and reflects meaning in the face of death.

It may be helpful to remind readers of the particular perspective with which many of the essays in this volume are making their argument. The editors have chosen to explore how Scripture is received through the liturgy in many ways, with introductory guidance given by the framework of Paul Bradshaw's 1992 article, "The Use of the Bible in Liturgy: Some Historical Perspectives."[1] Bradshaw's five approaches to historical uses of Scripture in liturgy include the didactic, kerygmatic, anamnetic, paracletic, and doxological. Funerals could fit into each of these categories, depending on how Scripture is proclaimed, adapted, interpreted, emphasised and even distorted

[1] Paul F. Bradshaw, "The Use of the Bible in Liturgy: Some Historical Perspectives," *Studia Liturgica* 22, no. 1 (1992): 35–52.

in the actual pastoral practice of the order of Christian funerals. But for the sake of clarity, we will look at funerals and their paracletic use of Scripture. Bradshaw observes that:

> if the anamnetic approach [to the use of Scripture] begins with the liturgical rite and envisages the biblical texts as fulfilling an illuminating and interpretive function in relation to that action, then the paracletic ministry of the Word begins instead with the worshipping assembly and asks what needs the people have which may be met by the reading of appropriate biblical passages. Its function is . . . primarily . . . . pastoral.[2]

From the Funeral of the Church to Personally Curated Funerals: Changes in the Use of Scripture

As recently as the 1960s the funeral liturgy offered by many Christian churches for their deceased members had an (officially) fixed set of readings. Two examples of the historical evolution from no choices (or very limited) to endless choices follow, using Canadian Anglican and Roman Catholic funeral rites as exemplars.

Anglican

In the Anglican tradition, the 1662 *Book of Common Prayer* used 1 Corinthians 15:20-58 as the "lesson" for the burial office, a strongly christological reading focused on hope in the resurrection to come ("Now is Christ risen from the dead and become the first-fruits of them that slept."). The liturgy also contained many other Scripture passages, starting with three processional texts (John 11:25-26; Job 19:25-27; 1 Tim 6:7 together with Job 1:21). These were followed by two psalms (one could use either or both Ps 39 and 90, then the "lesson" from 1 Cor, followed by a sentence from the book of Revelation 14:13). In addition, many of the prayers were built around New Testament verses.

Turning to an adaptation of the 1662 prayer book in the 1962 *Common Prayer of the Anglican Church of Canada*, a few contextualizing comments may be helpful. British North America remained a series

[2] Bradshaw, "Use of the Bible," 42.

of English and French colonies (and then with English oversight) until 1867, when the Dominion of Canada was formed as a self-governing colony of the British Empire. Throughout the twentieth century a gradual movement toward sovereignty reached a resting place in 1982 with the Constitution Act and the Royal Assent, making Canada both a parliamentary democracy and a constitutional monarchy with Queen Elizabeth II as monarch of Canada. The first prayer book Eucharist was celebrated in what would become Canada in 1578 (in Nunavut). In 1893 the Church of England in the Dominion of Canada created the national body of General Synod. In 1955, the church changed its name to "The Anglican Church of Canada." This close alliance with the Church of England is important to note, as there is both continuity with and independence from the 1662 prayer book, which marked the long struggle to create a more inculturated prayer book in Canada.

Regarding the Office of Burial in the 1962 prayer book, there are similarities to the 1662 rite as well as options, starting with a greatly expanded choice of opening processional verses, several psalms to choose from (although no longer including Ps 39), and two alternatives to the 1 Corinthians 15 reading (that text alone, however, remains printed in the Burial Office liturgy). An alternative to the Burial Office was allowed to accommodate the circumstances envisaged in one of the opening rubrics: "The Office ensuing is not to be used for any that die unbaptized, or excommunicate, or by their own wilful act while in a sound state of mind."[3] The 1962 prayer book also offers an "Order of Holy Communion" to be used either with the "Order for the Burial of the Dead" or as a "separate and additional service."[4]

It is interesting that the dropping of Psalm 39 ("Lord, let me know mine end, and the number of my days: that I may be certified how long I have to live . . .") removes the ancient Christian practice of lament in the voice of the deceased, often during a ritual of procession (although the rarely chosen Ps 130—which comes last in the options—draws close to that imagery). In addition, the change in the processional verses from Job (Job 19:25-27 to Job 19:25) drops the verses about the decay of the human body and the physicality of

[3] General Synod of the Anglican Church of Canada, *The Book of Common Prayer and Administration of the Sacraments* (Toronto: Anglican Book Centre, 1962), 591.

[4] *Book of Common Prayer* 1962, 608.

resurrection ("And though after my skin worms destroy this body; yet in my flesh shall I see God: whom I shall see for myself, and mine eyes shall behold, and not another.") and suggests that over the course of three hundred years, Anglicans became much more squeamish regarding the destruction and the resurrection of the body.

There is, in addition, a new rite for the Anglican Church of Canada in 1962, "At the Burial of a Child," with very different Scripture and prayer texts, no doubt influenced by the rite introduced in the proposed 1928 *Book of Common Prayer* for the Church of England as well as the approved 1928 Prayer Book of the Episcopal Church in the United States. In this liturgy the three opening sentences include John 11:25-26 (the same as with an adult); Isaiah 40:11, "He shall feed his flock like a shepherd: he shall gather the lambs with his arm, and carry them in his bosom," which begins a recurring scriptural theme of the Lord as shepherd and the deceased children as lambs; and lastly Matthew 5:4, "Blessed are they that mourn: for they shall be comforted." Here in the third verse the focus shifts to those who mourn. The psalm following the processional verses is appropriately Psalm 23, followed by Matthew 18:1-5, 10, focused on children being presented to Jesus, who proclaims them as examples to be emulated. The addition of the discontinuous verse 10 is clearly to include a new idea, "I tell you, in heaven their angels continually see the face of my Father in heaven," which is also quite ancient—it was a common medieval practice to use the *missa de angelis* for the burial of children along with the common use of angel images on children's gravestones.[5] For the service at the grave, the verses are again quite different from the service for adults: Isaiah 66:13, "As one whom his mother comforteth, so will I comfort you." And Psalm 103:13, "Like as a father pitieth his own children, even so is the Lord merciful unto them that fear him." At the casting of dirt on the coffin, Matthew 19:14 is "said or sung" ("Let the little children come unto me, and forbid them not; for of such is the kingdom of God.").

Here in the addition of a burial for children are the clearest indications of pastoral shifts in the use of Scripture, reflecting Bradshaw's "paracletic ministry of the Word," with its concerns for what may be needed by those gathered to worship. To this end, several of the read-

[5] Children's funerals are discussed in more detail below.

ings turn to comforting the mourning parents and family, along with imagery of Jesus' own regard for children and their innocence.

The 1962 *Book of Common Prayer* was, as Canadian liturgical historian William Blott describes, "the last revision of the old Anglican liturgy before the impact of modern scholarship and contemporary language created a whole new school of revisions; and it was the only modern revision of the 1552 type [of *BCP*]."[6] While remaining the official prayer book for Canada, there is also an official supplement, the 1985 *Book of Alternative Services* (hereafter *BAS*), which has surpassed the *BCP* in volume and use. The 1985 book is a product of the ecumenical liturgical movement, with its sights on a different liturgical inheritance than that of the "old Anglican liturgy." It is modelled on the 1979 *Book of Common Prayer* of the Episcopal Church in the United States (although less so in the funeral liturgies than elsewhere, the funeral liturgies are beholden to the Roman Rite's *Order of Christian Funerals*) and draws on the twentieth-century scholarship on early church liturgy as well as the desire for flexibility and variety in all its liturgies.

"The Funeral Liturgy," significant even in its title shift, offers three different patterns:

A. A funeral composed of three events separated by two processions. Prayers are provided for use in the home or in an undertaker's premises; a liturgy is provided for use in church; a committal is provided for use at the grave or other appropriate place.

B. A funeral composed of two events: a liturgy in a chapel and a committal at the grave.

C. A funeral which takes place entirely in a home or other suitable place. (This form would usually be observed in special circumstances, e.g., when a committal must be deferred because of inclement weather or the distance of the grave).[7]

[6] William R. Blott, *Blessing and Glory and Thanksgiving: The Growth of a Canadian Liturgy* (Toronto: Anglican Book Centre, 1998), 137–38.

[7] General Synod of the Anglican Church of Canada, *The Book of Alternative Services of the Anglican Church of Canada* (Toronto: Anglican Book Centre, 1985), 568–69. Hereafter *BAS*.

Because of the plethora of ritual patterns and readings, we will focus primarily on form A, and within that the "Funeral Liturgy for Use in Church." Before listing Scripture passages suggested there, it is worth noting that the second form (B) is the only one with the rubric "the celebrant then says," instructing the use of three opening Scripture passages: John 11:25-26; John 14:1-3; Romans 8:38-39. This appears to be the only place where the Scripture passages written out in the rubric must be used. The psalms which follow include many options, as do the Scripture readings. In the funeral liturgy proper, the Proclamation of the Word recommends "two or three readings" with a gospel required at a Eucharist. Not until the end of the layout of all three forms for ordering a funeral does the book present a page and a half of "readings and psalms suitable for funeral liturgies," to be used in this liturgy as well as an option for the other forms.[8] These include six Old Testament readings; eleven psalms (with suitable refrains); fourteen New Testament choices; and ten gospel passages. Following these there is a rather surprising category of "non-biblical readings" allowed, with the following instructions: "A short, appropriate reading from a non-biblical source may be read instead of one of the readings before the gospel, or at the time of the sermon, or at another suitable point in the service."[9]

In the span of twenty-three years between the 1962 *Book of Common Prayer* and the 1985 *BAS*, the explosion of choices for Scripture readings is remarkable, as is the choice of pattern for the funeral liturgy. Also noticeable is that the proportion of the liturgy composed of direct quotations from Scripture has diminished at the same time as the choices for which Scripture can be used have expanded.

Roman Catholic

The funeral liturgies of the Roman Rite developed over many centuries, with local variations gradually being consolidated so that greater similarities existed in particular geographical areas, with greater differences between those areas (in addition to monastic patterns). The stages of a funeral (hence "The Order of Funerals") were the preparation of the body and prayers (normally at home); the

[8] *BAS*, 604–5.

[9] *BAS*, 605.

funeral liturgy in the church (the funeral Mass), and the burial liturgy around the grave, with two processions from home to church, and from church to grave, being important rituals with their own psalmody and liturgical texts. Between the ninth and thirteenth centuries, a number of these traditions merged until a distinctive (and proper) funeral Mass emerged in the thirteenth century under the guidance of the Franciscans and in use at the papal court, with its own liturgical texts, Scripture readings, and prayers for the deceased before burial, as opposed to simply using the daily Eucharist of the parish church. It is this "Requiem Mass" which "became the normative funeral Mass for adults in the Tridentine *Missale Romanum* (1570)"[10] and to which we turn to look at the liturgical Scripture choices.

With the suppression of official diversity in funeral liturgies (as a consequence of the publication of 1570, the homogenising tool of the printing press, and its solidification in 1614), the "Funeral Mass and Burial Service for Adults" began with "Meeting the Corpse" (if the priest could not go to the house of the deceased). The corpse is sprinkled with holy water and Psalm 130 (129) is recited ("Out of the depths have I cried unto Thee, O Lord! Lord, hear my voice"). The procession into the church is accompanied with Psalm 51 (50) ("Have mercy on me, O God; according to Thy great mercy"). Upon arriving, the Office of the Dead may be said, or the liturgy may continue straight into the Mass. The appointed Epistle is 1 Thessalonians 4:13-18 ("But we do not want you to be uninformed . . . about those who have died, so that you may not grieve as others do who have no hope") and the gospel reading is John 11:21-27 ("Jesus said to Martha, 'I am the resurrection and the life. Those who believe in me, even though they die, will live' "). The Mass was concluded with the reading of the last gospel (John 1:1-14), followed by the absolution service. At the burial service (at the grave) the *Benedictus* is recited (Luke 1:68-79) using the antiphon, "I am the resurrection and the life" from the gospel reading.

Minor changes occurred in the years between 1614 and 1969, but the rite remained consistent, with a couple of exceptions, most notably the burial of infants and young children. Separate texts for children begin to emerge in the thirteenth century, widespread but of unknown

[10] Richard Rutherford (with Tony Barr), *The Death of a Christian: The Order of Christian Funerals* (Collegeville, MN: Liturgical Press, 1990), 59.

origin.[11] Several different versions are contained in fourteenth-century manuscripts, with one, Sanctorius' *Ritual*, making its way into the *Roman Ritual* of 1614.[12] The earliest of these funeral Masses (for baptized children) mixed New Testament Scripture mentioning children with prayers that focused on "joy and thanksgiving," with no reference to the "pain of the bereaved," which is often a surprise to our contemporary ears.[13] By the fourteenth century, however, it was rare that the funeral Mass would be used for children at all because of the theological assumption that the Mass was for the forgiveness of sins (of the deceased), and children under the age of reason had not yet sinned. Instead, the texts and readings were from the "Mass of the Angels," one of the votive Masses of 1570 and 1614. The Scripture readings seem at first off-topic for a funeral (Rev 5:11-14, "I heard the voice of many angels surrounding the throne, singing with full voice 'Worthy is the Lamb,'" and John 1:47-50, "Very truly I tell you, you will see heaven opened and the angels of God ascending and descending"), until one puts them in the context of the multiple liturgical texts (using short Scripture texts) which "interpret" the Mass of the Angels as a celebration of all Christians praising God with the angels, and young children joining those angels.

In a number of changes to the 1614 ritual, the "Order of Burying Children" (*Ordo Sepeliendi Parvulos*) came to include the various stations and patterning of adult funerals (without the absolution service) but with the use of Psalm 149 or the first section of Psalm 119 at the entrance to the church, and Psalm 24 at the time when the absolution service for an adult would take place. Psalm 148 was used at the graveside service, and several adapted prayers continuing the theme of joy in heaven were added, but even with these adaptations, many bilingual Mass books (Latin and English) were printed with the following rubric: "Where it is the custom, the votive Mass of the Angels is celebrated, but in accordance with the rubrics."[14] In spite of the appearance of outward uniformity, many diocesan instructions added words of consolation (in the vernacular) to the ending of funeral litur-

[11] Rutherford, *Death of a Christian*, 90.

[12] Rutherford, *Death of a Christian*. The *Roman Ritual* of 1614 contained the 1570 funeral liturgy with some minor changes.

[13] Rutherford, *Death of a Christian*, 91.

[14] *Collectio Rituum pro Dioecesibus civitatum foederatarum americae septentrionalis* (Collegeville, MN: Liturgical Press, 1964), 349.

gies, as well as adaptations to urban life throughout the twentieth century.

Following Vatican II and its blueprint for liturgical renewal, the first of the new funeral liturgies was promulgated in 1969 as the *Ordo Exsequiarum (Order of Funerals)*, with the English translation known as the *Rite of Funerals*, in place between 1970 and 1989. Aside from several minor changes, that provisional rite was used until the promulgation of the *Order of Christian Funerals* in 1989. While the Requiem Mass had layers of historical emphases within it, the forgiveness of sins (effected and represented by the absolution service) dominated. That shifted after 1969 to an overarching theology of the paschal mystery, the life, passion, death, and resurrection of Jesus Christ, and the passage through the same for the deceased individual. The most noticeable ritual change was the replacement of the absolution service with the rite of commendation, and the return of many first millennium prayers and images to the various liturgies contained within the order.

The *Order of Christian Funerals* is a tripartite series of liturgies with the deceased: the vigil (or wake), the funeral liturgy proper (with or without a Eucharist); and the rite of committal. In addition there is a full set of funeral rites for children; a whole chapter of scriptural options for adults, baptized children, children who died before baptism, and antiphons and psalm texts; the office for the dead; and additional texts (prayers and ritual gestures). The standardised English language version was then published with variables for each national church.[15] The Canadian (English language) version added to the International Commission on English in the Liturgy (ICEL) publication several more options for the vigil (there are eleven thematic vigil options), committal options in inclement weather, and several other minor variations. The large number of Scripture options for the multiple ritual occasions led to a further publication as a way to gather together the many scriptural choices to assist in planning funerals. Titled *Sacred Scripture Selections for a Funeral Liturgy* (2014), this pastoral volume brings together appropriate Scripture choices from the *Lectionary: Ritual Masses, Masses for Various Needs and Occasions, Votive Masses, Masses for the Dead* and contains an extensive

[15] The English translation of the *Order of Christian Funerals* was done through the International Commission on English in the Liturgy, 1985.

listing of Scripture for a variety of situations (different people, different liturgies, different liturgical seasons, different circumstances of death and life).[16]

To provide one example, the first category of readings in the 2014 collection comprises general readings at the funeral Mass (for an adult). Within this category there are eleven Old Testament readings (five New Testament readings to use as the first reading within Easter), thirteen psalm choices, eighteen New Testament readings to use as the second reading, and twenty choices for the gospel reading. The funeral liturgy proper (here with Eucharist) does not include any Scripture readings within the rite itself, only the rubric: "after the introductory rites, the liturgy of the word is celebrated. Depending upon pastoral circumstances, either one or two readings may be read before the gospel reading."[17] The same follows for the vigil options, and funerals for children. With regard to non-biblical readings, the introduction states clearly: "In the celebration of Funerals and Masses for the Dead, only Biblical readings may be used. Readings from other sources are not permitted. If appropriate, they might be incorporated into the Vigil service."[18]

The Pastoral Theologies of Choice

The "traditional" funerals in Anglicanism and Roman Catholicism, with their fixed Scripture readings of 1 Corinthians 15:20-58 and John 11:21-27 respectively, probably fit better with Paul Bradshaw's category of the kerygmatic or anamnetic ministry of the Word, in which the central reading "was not simply to advance people's knowledge of the Bible, but to provide the biblical warrant and foundation for the liturgical rite being celebrated."[19] Like an archeological dig, the fundamental stratum of a theology professing "in sure and certain hope of the resurrection" shaped the inclusion of Scripture inter-

[16] Canadian Conference of Catholic Bishops, *Sacred Scripture Selections for a Funeral Liturgy* (Ottawa: Concacan, 2014). With particular thanks to Christina Ronzio, director of the National Liturgy Office (English Sector), Ottawa, Ontario.

[17] *Order of Christian Funerals* 84.

[18] *Lectionary: Ritual Masses, Masses for Various Needs and Occasions, Votive Masses, Masses for the Dead*. Cited in *Sacred Scripture Selections for a Funeral Liturgy*, ix.

[19] Bradshaw, "Use of the Bible," 39.

mingled with adopted and adapted cultural rituals of death to proclaim that with the death of a Christian, "life is changed, not ended." As doubts in that confidence of salvation enter into Christian funerals over the centuries, the liturgies become depositories of virtually opposing theologies, professing both that "death has lost its sting" (1 Cor 15:55) and praying "spare us, Lord most holy, O God most mighty, O holy and merciful Saviour, thou most worthy Judge eternal, suffer us not, at our last hour for any pains of death, to fall from thee" (the collect at the grave, *The Burial of the Dead*, 1962). Far more dramatically, hope in the resurrection and fear of judgement resided in the Roman Catholic Requiem Mass until 1969, remaining together in theological tension.

But funerals reimagined after the ecumenical liturgical movement do not only return to what we know of early church funeral patterns and Scripture readings focused on the paschal mystery: they also differ in the relationship to Scripture. As the brief survey above of Anglican and Roman Catholic funeral history for the past sixty years reveals, it is no longer possible to propose that Scripture in these pastoral offices functions primarily as a kerygmatic or anamnetic ministry of the Word. While that may be the received understanding of some who hear the Scripture in these liturgies, the shaping of individualised funerals means that Scripture passages meaningful to the deceased and the mourners can be chosen, and conversely problematic theological concepts for those attending the funeral can be avoided. Hence, contemporary funerals almost across the ecumenical board offer what Bradshaw terms "the paracletic ministry of the Word," beginning with the "worshipping community and . . . what needs the people have which may be met by the reading of appropriate biblical passages."[20]

What are the needs of "the people" with regard to Scripture in funeral liturgies today? The answer is varied, and often less influenced by ecclesial or theological directions than by the reality of living in a consumer culture, and family dynamics of continuity and beliefs. The experiences of preparing funerals, leading funerals, attending funerals, and reflecting on funerals has increasingly led both scholars and pastoral leaders to a growing unease about the dynamics of the

[20] Bradshaw, "Use of the Bible," 42.

many choices (in relation not only to Scripture, but also to ritual elements and patterns of liturgy).[21]

Before looking more closely at the three categories of influence mentioned above, it will be helpful to review what the official funeral rites from the examples laid out above (Canadian versions of Anglican and Roman Catholic) say about the meaning of Scripture in contemporary funeral liturgies. The 1985 *BAS* mentions Scripture in its theological introduction, primarily pointing out the "many attitudes to death" found in Scripture (and, by extension, in the funeral liturgy). It goes on to say:

> [a] Christian attitude to death is inseparable from the biblical accounts of the resurrection of Jesus Christ and his followers' experience of the saving power of his renewed presence . . . [but] there is no single biblical attitude to death, not even to the death of Jesus. The biblical narratives and letters reflect a mixture of grief and hope, suffering and glory . . . it is entirely fitting that Christian funerals reflect these various dimensions of the experience of death.[22]

The Canadian Roman Catholic collection of Scripture for funerals described above (*Sacred Scripture Selections for a Funeral Liturgy*) reiterates the role of Scripture in the funeral liturgy by quoting the "General Introduction" of the English language *Order of Christian Funerals*:

> In every celebration for the dead, the Church attaches great importance to the reading of the word of God. The readings proclaim to the assembly the paschal mystery, teach remembrance of the dead, convey the hope of being gathered together again in God's kingdom, and encourage the witness of Christian life. Above all, the readings tell of God's designs for a world in which suffering and death will relinquish their hold on all whom God has called his own. A careful selection and use of readings from Scripture for the funeral rites will provide the family and the community with an opportunity to hear God speak to them in their needs, sorrows, fears, and hopes. (22)

[21] Of particular note are Louis van Tongeren, "Individualizing Rituals: The Personal Dimension in Funeral Liturgy," *Worship* 78 (2004): 117–38, and Bénédicte Marie de la Croix Marolle, "Funerals as Paschal Remembrance and Incorporation into the Risen Christ," *Studia Liturgica* 50 (2020): 69–85.

[22] *BAS*, 565–66.

The Roman Catholic summary points to the multiple purposes of a funeral liturgy and the pastoral hope that those gathered for the funeral will hear the voice of God in their own "place" of sorrow, fear, and hope through the choices of Scripture. The Anglican introduction emphasises the variety of images of death in both Scripture and funerals, but at the same time acknowledges that while doubt is part of faith, the resurrection of Jesus remains central to the hope of the death of a Christian. Both traditions see the value of choice in Scripture readings primarily as a way to offer this both/and understanding of the inherent ambiguity of the death of a Christian.

Turning to the first of the issues raised above, the ecclesial and theological emphases of both churches also acknowledge that there are individual and corporate tensions in how death is understood that must be maintained in the funeral liturgy (by the juxtaposition of the Scripture readings one to another and the juxtaposition of liturgical texts and Scripture).[23] This tension is at the heart of hopes and fears, faith and doubt, but above all it is the reality of unanswerable questions regarding the specifics of life after death. *Where exactly do we go when we die and for how long?* is a question whose answer is known to God alone and asked by humans through concepts of known spatial and temporal understanding. The ecclesial reality is that a death rooted in Scripture and the contemporary adoption of tradition in the two ecclesial communities involves both a moment of individual death, and a participation in the second coming of Christ. The eschatological tension of the already/not yet (the reign of God here and now *and* its fullness yet to come) is a central aspect of Christian faith and funeral liturgies. With regard to maintaining eschatological tension, John P. Meier writes, "how can this New Testament data be applied to the problem of a Christian funeral? The basic question to raise of any Christian funeral liturgy is: Does this liturgy reflect the New Testament tension between already and not-yet? Is the present funeral liturgy in danger of expressing an overrealized eschatology?"[24] With regard to the eschatological question about the individual deceased, he says that "the exact state of the deceased right

[23] See the treatment of juxtaposition in liturgical use of Scripture by Matthew S. C. Olver, "A Classification of Liturgy's Use of Scripture: A Proposal," *Studia Liturgica* 49, no. 2 (2019): 220–45, esp. 243–44.

[24] John P. Meier, "Catholic Funerals in the Light of Scripture," *Worship* 48 (1974): 206–16, 214.

now is not known to us fully. We may speculate all we want on the relation or nonrelation of the deceased to time and ongoing history, or on whether he is present at the last day as soon as he dies. But the truth is: we simply do not know."[25]

In the theological introduction of the *BAS*, the authors approach the same necessary tension in discussing the assumed and varied pieties of all involved in the funeral:

> These nuances of piety can be helpful if they are held in some kind of balance and with a strong sense of their symbolic structure. They are less helpful, and even destructive, when they are held with conviction in their exact and literal correspondence to an unseen reality. For the truth is that we do not know the condition of the dead, and while faith may consign their well-being to the creative and redemptive remembrance of God, everything we say about them remains, as thing said, at the level of symbol. . . . It is important that funeral liturgies enable people to act at this poetic and symbolic level of their being.[26]

Second, while this eschatological tension features prominently in the official rituals of the church, it does not necessarily match the primary concerns of many people involved in the preparations of funerals. The reality of being immersed in a consumer culture has clearly affected all aspects of funerals. The phrase "consumer culture" refers to a commodification of everything as a primary worldview—everything is for sale—including tradition, spirituality, and liturgy. A key hallmark of this commodification is the fragmentation of things, rituals, and texts, all divorced from their systemic contexts, to be used as desired, including the multiple choices for constructing funerals. The readings and rituals are "detached from religious institutions and communities" so that believers can "construct their own religious syntheses from diverse traditions and sources."[27] This overarching cultural perspective means that many people who meet with clergy to plan a funeral do not understand why a set of non-biblical readings is not appropriate (although one is allowed in the Canadian

[25] Meier, "Catholic Funerals," 214.

[26] *BAS*, 567.

[27] Vincent J. Miller, *Consuming Religion: Christian Faith and Practice in a Consumer Culture* (New York: Continuum, 2003), 6.

Anglican tradition, none are permitted in the funeral Mass for Canadian Roman Catholics). They are culturally conditioned to create their own spirituality. This is even more the case with people who are "digital natives" (who have grown up with the internet and social media). They "envision themselves as creators of their own bespoke religions, mixing and matching spiritual and aesthetic and experiential and philosophical traditions."[28] Above all, this is a series of systems which circle around the individual or occasionally a small group of like-minded individuals. It is the hegemony of the "subjectification of reality" in which conflicting views need not be included.[29]

Third, the family dynamics of continuity and actual beliefs is a catch-all category which dominates how people plan funerals. In some cases, the deceased individual has left choices for Scripture readings, music, and perhaps ritual elements. But most clergy have had the task of sitting down with family members who have no belief or different beliefs than their deceased relative. One often hears, "Could we plan a church funeral with no mention of God?" or other strange requests. Part of this is the impact of consumer culture and individualization mentioned above. Louis van Tongeren writes that "the personalized funeral appears to hang together with the privatisation and individualisation that are characteristic of the lifestyle and thinking in postmodern culture, which distance themselves from institutional forms of religion. Religion and belief are no longer obviously related to the church. Not what a church believes, but the personal relation with God is central."[30] Not unlike weddings, funerals are often shaped by what people have seen, consistent with their self-constructed beliefs. This has led to repeated requests for a "Celebration of Life," which looks back at the life lived by the deceased, rather than a Christian funeral which looks forward to the life to come—an act of faith beyond the present understanding of many gathered to mourn (and their request is often granted by misguided clergy, adding to the problems). There is also a popular presumption

[28] Tara Isabella Burton, *Strange Rites: New Religions for a Godless World* (New York: Public Affairs, 2020), 9.

[29] The "subjectification of reality" was M. Francis Mannion's phrase from an important 1988 article in which he talked about the insidious and seemingly invisible inculturation of liturgy all around us. "Liturgy and the Present Crisis of Culture," *Worship* 62 (1988): 98–123.

[30] van Tongeren, "Individualizing Rituals," 137.

that a Christian funeral is only about the mourners, whereas the primary theological focus is on the dead (one might also argue that it is, as liturgy, first about the worship of God). Here, the guiding principle for choosing Scripture becomes a survey of the choices for the least offensive passage—preferably one with no disturbing talk of judgement or even overt assurance of eternal life—it is this life (and the remaining memories) which is "real" for many people. The result is often a type of "canonisation" event, rather than a commendation of the dead to God.

Conclusions

These three factors (omitting many others for lack of space) influence the use of Scripture readings for a funeral from the many choices available. Sometimes the readings are directly linked to the preaching: they are consequently often in tension with the theology of the liturgical texts and the chosen music—all of which may be part of a positive tension. It is interesting that of the ten gospel choices offered in the Anglican *BAS*, the most commonly chosen is John 14:1-6 ("In my Father's house are many rooms"). It is both familiar to many people who have little familiarity with Scripture and provides a somewhat concrete image of room in heaven for all. It also supports what many surveys have discovered, a common popular belief that all good people go immediately to heaven, held by those active in a Christian community or not.[31] The same can be said for the use of Psalm 23 (familiar to mourners who have encountered it at other funerals), and for Roman Catholics and Anglicans alike the choice of Wisdom 3:1-6 ("the souls of the righteous are in the hand of God") for an Old Testament reading with a poetic image of comfort and embrace by God is popular (although many in many Anglican planning sessions there is a request to shorten it so that the image of "being tested in fire" can be omitted).

[31] A 2014 Pew Research Survey found that 72 percent of Americans believed in heaven (basically unchanged from 2007 survey). The US represents a higher percentage of belief than other countries, but is also the most recent accredited survey of beliefs. https://www.pewresearch.org/fact-tank/2015/11/10/most-americans-believe-in-heaven-and-hell/.

The liturgical developments of the 1960s, which opened up many official choices for Scripture at funerals, resulted in a situation where the impact of Scripture on the understanding of the funeral liturgy really cannot be assessed because different passages of Scripture tie the liturgy together in different ways. The emphases are quite different between readings with a strong eschatological hope, versus readings focused on a time of trial and judgement, versus non-biblical readings about memories and the life that was. Each of these sets of choices impacts the overall theological communication of the liturgy. It is not the case that Scripture ceases to have an effect on funeral liturgies—that continues—but the effects are diverse depending on the choices which can provide a uniform theological view over the juxtaposition of two or three readings, or a roiling tension between the readings. It also raises the question of the essential tension between Scripture readings and liturgical texts (many of which are now also variable) and future revisions of funeral liturgies in the two traditions used as examples above. What do people "need" in the pastoral choices of Scripture at funerals? Perhaps ongoing catechesis with regard to the eschatological promise of resurrection, and a more counter-cultural church will assist in helping people commend their dead to God "in sure and certain hope of the resurrection" and know the comfort of God in their mourning.

Chapter 9

Bible, Liturgy, and Doxology

Bridget Nichols

Introduction

Previous chapters have considered the Bible as kerygma, proclaimed and preached in the liturgical assembly to informed listeners and to those with little biblical literacy. They have reflected on the power of Scripture to make anamnesis, recalling and illuminating the themes of the major seasons of the Christian year, and in the great remembering which takes place each time the Eucharist is celebrated. They have also pointed to the accompanying or paracletic role of Scripture in liturgy that encounters human life at points of profound loss and joy. The present chapter turns to Scripture used doxologically, as the inspiration for liturgical praise and the direct source of much of its content.

Paul Bradshaw, who identifies these four functions of a "Ministry of the Word", also reminds us that there is a necessary porosity between them, preventing the kinds of over-emphasis that would distort the offering of worship.[1] In the case of the doxological function, the danger is performance for its own sake:

> When . . . giving glory to God becomes such an important aspect of the activity that little or no attention is paid to whether the congregation can hear, understand, or make use of what is being read,

[1] Paul F. Bradshaw, "The Use of the Bible in Liturgy: Some Historical Perspectives," *Studia Liturgica* 22 (1992): 35–52, 42.

> then the line separating the doxological from the other functions of the public reading of scripture has certainly been crossed.[2]

While keeping this delicate balance, though, there is one significant difference to be borne in mind. Where proclamation, the retelling and lively recollection of the narrative of salvation, and the consolation and encouragement of Christians in all situations depend chiefly on selections from Scripture with defined positions in the structure of liturgical rites, the scripturally inspired glorifying of God is the substance of almost every element of the rite—prayers, psalms, antiphons, songs, and acclamations. My approach is therefore broad and at some points eclectic. It rests on five preliminary assumptions: first, the presence of Scripture in the liturgy stands as a pledge that God and the glory of God are present in God's word proclaimed. It is, pre-eminently, the *response* to that glory that provides a focus. Second, this central role of Scripture is the gift of a living tradition, constantly renewed in liturgical action. Third, in making scriptural words their own, worshippers associate themselves with their forerunners in faith and with the "whole company of heaven" in the regular round of prayer and praise. Fourth, these doxological texts have a credal aspect. Each time God is praised as supremely glorious, or the author of light, or the giver of gifts, or the architect of salvation, or the forgiver of sins, or the one who confers blessing; each time God is named relationally as one of the persons of the Trinity—Father, Son, and Holy Spirit—a statement is being made about who God is and what God does.[3] Fifth, Scripture becomes an authoritative source and inspiration for the ongoing poetic and literary creativity that adds to the corpus of liturgical praise and thanksgiving.

I begin this tentative exploration of an enormous subject with the physical, audible, and symbolic presence of the Bible in the liturgy. Didactic and homiletic in one sense, in another sense the reality of the book also stands for the living Word in our midst. In yet another

[2] Bradshaw, "Use of the Bible," 42.

[3] Naming the Trinity is an increasingly controversial question in debates about gendered language and God. Janet Martin Soskice's work on metaphors for God is indispensable. See the essays "Calling God Father," in *The Kindness of God* (Oxford: Oxford University Press, 2007), 66–83, and "Naming God: Or Why Names Are Not Attributes," *New Blackfriars* 101, no. 1092 (2020): 182–95.

sense it is an eschatological sign, occupying the place it will vacate when Christ appears in glory.

Following this, the main body of the discussion turns to doxology itself, the business of praise. Here, I draw on Michael Ramsey's fruitful insights into the nature of glory, developed in his study of the transfiguration.[4] This offers a threefold scheme of approach, through the themes of creation, salvation, and eschatology. While the scheme assists us to see the familiar texts of liturgical rites through new lenses and allows them to declare their own distinctive contribution to the total offering of praise, its categories are always penultimate. In the end, they are subservient to the whole act of worship, and then to the cycles of time, of feasting and fasting, of the renewal of thanksgiving, memory, and hope in the sacraments. A final section considers a creative flowering out of the liturgy itself—the generation of biblically inspired compositions both within the regular provision, for example, *Gloria in Excelsis* and *Te Deum*, and the corpus of hymns and songs which stretches from at least the third century to the present.

Most of the illustrations used in what follows are part of the prayer and praise of all Christian traditions. Although I often cite them from the Anglican sources most familiar to me, it is always in the consciousness that no tradition has exclusive claims to the text of Scripture, and that all traditions, especially in the decades of liturgical revision, have benefited greatly from one another and from the work of historians, archaeologists, and textual specialists.

The Presence of the Word

Presence requires conscious acknowledgment. Simply being able to understand the words at a lexical level may still not be enough to count as giving glory to God in the public performance of God's word. Bradshaw quotes Richard Hooker's description of reading the Bible in church—"that special act of service which we do to God"—as part of the general purpose of glorifying God which is the rationale of our worship.[5] The later sixteenth-century context in which Hooker

[4] Arthur Michael Ramsey, *The Glory of God and the Transfiguration of Christ* (London: Longmans, Green, 1949), 28.

[5] Richard Hooker, *The Laws of Ecclesiastical Polity*, vol. III (book V.xix.5), ed. John Keble (Oxford: Oxford University Press, 1836), 88–89. Available online at http://anglicanhistory.org/hooker/5/5.060-069.pdf.

makes this statement is significant. He contrasts the English church's practice with the habits of others (probably Presbyterians and Puritans in the Elizabethan understanding of both those words[6]) of reading the Scriptures to occupy the time while people were gathering for worship. He pays tribute to a liturgy that consciously and deliberately makes space for serious engagement with Scripture, rather than using it as preparation for the main act of worship.

Christian traditions have a variety of ways of honouring the Bible as a material presence in the assembly.[7] This begins even before the book is opened and its contents proclaimed, as evidenced by the decorated gospel books that were being created for liturgical use, perhaps as early as the fourth century, according to radiocarbon dating of the oldest of the Ethiopian Garima Gospels.[8] The Irish Book of Durrow, produced in the late seventh century, is the earliest surviving example of the insular tradition and displays the characteristic canon tables, carpet pages, and illuminations which serve not just as ornamentation, but also as highly sophisticated commentary on the text.[9] The Book of Kells and the Lindisfarne Gospels belong to the same style of manuscript illumination.[10] Richly decorated gospel books are also found in the Byzantine tradition. Produced in monastic scriptoria, where the artistic and literary skills required for work of this sophistication were fostered, the books would have been used in the liturgy, perhaps on feast days rather than in the daily round of prayer.

[6] See Stephen Tomkins, *The Journey to the Mayflower: God's Outlaws and the Invention of Freedom* (London: Hodder and Stoughton, 2020); Patrick Collinson, *The Elizabethan Puritan Movement* (Oxford: Clarendon Press, 2004).

[7] Bradshaw, "Use of the Bible," 32. Bradshaw begins his article with a tantalisingly brief example from the Council of Ephesus in 431.

[8] Judith S. McKenzie and Francis Watson, *The Garima Gospels: Early Illuminated Gospel Books from Ethiopia*, Manar Al-Athar Monograph 3 (Oxford: Ioannou Centre for Classical and Byzantine Studies, 2016), 1.

[9] Bernard Meehan, *The Book of Durrow: A Medieval Masterpiece at Trinity College Dublin* (Dublin: Town House and Country House, 1996); Laura McCloskey, "Exploring *Meditatio* and *Memoria* in Ireland through the Book of Durrow: Manuscript Illumination as the Intersection of Theological and Artistic Traditions," *Eolas* 11 (2018): 32–59.

[10] See Bernard Meehan, *The Book of Kells* (London: Thames and Hudson, 2012); Carol Farr, *The Book of Kells: Its Function and Audience* (London: British Library & Toronto: University of Toronto Press, 1997); Janet Backhouse, *The Lindisfarne Gospels* (London: Phaidon Press, 1994).

Orthodox Christians have historically incorporated the ceremonial entry of the gospel book into their liturgy. The Little Entrance in the Divine Liturgy of the Orthodox Churches prefaces the Liturgy of the Catechumens and sees the priest (or the bishop) and the deacon processing round the altar with the book, elevating it, and calling on the people to be attentive. Roman Catholics and Anglicans have recovered the practice of processing the gospel book into church at the beginning of the eucharistic liturgy, and some very beautiful modern examples of gospel books can be found.[11] In Presbyterian worship, it has been customary for an elder to bring the Bible into church at the beginning of the act of worship and lay it on the altar. A modern commentator notes that there is something anomalous about leaving the prominent edition of the Bible there, while the readings are delivered at the lectern from a less impressive-looking volume.[12] This is a pastoral-performative question and in some ways beyond the remit of the present discussion, yet it may say something about the living status of the Word, as opposed to its rather monumental and statuesque function.

Scripture's role as both lively word, and an instrument and medium for glorifying God when performed, is "marked" or emphasised by the actions that surround it. Formulae of thanksgiving usually end the reading of the Old and New Testament lections. The proclamation of the gospel is framed in announcements and responses, calling for attention before the reading and reaffirming its status as "the Gospel of the Lord" at its conclusion. Alleluias, often textually and musically elaborated, precede the reading, except in Lent and Advent when "Praise to you, O Christ, King of eternal glory," replaces "Alleluia." Further actions, including blessing the designated reader, carrying the book in procession to the place of proclamation with cross and candles leading, censing of the gospel book, and kissing the book at the end of the reading add dignity. They also suggest the

[11] *The Saint John's Bible*, commissioned by Saint John's Abbey and University in Collegeville, Minnesota, is a signal example of the tradition of manuscript illumination recovered in a new idiom. Printed Bibles and individual books containing selections of the illuminations make the work widely available. https://saintjohnsbible.org/.

[12] Peter C. Bower, ed., *The Companion to the Book of Common Worship* (Louisville, KY: Geneva Press, 2003), 53.

love that comes with veneration of God present in the Word. Any part of this can be disturbed and rendered less effective and eloquent by poor performance.[13] How the biblical text, woven into the whole texture of prayer and praise, becomes the church's own voice each time the assembly gathers forms the next part of this enquiry.

Praising God for Being God

With good reason, St. Benedict prescribed Psalms 148, 149, 150 to be recited as the last part of the office of Lauds, the office specially dedicated to the praises of God, every day (RB 12–13). Psalm 148 recognises God as Lord of creation in its summons to the whole population of heaven and earth, including the celestial bodies and the natural world, to give praise; Psalm 149 praises God who has been faithful to a faithful people and defended them from their enemies; Psalm 150 summons musical instruments and every living creature to praise the Lord. This adds to the call to praise the reminder that breath determines the ability to praise, and elsewhere the psalmist warns that those who go down to Sheol cannot praise God (Ps 6:5; Ps 30:9; Ps 115:17. See also Job 10:21-22 and Isa 38:18).[14] It is always God who "opens the lips" of the worshipper (Ps 51:16).

The patterning of psalmody in contemporary monastic settings follows a variety of systems, not all of them retaining Benedict's distribution, but the priority of praise in the morning and evening offices survives. Anglicans accustomed to the *Book of Common Prayer* of 1662 have encountered Psalm 95 each morning, with its call to "sing unto the Lord" and "rejoice in the strength of our salvation."[15] This varied in the Prayer Book order only on Easter Day, when the Easter anthems (*Pascha Nostrum*) were recited, or on the nineteenth day of the month, when it formed part of the regular daily psalmody and a rubric directed the use of an alternative. Current forms of morning and evening prayer have moved away from this strict uniformity, instead

[13] See Juliette Day, "Liturgical Competence," *Anaphora* 2, no. 2 (2008): 61–72.

[14] See the exposition of this theme in Robert Alter, *The Art of Biblical Poetry* (Edinburgh: T&T Clark, 1985), 133–35.

[15] Brian Cummings, ed., *The Book of Common Prayer: The Texts of 1549, 1559, and 1662* (Oxford: Oxford University Press, 2011), 242.

providing a selection of psalms and biblical songs, and giving more scope for observing the seasons and feasts of the Christian year.[16]

Psalm 148 has already alerted us to the whole creation's involvement in responding to God. That vocation finds more developed expression in the morning canticle *Benedicite*, the Song of the Three Young Men, which Daniel and his companions sang in the furnace (Dan 3:35-65).[17] The song is a triumphant assertion in the face of persecution that everything in existence owes its being to the Lord. The heavens, the waters, the elements of the weather, day and night, the earth and its plants and rivers, the creatures of sea, land and air, and finally the people of the earth unite in the same purpose—to "praise the Lord and exalt him forever." In a move that was innovative at the time and remains striking, the Anglican Church of New Zealand produced its own *Benedicite Aotearoa* in 1989. This song is populated with ferns, dolphins, and other indigenous plants and creatures, as well as people of indigenous and settler descent, who have a variety of roles to play in maintaining the ecology of society at every level.[18]

As Christopher Irvine shows elsewhere in this volume, serious consideration has been given to rebalancing the place and role of humanity in the whole creation since the publication of the encyclical *Laudato Si'* in 2015. The evidence of human responsibility for the depletion of the earth's resources, extinction of species and the climate crisis has called dominance, once assumed as God-given (Gen 1:28), radically into question.[19] "Stewardship" and Kevin Irwin's preferred term, "service," now inflect the discussion.[20]

[16] For two Anglican Communion examples see Archbishops' Council of the Church of England, *Common Worship: Daily Prayer* (London: Church House Publishing, 2005); General Synod of the Anglican Church of New Zealand, *A New Zealand Prayer Book/He Karakia o Aotearoa*, new ed. (Auckland: General Synod Office, 2020), 30–53, http://anglicanprayerbook.nz/030.html.

[17] *Common Worship: Daily Prayer*, 602–3.

[18] Anglican Church of New Zealand, *A New Zealand Prayer Book*, 63 and 457.

[19] Anathea Portier-Young, "'Bless the Lord, Fire and Heat': Reclaiming Daniel's Cosmic Liturgy for Contemporary Eco-Justice," in *Full of Your Glory: Liturgy, Cosmos, Creation*, ed. Teresa Berger, 45–67 (Collegeville, MN: Liturgical Press, 2019).

[20] Kevin W. Irwin, "Sacramental Theology after Laudato Si'," in Berger, *Full of Your Glory*, 267–83; Richard Bauckham, "Joining Creation's Praise," *Ecotheology* 7, no. 1 (2002): 45–59.

Praising and Believing

Praise arises out of adoration, but Nicholas Wolterstorff's careful probing indicates why that claim by itself is insufficient. Adoration, he argues, takes on a "particular contour," both from "the object of adoration and from the worshipper's understanding of that object." In carefully nuanced language, he goes on to trace the shading of "contour" into belief:

> [P]rominent in the Christian's liturgical adoration of God is awed adoration of God for God's inestimably great glory, reverential adoration of God for God's inestimably great holiness, and grateful adoration of God for God's inestimably great love for us, God's human creatures.[21]

Three "hymns of the church" (the terminology of Renato de Zan, who distinguishes them from biblical hymns[22]) provide models of the kind of development of credal themes in response to the glory and majesty of God which can be taken as a legitimate extension and application of Wolterstorff's mapping of adoration.

The *Gloria in Excelsis*, a fourth-century composition, springing from Luke's record of the song of the angels at the birth of Jesus (Luke 2:13-14), exemplifies all three "contours": the glory of God the Father who is also "Lord" and "King"; the redemptive love of God the Son, the Lamb of God (John 1:29) who occupies a unique relationship to the Father; and the holiness of the unity of divine persons in the Trinity. It continues to be a morning hymn in a number of Eastern Rites, though it has migrated into the Eucharist in the West, where it is omitted in Advent and Lent.[23] This expresses something important

[21] Nicholas Wolterstorff, *The God We Worship: An Exploration of Liturgical Theology* (Grand Rapids, MI: Eerdmans, 2015), 163.

[22] Renato de Zan, "Criticism and Interpretation of Liturgical Texts," in *Handbook for Liturgical Studies: Introduction to the Liturgy*, vol. I, ed. Anscar J. Chupungco, 331–65, 341 (Collegeville, MN: Liturgical Press, 1997).

[23] See Josef Jungmann, SJ, "Doxology," in Paul F. Bradshaw, ed., *The New SCM Dictionary of Liturgy and Worship* (London: SCM Press, 2002), 156. Representative texts of the *Gloria in Excelsis*, *Sanctus*, *Te Deum*, *Benedictus*, *Magnificat*, and *Nunc Dimittis*, with commentary, can be found on the website of the English Language Liturgical Consultation, https://www.englishtexts.org/praying-together.

in the mood and atmospherics of Christian worship. While God is always to be praised, in seasons where glory is eagerly anticipated but eschatological or penitential themes are dominant, muting the ecstasy of the *Gloria* enhances its return at Christmas and Easter.

The *Te Deum*, also used in forms of morning prayer, takes on the cosmic frame of reference more explicitly than the *Gloria*, associating "all creation" with the praises of "all angels, all the powers of heaven, the cherubim and seraphim." The angels sing the song recorded by Isaiah (6:3), while the Church Triumphant—apostles, prophets, and martyrs—joins the church of earth in acclaiming God as the unity of the Trinity:

> Father, of majesty unbounded,
> your true and only Son, worthy of all praise,
> the Holy Spirit, advocate and guide.

The hymn then turns to acclaim Christ, "the eternal Son of the Father," who took human flesh, conquered death, and is now seated in glory. This Christ will "come and be our judge" and the final lines are a combination of longing for deliverance now, and anticipatory rejoicing in "glory everlasting."

The hymn has a majesty and substance which makes it a fitting centrepiece for special acts of thanksgiving, and this potential for impressive public performance continues to inspire musicians. In addition to chant forms, some pre-dating Gregorian chant, many composers have set the *Te Deum*. Palestrina, Tallis, Byrd, Purcell, Handel, Berlioz, Bruckner, Dvorak, Stanford, Elgar, Howells, Britten, and Vaughan Williams by no means exhaust the list. Coronations and royal events have provided an obvious occasion for the hymn to be sung, Sir William Walton's Coronation *Te Deum* for the coronation of Queen Elizabeth II in 1953, and Sir James Macmillan's setting for the Queen's Golden Jubilee in 2001 standing as notable examples. Papal elections, the consecration of bishops, the canonisation of saints, and even military victories are marked by the *Te Deum*. Outside of liturgical or liturgical-civic contexts, the hymn makes an operatic appearance in Puccini's *Tosca*, but we can only imagine the setting Shakespeare's Henry V had in mind when he commanded at the final counting of the dead on both sides after the Battle of Agincourt:

Let there be sung *Non nobis* and *Te Deum*,
The dead with charity enclosed in clay;
And then to Calais, and to England then,
Where ne'er from France arrived more-happy men.[24]

Pre-dating both the *Gloria* and the *Te Deum*, the third-century evening hymn, *Phos Hilaron*, well known in John Keble's translation as "Hail, gladdening light," was, according to John Hale, sung at the lighting of the lamps in the catacombs.[25] It is principally a hymn in praise of Christ, though always in relation to the Father and then to the whole unity of the Trinity. The natural rhythm of the day, from sunset to darkness, establishes a temporal cycle—"we have come to the setting of the sun and see the evening light"—into which Christ, the true and "gladdening light of the holy glory of the immortal Father," always shines.[26] If the Johannine prologue suggests itself as a primary reference, the web of allusions to light is almost certainly more complex, with Psalm 18:29, Psalm 36:9, and Psalm 141 as only three candidates for consideration. Like the *Te Deum*, it recalls the praise of a much earlier time in the life of the church, though here the connection is more secure than the now discredited attribution of the *Te Deum* to Ambrose and Augustine.

Praising, Remembering, and Hoping

From the praise of God simply (though never really simply once doctrinal assertions enter the picture) for being God, we move to the praise of God who acts in history. Here, the outstanding witnesses are the Gospel canticles: the *Benedictus*, *Magnificat* and *Nunc Dimittis*. In the Lukan narrative, these songs are identified with individuals. Zechariah, Mary, and Simeon give thanks because they have all "seen salvation." All three speak in the perfect tense, signifying actions performed in the past but with ongoing consequences. For Zechariah, it is the promise of the freedom originally promised to the ancestors

[24] Shakespeare, *Henry V*, act 4, scene 8, lines 123–26, in *The Oxford Shakespeare: The Complete Works*, ed. Stanley Wells and Gary Taylor, 592 (Oxford: Clarendon Press, 1994).

[25] John K. Hale, "'Hail! Gladdening Light': A Note on John Keble's Verse Translations," *Victorian Poetry* 24, no. 1 (1986): 92–95, 92.

[26] Text of the *Phos Hilaron* in *Common Worship: Daily Prayer*, 635.

of the nation; for Mary, it is the raising up of Israel out of humiliation and poverty, again according to an ancient promise; for Simeon, God has fulfilled the promise of salvation, restoring glory to Israel and extending knowledge of God to all nations.

Christians who have adopted their words as part of the cycle of daily prayer in the morning, evening, and last thing at night sing these songs of salvation from a perspective adjusted by history. Promises have been fulfilled, but just order seems no less elusive than it might have been for a first-century audience. The canticles, in their liturgical setting, locate history in hope, on the basis of the enduring faithfulness and saving purpose of God. The church, in appropriating these biblical songs verbatim, strives for its own vision of salvation and the need for salvation, and in that light, associates itself with God's action in the world. Particularly in the case of the *Magnificat*, some twentieth-century metrical versions have emphasised the turn to the world at the expense of the shape and sweeping vision of the whole song. Timothy Dudley Smith's perennially popular "Tell out, my soul, the greatness of the Lord" takes a faithful approach to the original, but Fred Kaan's "Sing we a song of high revolt" and Rory Cooney's "Canticle of the Turning" call more urgently for upheaval in the world order towards a just dispensation for all.[27]

These striking, though partial, renderings are a reminder of what Kevin Irwin has called the "surplus of meanings implicit in such texts [which] . . . cannot be exhausted by one act of proclamation; their repetition in varying contexts actually serves to help uncover their many meanings." It is here that antiphons can be of immense importance as primary shapers of liturgical theology. Directing the way the text is received in different seasons of the church's year, and on particular festivals, they "help to shed light on a particular aspect of a text so filled with meanings."[28] Margaret Daly Denton shows how ingeniously they engage worshippers by first defamiliarising the familiar text of the canticle, and then revealing new layers of mean-

[27] Fred Kaan, "Sing We a Song of High Revolt," *Hymns Ancient and Modern New Standard Edition* (Norwich: Canterbury Press, 1983), no. 419; Timothy Dudley Smith, "Tell Out, My Soul, the Greatness of the Lord," *Hymns Ancient and Modern New Standard Edition*, no. 422; Rory Cooney, "The Canticle of the Turning," *The Presbyterian Hymnal* (Louisville, KY: Westminster John Knox Press, 1990), no. 100.

[28] Kevin W. Irwin, *Context and Text: A Method for Liturgical Theology*, rev. ed. (Collegeville, MN: Liturgical Press), 209–10.

ing through the interpretative dialogue between canticle and antiphon.[29]

Creation, Redemption, Eschatology: The Great Thanksgiving

All the themes of praise we have traced so far—creation, covenanted faithfulness, history, memory, and redemption, and the unseen presence of "angels, archangels, and all the company of heaven"—come together in the Great Thanksgiving of the Eucharist. Here it is only possible to gesture at the immense body of prayers from all parts of the Christian tradition, with its multiple vision of memory becoming hope. In a prayer which is all praise, two moments stand out: First, the climactic response to the story of salvation in the words of the cherubim and seraphim of Isaiah's vision in the temple (Isa 6:1-3); second, the offering of the people's own "sacrifice of praise" as witness to unity in Christ now, and anticipation of the worship of heaven at the end of time.[30]

Although these prayers are performative in that they effect something by their utterance, they resist the kind of analysis that a speech act theorist might apply.[31] There is nothing utilitarian about them, and their power to draw worshippers into the mystery of faith owes a great deal to a literary beauty that is deeply rooted in Scripture and in patristic sources.[32] In liturgical traditions which allow the "com-

[29] Margaret Daly-Denton, "Amen Corner: Apprenticing Ourselves to the Antiphonal," *Worship* 93 (2019): 4–11, 7.

[30] See Achille M. Triacca, "La Strutturazione Eucologia dei Prefazi," *Ephemerides Liturgicae* 86 (1972): 233–79; Stephen Beall, "*Mirabilia Dei*: Style and Translation in the Prefaces of the *Missale Romanum*," *Antiphon* 8 no. 1 (2003): 10–12; and Bridget Nichols, "Scripture, Time and Narrative in the Proper Prefaces of the Church of England's 'Common Worship,'" *Studia Liturgica* 39 (2009): 122–28.

[31] This is too complex a question to be pursued here. Eucharistic prayers cannot be said to succeed or fail, for example, and any consideration of their illocutionary and perlocutionary effects must take into account that this is the prayer of the church, though spoken by a single voice. Obvious primary references are J. L. Austin, *How to Do Things with Words*, 2nd ed., ed. J. O. Urmson and M. Sbisá (Cambridge, MA: Harvard University Press, 1962), and John Searle, *Speech Acts: An Essay in the Philosophy of Language* (Cambridge: Cambridge University Press, 1969).

[32] Demonstrated in detail in Anthony Ward, SM, and Cuthbert Johnson, OSB, *The Sources of the Roman Missal* (1975) II: Prefaces (Rome: Libreria Editrice Vaticana, 1987).

mon preface," with its rehearsal of events from creation to redemption, to be replaced during certain seasons and on feast days, there are opportunities to intensify the focus of praise on distinctive aspects of the *mirabilia dei,* the mighty acts of God. This preface for use from Easter Day until the eve of the Ascension is an example:

> It is indeed right, our duty and our joy,
> always and everywhere to give you thanks,
> almighty and eternal Father,
> and in these days of Easter
> to celebrate with joyful hearts
> the memory of your wonderful works.
> For by the mystery of his passion
> Jesus Christ, your risen Son,
> has conquered the powers of death and hell
> and restored in men and women the image of your glory.
> He has placed them once more in paradise
> and opened to them the gate of life eternal.
> And so, in the joy of this Passover,
> earth and heaven resound with gladness,
> while angels and archangels and the powers of all creation
> sing for ever the hymn of your glory . . . [followed by the Sanctus][33]

One of the striking features of this richly referenced composition is its reordering of time. "In these days of Easter" both defines the present season and recapitulates the consequences of Christ's death and resurrection as if they were realised events. The creation and fall narrative of Genesis finds its ultimate reversal: God's image has been restored in human beings; they have been reinstated in paradise; and they have been invited into eternal life. Where an angel once ushered humanity out of paradise, the preface concludes with the joy of the whole angelic host at humanity's restoration.

There are other occasions, though, when the eschatological hope is modified by shadows that fall across the present. Two prefaces for

[33] *CW* 317. The prayer is closely modelled on the Ambrosian preface for the second Wednesday after Easter and translated in Alan Griffiths, trans., *We Give You Thanks and Praise: The Ambrosian Eucharistic Prefaces* (Norwich: Canterbury Press, 1999), 122. Griffiths bases his translation on the 1981 Ambrosian Missal.

feasts celebrating the glory of Christ as Lord also reckon with the historical and temporal aspects of suffering. Thus, on the feast of the Presentation, the church recalls that the infant presented in the temple, wearing human flesh, also "[comes] near to us in judgement," that "he was lifted high upon the cross," and that "a sword of sorrow pierced his mother's heart." And yet we may still join the angels "in their unending hymn of praise," because with the eyes of faith "we too have seen his salvation."[34]

On the feast of the Transfiguration the emphasis is on strengthening the whole people of God for trials that lie ahead. The glory of the incarnate and transfigured Christ, who "revealed his glory before his chosen witnesses" both "prepared his disciples to bear the scandal of the cross," and enacted the hope for the church, "his body." Confidence in that promise of glory enables worshippers to "echo on earth the song of the angels in heaven."[35] Where churches read one of the Synoptic accounts of the transfiguration (the RCL provision) on the last Sunday of the season of Epiphany, this preface might be used with striking effect to draw worshippers into the convergence of glory and suffering as Lent approaches.[36]

In both the examples just mentioned, the preface specifies that the events occurred "on this day." Anthony Ward and Cuthbert Johnson draw attention to its Latin equivalent, *hodie*, in many of the *Roman Missal*'s prefaces for particular days in the calendar. The preface, they insist, is not "a commemorative plaque to past events viewed solely under the aspect of human history, but an entry into the reactualisation of salvific events in a mode that brings the church across the threshold of God's eternal now."[37]

[34] *CW* 317, in Griffiths, *We Give You Thanks and Praise*, 122.

[35] Archbishops' Council of the Church of England, *Common Worship: Festivals* (London: Church House Publishing, 2008), https://www.churchofengland.org/prayer-and-worship/worship-texts-and-resources/common-worship/churchs-year/festivals-0. Accessed 10 April 2021.

[36] Richard Buxton, "Transfiguration," in Paul F. Bradshaw, ed., *The New SCM Dictionary of Liturgy and Worship* (London: SCM Press, 2002), 459.

[37] Anthony Ward, OM, and Cuthbert Johnson, OSB, *Fontes Liturgici: The Sources of the Roman Missal (1975): Prefaces* (*Notitiae* 24 nos. 252, 253, and 254) (Rome: Libreria Editrice Vaticana, 1987), 421 [13].

Praise, Creativity, and Innovation: Hymns and Songs

The expressions of praise and thanksgiving introduced so far have been drawn from what might be thought of as the core provisions for daily prayer and the Eucharist, most of them the shared property of a number of ecclesial traditions. The psalms, canticles, hymns, acclamations, responses, and prayers that constitute this repertoire not only lend themselves to sung as well as spoken performance: in their earliest lives they were very likely to have been sung by default. That continues to be the custom where choral and instrumental resources are available and the choice of Mass setting and psalm chants receives as much attention as the choice of hymns and songs.[38] The contrast with contexts where the musical provision might be an organist or keyboard player, and congregational hymn-singing the primary musical experience, or where the liturgy is largely improvised and led by a worship band with vocalists, is marked. So too is the traditional understanding of sung praise as an element interspersed with other parts of the liturgy, perhaps with a thematic or seasonal development in mind, and the "time of worship" prefacing Scripture reading, preaching and prayer and taking the form of a series of songs choreographed or "curated" by the musicians.[39]

The brief readings that follow look at some examples of this extraordinarily diverse phenomenon, widely separated in the history of the church, but broadly constellated around incarnational themes. They do this in full awareness of the vast specialist literature by musicologists, music historians, hymnologists, and theologians addressing all areas of church music, including the fast-expanding world of contemporary Christian music, which should be consulted by any serious enquirer.[40] My interest here is in strategies of praise and in particular, the interplay of the theological and poetic imagina-

[38] The chanted liturgy of the Orthodox Churches demands discussion in its own right and is not treated here.

[39] See Stephen R. Holmes, "Listening for the *Lex Orandi*: The Constructed Theology of Contemporary Worship Events," *Scottish Journal of Theology* 66, no. 2 (2013): 192–208.

[40] On liturgical music see Jan Michael Joncas's excellent survey chapter, "Liturgy and Music," in *Handbook for Liturgical Studies: Fundamental Liturgy*, vol. II, ed. Anscar J. Chupungco (Collegeville, MN: Liturgical Press, 1998), 279–321. For a magisterial survey of English language hymnody see J. R. Watson, *The English Hymn: A Critical and Historical Study*, rev. ed. (Oxford: Oxford University Press, 1991). On contempo-

tions with fidelity to doctrine and concern for Christian formation. Geoffrey Wainwright expressed the relationship like this: "In virtue of their greater flexibility, hymns fulfil a complementary function to creeds; they also allow the expression of 'ecstatic reason.'"[41] Just over twenty years later, Randall Bradley would stake a claim for the worship song alongside the hymn:

> The church needs hymns and choruses, texts (and their musical counterparts) that speak deeply and comprehensively to the mind and the heart. Biblically, neither pole is exclusive. Worship with developed theological content such as hymns keeps worship solidly connected to the community of faith in history and the tradition borne out by centuries of reflection, study, research and prayer. Texts and music that have an unapologetic appeal to the emotions connect with our feelings and intuitions—our affective side.[42]

The sixth- or seventh-century Ambrosian hymn, *Conditor Alme Siderum*, is a much-loved part of Advent processions, often in J.M. Neale's version (1851), "Creator of the starry height." Addressed to Christ, it begins with Johannine imagery of light and describes the divine response to the cry of fallen humanity in the incarnation. Its central verses beautifully demonstrate the art of turning biblical and doctrinal density into poetry:

> When earth was near its evening hour,
> Thou didst, in love's redeeming power,
> Like bridegroom from his chamber, come
> Forth from a Virgin-mother's womb.
>
> At thy great Name, exalted now,
> All knees in lowly homage bow;
> All things in heaven and earth adore,
> And own Thee King for evermore.[43]

---

rary Christian music see Pete Ward, *Selling Worship: How What We Sing Has Changed the Church* (London: Church House Publishing, 2005).

[41] Geoffrey Wainwright, *Doxology: The Praise of God in Worship, Doctrine and Life* (London: Epworth Press, 1980), 7.

[42] C. Randall Bradley, "Congregational Song as Shaper of Theology: A Contemporary Assessment," *Review and Expositor* 100 (2003): 351–73, 361.

[43] General Synod of the Church of Ireland, *Church Hymnal*, 5th ed. (Oxford: Oxford University Press, 2000), no. 121.

The first of these verses invokes the exuberant description of the daily course of the sun in Psalm 19:5 as an image of Christ's birth. Unlike that triumphant progress, however, this one happens in the "evening hour," and God enters the descending darkness of a doomed world as a human infant.[44] At the same time, the hymn-writer has drawn on New Testament depictions of Christ as the "bridegroom," initially in his doubly paradoxical emergence "*from* a virgin-mother's womb," and then as the one whose presence among the wedding guests prevents them from mourning (Matt 9:10-20, Mark 2:19-20, Luke 5:35), the bridegroom anticipated in the wedding feast parable of Matthew 25:1-13, who is a figure of finality and judgement, and finally as the true bridegroom hailed by John the Baptist (John 3:29), who comes to claim God's people (the "bride"). The next verse sums up all these allusions, celebrating Christ glorified in a paraphrase of the credal claim of Philippians 2:9-11. In a response to the previous verse, the direction of Psalm 19:5 is definitively, and again paradoxically, reversed as nightfall gives way to everlasting glory.

The tension between divine glory and divine humility is a recurrent one in hymnody, and Graham Kendrick's composition, "The Servant King," has been one of its most prominent exemplars since its debut in 1984. A perennial favourite in liturgical gatherings in a variety of idioms, and now institutionalised in published hymnals, it draws into a single, simultaneous view the incarnation of Christ as "helpless babe," his agony in Gethsemane ("the garden of tears"), and the crucifixion still visible in "the scars that speak of sacrifice."[45] Worshippers are invited to meditate on "hands that flung stars into space" transfixed by "cruel nails." Whether or not this is a strictly orthodox understanding of the persons of the Trinity, the image has maintained a powerfully evocative hold on the congregational imagination, epitomising the "Servant King" who is best worshipped in lives presented as a "daily offering." Kendrick's "Meekness and Majesty," written a few years later and also firmly part of the canon of modern hymnody, is a more theological treatment of the mysteries of incarnation and redemption. Arguably more assured poetically,

[44] Much later, Charles Wesley would contemplate the same mystery in the hymn "Let Earth and Heaven Combine": "Our God contracted to a span, incomprehensibly made man." *Singing the Faith* (Norwich: Canterbury Press, 2011), no. 208.

[45] Church of Ireland, *Church Hymnal*, no. 219.

its preponderance of abstract nouns nevertheless makes it less emotionally accessible than "The Servant King." In one sense, it seems obvious that graphic verbal images should have immediate impact, an observation borne out by the durability of hymns like "The royal banners forward go" and "When I survey the wondrous cross." Nevertheless, Bradley's reflection on their potential longer-term effects is telling:

> Worshippers in traditions that lack formal symbol and ritual . . . often depend on the texts of congregational song to fill the void in their religious imaginations. For this reason, we need to be particularly discerning of what in our song is acceptable imaginative development of the biblical narrative and what departs from sound doctrine.[46]

"[A]cceptable imaginative development" and Wainwright's "ecstatic reason" converge in the radiant vision of Charles Wesley's "Love divine, all loves excelling" (1747).[47] The hymn begins by describing the "[crowning]" of "all [God's] faithful mercies" in the incarnational movement of "love divine" into the "humble dwelling" of human lives (John 1:14; Phil 2:6-8). In 1761, Wesley republished the hymn, omitting the original second stanza, which had become a source of dispute with his brother John on the nature of Christian perfection. The revised text calls on God as deliverer and alludes to Malachi 3:1-2, appropriated in the Christian tradition as a prophecy of the Messiah, this time to anticipate the second coming. Until that time, earth strives to mirror heaven: the Christian vocation is to "be always blessing" and serving God "as thy hosts above," absorbed like them in ceaseless praise and rejoicing in God's "perfect love." The third stanza takes a wholly eschatological perspective, as it looks for the "new creation" that will be completed when God's "great salvation" is "perfectly restored." As part of that new act of creation, human beings will be made "pure and spotless" (Eph 5:27, 2 Pet 3:14)

[46] Bradley, "Congregational Song," 364–65.

[47] For a succinct account of the hymn's genesis and theological development, and its part in the controversy over Christian perfection between the Wesley brothers, see Roger D. Duke and Chris Fenner, "Love Divine, All Loves Excelling," in Chris Fenner and Brian G. Najapfour, eds., *Amazing Love! How Can It Be: Studies on Hymns by Charles Wesley* (Eugene, OR: Resource Publications, 2020), 86–94.

and changed "from glory into glory" (2 Cor 3:18) until they "take their place" in heaven. The last four lines of the stanza describe the eternal vocation of the Christian life: to be part of the ecstatic praise of heaven (Rev 4:10) and to find the greatest joy only when "lost in wonder, love and praise." Wesley's achievement is to turn doctrine into vision, and the enacted praise of the church into a rehearsal for the praise of eternity. The hymn is self-transcending in its movement towards immersion in the life of God.

The Bible and Liturgical Praise: Prospects

Addressing the question, "What makes the liturgy biblical?" in an article published in 1992, Louis-Marie Chauvet expressed confidence in the ability of the Bible to be "inspiring for the liturgy even to the extent that it allows it to draw from its treasure 'of the new and the old' (cf. Matt 13:53), from the cultural sensibility and the problems of a certain period." He saw this flowering in new liturgical texts, and hymns in particular, following the Second Vatican Council. Here was a paradigm of the ambition of *Sacrosanctum Concilium* 24: disciplined attention to Scripture and the resources of imagination working together, to produce an "exacting creativity" that could instigate a fresh "savouring of the Bible in the culture of our time."[48]

Forty years later, liturgical creativity continues in dialogue with Scripture, and biblical literacy continues in dialogue with liturgy, but realists acknowledge that less and less can be taken for granted. This may have positive outcomes when newcomers to ordered liturgical practice find that its unfamiliar language leads them directly into new encounters with Scripture. The memory of a young greengrocer who found himself taking a liturgy course as part of his retraining as a teacher and met Psalm 17:8 ("Keep me as the apple of your eye") in Compline with the class comes to mind. His exclamation of surprise that this homely idiom was in fact in the Bible met the riposte from a classmate, "It's the greengrocer's psalm." For others, unfamiliarity might be alienating, for reasons that are increasingly complex. Further chapters will describe some of the expectations now placed on any endeavour to praise and glorify God in the liturgical

[48] Louis-Marie Chauvet, "What Makes the Liturgy Biblical?—Texts," *Studia Liturgica* 22, no. 1 (1992): 121–33, 132.

assembly. Those charged with making a tradition speak freshly each time the liturgy is celebrated, and those responsible for producing new texts to be appropriate by worshippers in speech and song do this with due regard to human diversity and its darker side of exclusion and marginalisation, the liturgical formation of children, and the precious and threatened world we inhabit. The official overseers of liturgical composition and authorisation, and the burgeoning number of untrained "grassroots" theologians who are writing the songs that express much contemporary praise[49] are challenged to find in Scripture the "lively oracles" that can meet these immense opportunities.

[49] Bradley, "Congregational Song," 355.

Chapter 10

Limping with the Living God: Reimagining Centre and Margins in the Liturgy

Armand Léon van Ommen

Introduction

Janet has not attended the worship service for three months because of a depression; Chris, who identifies as autistic, does not feel welcome; Mary and John feel judged by the community because Aaron, their son, who has a learning disability, does not conform to standards of sitting still and being quiet; teenager Madeleine has declared the service boring; Dora feels excluded because of her skin tone; Peter is divorced from Carla, but everyone sides with Carla, so Peter feels excluded and not understood; Beatrice hates Communion because she can't go up to the altar rail because of the steps; Jason feels he cannot be open about his sexual identity; Grace is excluded from preaching because she is a woman. The examples of people who feel excluded by the worshipping community abound, and often certain characteristics overlap; for example, someone may be black and gay, or disabled and a woman.[1] Why is it that people who are often pushed to the margins by society do not find the church a more

[1] This overlapping is called "intersectionality."

welcoming place, despite the fact that churches sing that "All Are Welcome?"[2]

This chapter does not focus on one particular group of people or intersection, but rather reflects on the general dynamic of exclusion in the practices of worshipping communities, whilst realising that for each individual and community the situation will be different. However, I trust that the arguments presented here will resonate with many who feel marginalised. The first aim of my exploration is to become more aware of the centre-and-margins dynamic in the liturgical practices of Christian communities, in other words, how communities can be exclusive to some people. The second aim is to understand how both Scripture and liturgy are part of the problem, to offer a critique of this problem, and to suggest how they can be part of the solution. The chapter starts with a brief discussion of the critical dialogue between Scripture, liturgy, and practice. The two middle sections argue that liturgy and Scripture can be used to reinforce but also to reimagine unhealthy centre-and-margin dynamics. The final section claims that a revision of the liturgy's use of Scripture, as part of such reimagining, should be juxtaposed with the biblical injunctions for ethical living.

Scripture, Liturgy, and Practice in Critical Dialogue

Scripture and liturgy are interrelated in important ways. The liturgy celebrates the God of Scripture, just as Scripture tells about the God whom the Israelites and the first Christians met in worship. Parts of Scripture seem to be based on early liturgical use, such as the hymn about Jesus Christ's kenosis in Philippians 2.[3] Other texts might have made their way into the liturgy only after they were included in the gospels or letters of the New Testament. What Christians came to call the Old Testament was read in the liturgical gatherings of the early

[2] Marty Haugen, 1994, Chicago: GIA Publications. For some critical reflections on this song, see Teresa Berger, "'All Are Welcome?': A Sermon," in *Liturgy with a Difference: Beyond Inclusion in the Christian Assembly*, ed. Stephen Burns and Bryan Cones, 139–42 (London: SCM Press, 2019).

[3] Larry W. Hurtado, *At the Origins of Christian Worship: The Context and Character of Earliest Christian Devotion* (Carlisle: Paternoster Press, 1999), 86–89.

Christians (cf. 2 Tim 3:15-17), later to be followed by writings from St. Paul and others.[4]

Liturgy uses Scripture in various ways. In liturgy, the Bible is read and commented upon (the sermon or homily). Liturgy also sings Scripture, in hymns directly derived from the biblical texts, such as the *Magnificat*, *Gloria*, *Benedictus* and *Nunc Dimittis*. It sings Scripture in the rich tradition of singing that has developed over the centuries, and contemporary songwriters continue to work creatively with the Bible.[5] Finally, liturgical texts are based on Scripture throughout. Sometimes this results in verbatim/direct quotations, at other times in explicit or implicit allusions. Some scholars have proposed fine-grained categorisations of the use of Scripture in liturgy.[6] This chapter does not offer a detailed analysis of every instance of explicit, implicit, or other use of the Bible. The point here is to affirm the ubiquitous use of Scripture in liturgical texts. Even churches which use fewer prescriptive liturgical texts, or none at all, will usually include or allude to passages and stories from Scripture.

At the same time, some scriptural texts are critical of the gathering of the people of God. The priest Eli's misinterpretation of Hannah's prayer in the "Lord's house" can be read as an implicit criticism of what priesthood, as part of Israel's liturgical setup, had become at the time (1 Sam 1). The prophet Amos offers a devastating critique of Israel's worship at a later time:

> I hate, I despise your religious festivals;
> your assemblies are a stench to me.
> Even though you bring me burnt offerings and grain offerings,
> I will not accept them.

[4] Andrew B. McGowan, *Ancient Christian Worship: Early Church Practices in Social, Historical, and Theological Perspective*, Alcuin Club Collections 91 (Grand Rapids, MI: Baker Academic, 2014), 78–93.

[5] For some reflections on the intersection of music, liturgy, and theology, see Don E. Saliers, *Music and Theology*, Horizons in Theology (Nashville: Abingdon Press, 2007).

[6] For a fine-grained classification of the various uses of Scripture in liturgy, and a review of other classifications, see Matthew S. C. Olver, "A Classification of a Liturgy's Use of Scripture: A Proposal," *Studia Liturgica* 49, no. 2 (2019): 220–45, https://doi.org/10.1177/0039320719863593; see also Juliette J. Day, *Reading the Liturgy: An Exploration of Texts in Christian Worship* (London: Bloomsbury, 2014).

Though you bring choice fellowship offerings,
I will have no regard for them.
Away with the noise of your songs!
I will not listen to the music of your harps.
But let justice roll on like a river,
righteousness like a never-failing stream! (Amos 5:21-24, NIV)

The apostle Paul likewise is very critical of the Christian assembly in Corinth, when they fail to share with the poor or when spiritual gifts are used in ways that lead to chaos (e.g., 1 Cor 11, 14). James similarly criticises favouritism in the assembly. Many more examples can be given,[7] but these suffice to make the point that Scripture criticises worship practices and encourages the believers to adhere to the "royal law" of loving your neighbour as yourself (James 2:8). In the light of worship wars and liturgical differences, it should be noted that the critiques which biblical writers have made of the liturgies of the people of God have little to do with what songs to sing, which liturgical style to employ, or drinking communion wine from a shared or individual cups. When the assembly is criticised, it is because of how the believers treat each other and whether their commitment is fully to God. Liturgical criticism in Scripture, therefore, can all be brought back to Jesus' summary of the law: love God above all, and your neighbour as yourself.

Insofar as liturgy is based on Scripture, with all its references, allusions, and explicit uses, it is not unlikely that we can hear the same kinds of criticism even in the liturgy itself. For example, the "sharing of the peace," especially when it comes just before the eucharistic prayer, reminds us of Jesus' critical comment about offering: "If you are offering your gift at the altar and there remember that your brother or sister has something against you, leave your gift there in front of the altar. First go and be reconciled to them; then come and offer your gift" (Matt 5:23-24, NIV). For Jesus, it is unthinkable to love and worship God without loving one's neighbour. Through the liturgy we are seeing our lives, our community, and the world, in the light of God's reign.

[7] See Gordon W. Lathrop, *Saving Images: The Presence of the Bible in Christian Liturgy* (Minneapolis: Fortress Press, 2017), 75–77.

A community's self-criticism in liturgy can also result from a critical engagement with the history and theology of liturgy and worship. Don Saliers refers to liberationist critiques (e.g., by feminists Marjory Procter-Smith and Rosemary Radford Ruether, and we can add Black theologian James Cone, as well as many others) who have demonstrated how liturgy "actually *malforms* a community of moral discourse." Saliers quotes the poignant words from Johann Baptist Metz: "Christian worship is often a kind of 'eulogistic evasion of what really matters.'"[8] We need to engage in deep and active listening to our own liturgical texts to see in what ways the very celebration of liturgy and reading of Scripture might criticise the practices of our own liturgical communities, and to hear whether our communities are marked by the love of God and neighbour.

Scripture and Liturgy as Part of the Problem: Reinforcing the Centre

The dynamic of the centre-and-margins is one of dominant voices becoming oppressive of voices (or indeed the voiceless) at the margins. Scripture itself is not flawless in this regard and reading Scripture uncritically can reinforce this problematic dynamic. Examples abound. We have referred to liberationist readings that expose this dynamic in particular contexts. For example, feminist readings of Scripture have pointed to the fact that the Bible has been used to deny women equality in the church. Black theologians and others have identified how racism, abuse, and marginalisation have been defended with the Bible in hand. Ethical burdens can be placed wrongly on the shoulders of women and men suffering from domestic violence, one-sidedly and wrongly citing Jesus' imperative to "turn the other cheek," and suffering people are insensitively being told to "rejoice always." Spiritual abuse can occur when autistic people or people dealing with mental health issues are thought to have evil spirits that need to be exorcised. More subtly, by a narrow reading of healing stories, cultural ideas of normalcy and perfection can be imposed on people who somehow deviate from those cultural norms by the way they look or are physically, neurologically, or otherwise

[8] Saliers, *Music and Theology*, 214.

different. Even more subtly, people can be marginalised or excluded from the worship service by the selective use of texts in liturgy, including readings and the sermon. For example, Kathleen Billman and Daniel Migliore comment: "The exclusion of the lament screens out people who find the services shallow or harmful and provides no theological and liturgical way to come to terms with disturbing human experiences."[9] In sum, Scripture and the way it is used, interpreted, and selected, can be part of the problematic dynamic that sidelines certain people and reinforces notions of dominance and power.

It might be helpful to explore how Scripture and liturgy are part of the problem by looking at one particular example. Here I will comment on the book of Lamentations and the (lack of) use thereof, as part of the problem but also, in the next section, as part of a potential solution. The book of Lamentations is a good example because it speaks to various issues when it comes to the centre-and-margins. It is an example of a book typically less used than others in lectionaries, songwriting, and other worship practices,[10] except, of course, for the one part that is familiar to many: "The steadfast love of the Lord never ceases, his mercies never come to an end; they are new every morning; great is your faithfulness" (3:22-23, NRSV). The fact that exactly these two verses are so well-known illustrates the problem of highlighting texts we like, neglecting the surrounding verses that speak very differently (and in the light of which the meaning of verses 22-23 gains incredible depth, but must also be seen as strange and abrupt[11]). The bold claim at the start of the chapter that God has brought unspeakable affliction upon the poet is much less known. The liturgical use—through song or otherwise—of a narrow selection of verses can therefore render the meaning of the texts shallow, or at least lose the depth of Scripture. One might argue that this violates Scripture. One may also argue in another direction, that is, such cherry-picking leads pastorally to the violation of lived experience,

[9] Kathleen D. Billman and Daniel L. Migliore, *Rachel's Cry: Prayer of Lament and Rebirth of Hope* (Eugene, OR: Wipf and Stock, 1999), 14.

[10] Lester Meyer, "A Lack of Laments in the Church's Use of the Psalter," *Lutheran Quarterly* (1993): 67–78.

[11] Emmanuel Katongole, *Born from Lament: The Theology and Politics of Hope in Africa* (Grand Rapids, MI: Eerdmans, 2017), 52–57.

either within our own communities or across the wider world. Does the description of the horrific situation of Jerusalem not resonate with cities bombed and torn by conflict in our own time? Does the desperate question that ends the book of Lamentations not resonate with many who struggle for justice but find none?

> But you, O Lord, reign forever;
> your throne endures to all generations.
> Why have you forgotten us completely?
> Why have you forsaken us these many days?
> Restore us to yourself, O Lord, that we may be restored;
> renew our days as of old—
> unless you have utterly rejected us,
> and are angry with us beyond measure (Lam 5:19-22).

Neglecting texts like these—and there are many!—means a silencing of an important part of God's revelation through Scripture. The relational struggles of God and Israel, which are continued in Jesus and the early church, are part and parcel of the stories of Israel and the early church. I would argue that neglecting texts like these means silencing the doubts, fears, and desperation believers can have today, individually and as communities. Such neglect risks the forging of communities that centre on a superficial "happy-clappy" spirituality and marginalise experiences that ask hard questions of their feel-good theology. It risks resulting in intercessions that politely ask God's help without necessarily believing God will come to the aid of the petitioners,[12] and that avoid dealing with difficult questions in any depth.[13] I contend that dealing with difficult texts that express pain, doubt, accusation, and that dare to ask hard questions will create space for those who are marginalised by the church, whether that is because of their differing abilities, skin tone, ethnic background,

[12] Walter Brueggemann, "Necessary Conditions of a Good Loud Lament," *Horizons in Biblical Theology* 25 (2003): 19–49, 38.

[13] Armand Léon van Ommen, "Taboo and Stigma in Praying for Mental Health: An Empirical-Theological Investigation into the Practice of Public Intercession," *Ecclesial Practices* 6, no. 1 (2019): 83–101; Armand Léon van Ommen, "Intercession and the Taboo and Stigma on Mental Health and Doctrinal Anomalies: Pastoral and Theological Implications of Public Prayer Practices," *International Journal of Practical Theology* 23, no. 2 (2019): 206–23.

sexual orientation, gender, mental challenges, or otherwise, or an intersection of several of these.[14]

However, Scripture itself can be problematic. In general, I would argue that dealing with difficult texts in Scripture engages the community in their relationship with God, even when God's ways are indeed beyond human understanding (Isa 55:8, Job 36:26). Nevertheless, some texts are rather offensive, without offering any obvious solution. For example, Leviticus 21:16-20, 23 reads:

> The Lord spoke to Moses, saying: Speak to Aaron and say: No one of your offspring throughout their generations who has a blemish may approach to offer the food of his God. For no one who has a blemish shall draw near, one who is blind or lame, or one who has a mutilated face or a limb too long, or one who has a broken foot or a broken hand, or a hunchback, or a dwarf, or a man with a blemish in his eyes or an itching disease or scabs or crushed testicles. . . . But he shall not come near the curtain or approach the altar, because he has a blemish, that he may not profane my sanctuaries; for I am the Lord; I sanctify them. (NRSV)

Commenting on this passage, John Hull points out how the Levitical laws reinforce a picture of perfectionism (cf. Mal 1:8—only the best of the best is to be offered to God, and therefore only the best of best are to offer to God). Moreover, blind people are not to be *misled* (Lev 19:14 "You shall not . . . put a stumbling block before the blind") but, as Hull highlights, nor are they to be *led*. Hull calls this "negative compassion." "Behind this apparent compassion, however, lies a deep failure to offer acceptance and inclusion"—a failure that haunts the church still today," Hull argues.[15] In many respects the Bible seems to have a negative view of disabilities,[16] although some strongly

[14] For more on the "costly loss of lament," see Walter Brueggemann, "The Costly Loss of Lament," *Journal for the Study of the Old Testament* 36 (1986): 57–71; see further A. L. van Ommen, *Suffering in Worship: Anglican Liturgy in Relation to Stories of Suffering People* (London: Routledge, 2017).

[15] John M. Hull, *In the Beginning There Was Darkness: A Blind Person's Conversations with the Bible* (London: SCM Press, 2001), 69–73, 73.

[16] See the collection of essays in Sarah J. Melcher, Mikeal C. Parsons, and Amos Yong, eds., *The Bible and Disability: A Commentary* (Waco, TX: Baylor University Press, 2017).

argue to see disabilities as part of God's creation, and people with disabilities as indispensable to the Body of Christ (1 Cor 12:22), not despite but because of their disabilities.[17] Our use of Scripture, and indeed Scripture itself, can be harmful and endorse dominance at the expense of others. At the same time, Scripture and the use thereof can also be part of revisiting the centre-and-margins dynamic, as the next section will demonstrate.

Scripture and Liturgy as Part of the Solution: Reimagining the Centre and Margins

Scripture and liturgy are rich resources for revisiting the centre-and-margins dynamic. Even if some parts of Scripture can be problematic, and certainly the (liturgical) use of Scripture can be misguided, Scripture is also clear about its liberative intent for those who are oppressed and many believers turn to it for comfort. Liturgy should use Scripture in such a way that it narrates this storyline of Jesus' establishment of God's reign of justice, peace, joy, and love—on earth as it is in heaven. I suggest the concept of "reimagining reality" is helpful to follow this storyline of Scripture, and thus to reimagine the centre and margins.

Underlying the concept of reimagining reality is Israel's faith in a living God. Scripture tells the story of God and God's people as they journey with each other. The believer's faith is in a living God who is committed to a covenantal relationship, with a "faithfulness that vetoes our faithlessness."[18] Faith in a faithful God is also the basis for the prayers of lament in which believers accuse God of unfaithfulness. The point is that God is a living God, who cares and is active in this world. The use of Scripture in liturgy, and liturgy itself, should be marked by such faith, lest it become a "eulogistic evasion of what really matters." When stories about life and the circumstances in which the storytellers find themselves start to include belief in such

[17] See, e.g., Thomas E. Reynolds, *Vulnerable Communion: A Theology of Disability and Hospitality* (Grand Rapids, MI: Brazos Press, 2008), 235–38; Brian Brock, *Wondrously Wounded: Theology, Disability, and the Body of Christ* (Waco, TX: Baylor University Press, 2019), chap. 9.

[18] Walter Brueggemann, *The Prophetic Imagination* (Philadelphia: Fortress Press, 1978), 68.

a living God, the stories change and start to "redescribe reality" with "prophetic imagination."[19]

Scripture itself contains examples of what reimagining the centre-and-margins might look like. Often the Bible highlights that which (or who) is seemingly insignificant and invests it with special dignity or restores its dignity. The reign of God is like a little bit of yeast: it looks insignificant, it becomes invisible in the bread, yet its impact is most powerful. The people of Israel itself is another example (Deut 7:7), as is the oft-repeated concern for the orphans, widows, and stranger (e.g., Deut 10:18). In the words of Paul: "the foolishness of God is wiser than human wisdom, and the weakness of God is stronger than human strength" and "God chose the foolish things of the world to shame the wise; God chose the weak things of the world to shame the strong. God chose the lowly things of this world and the despised things—and the things that are not to nullify the things that are, so that no one may boast before him" (1 Cor 1:25, 27-29, NIV). With these words Paul points to Christ's death on the cross, through which the Corinthians are saved. All that is valuable and important according to the cultural standards of their days, Paul says, vanishes in light of this "foolishness of God." Jesus' lifegiving death—a reimagination of reality—was preceded by his ministry in which he habitually went to those at the margins and restored their dignity, whilst sidelining the religious centre of his day. Jesus redescribed the perception of what centre and margin is according to God's order.

The prophetic imagination to redescribe our world and evaluate our practices brings us, remarkably, to the practice of lament. Above we saw that lament as a practice as well as the book of Lamentations are at the margins of many Christian communities. Yet lament is a practice that the great visionary prophets of Israel turned to regularly. Brueggemann argues that imagining an alternative reality or community starts with grief and lament. Only grief can break through the numbness that dominant powers create.[20] Grief takes seriously

[19] I borrow these terms from Walter Brueggemann. They both refer to the concept of imagining a different reality to the dominant one. That concept underlies much of my argument in this chapter. Walter Brueggemann, *Redescribing Reality: What We Do When We Read the Bible* (London: SCM Press, 2009); Brueggemann, *Prophetic Imagination.*

[20] Brueggemann, *Prophetic Imagination*, 51–61.

the reality as it is: ongoing discrimination; embittered relationships; opportunities not taken to improve a situation; communities excluding people by their practices, betraying false beliefs. Grief breaks open angered and resentful hearts and moves them into the realm of compassion. The task of the prophet is threefold: (1) to "*offer symbols* that are adequate to the horror;" (2) "to *bring to public expression those very fears and terrors* that have been denied so long and suppressed so deeply that we do not know they are there;" and (3) "to *speak metaphorically but concretely about the real deathliness that hovers over us and gnaws within us*, and to speak neither in rage nor in cheap grace, but with the candor born of anguish and passion."[21] This summary of the prophetic task shows that grief is not passive. Grief is born out of passion and moves into passion, which in turns leads to speak with imagination about newness of life.

Speaking with imagination, therefore, requires a counterpart for each of the three elements of the prophetic task: (1) "The *offering of symbols* that are adequate to contradict a situation of hopelessness;" (2) "to *bring to public expression those very hopes and yearnings* that have been denied so long;" and (3) to "*speak metaphorically about hope but concretely about the real newness that comes to us and redefines our situation*."[22] In the prophetic imagination horror, fear, and deathliness are lamented but contrasted with hope and newness of life. Note that the hope only gains its profound significance and depth in light of the grief for its opposite. Hence, Lamentations speaks of horror and deathliness first, and at length, before that well-known hope for God's new mercies is uttered. Hence, the psalms of lament do not skip over the raw reality of despair in order to move as quickly as possible to the upbeat choruses of hope, like so many contemporary worship songs do. To hope is to enter into grief first.

The book of Lamentations, then, can be seen as a book of hope in that it enters into grief. As Emmanuel Katongole says, commenting on this book, "The ability to name pain and voice grief is in itself a form of hope."[23] However, he continues by pointing out that hope is not a theme as such in the book of Lamentations, and that utterances of hope are sketchy and immediately contradicted by doubt and

[21] Brueggemann, *Prophetic Imagination*, 49–50, emphasis original.
[22] Brueggemann, *Prophetic Imagination*, 66–69, emphasis original.
[23] Katongole, *Born from Lament*, 52.

despair. Surely, there is hope, even in the songs of lament, but the going back and forth between hope and despair, as in the Book of Lamentations and in a good number of lament psalms, shows that there is no such thing as a linear movement from suffering to hope.[24] The grief and despair are dealt with by voicing the lament, but they are never fully overcome in Lamentations.

Lamentations also provides a link to disability. Disability is not an explicit theme in the book, but we can see disability in various ways in the poems and the situation they describe. First, enemies have destroyed Jerusalem. They have been ruthlessly murdering, and it is most likely that some people have been permanently injured as a result of violence. Second, the destruction of the city and many of its inhabitants has left the city disabled in the sense of not being able to function and flourish.[25] Third, the Book of Lamentations itself "limps." Even though there are no disabled characters in the book other than by implication, "Lamentations itself is disabled."[26] In an insightful reflection on Lamentations in relation to disability, Jennifer Koosed explains that the acrostic form of Lamentations' poetry functions as a brace.[27] Rendered speechless by the traumatic events, the poet is forced back to the basics of language, to the poet's "ABC." "The brace of the acrostic wraps around and holds up the wounded body of the text itself."[28] Yet not all the five poems follow this acrostic neatly: in three of the four acrostics two letters are swapped around, and the last one is not an acrostic, although it has 22 lines, the number of letters of the Hebrew alphabet. Koosed explains that on the one

[24] Katongole, *Born from Lament*, 52–56. Whilst it is often claimed that the lament psalms move from suffering to hope, not all of them do. See Federico G. Villanueva, *The "Uncertainty of a Hearing": A Study of the Sudden Change of Mood in the Psalms of Lament* (Boston: Brill, 2008).

[25] Social models of disability argue that often not the condition, but the way society treats people with certain conditions is disabling those people. Tom Shakespeare, "The Social Model of Disability," in *The Disability Studies Reader*, ed. Lennard J. Davis, 214–21 (New York: Routledge, 2013).

[26] Jennifer L. Koosed, "Psalms, Lamentations, and Song of Songs," in Melcher et al., *Bible and Disability*, 200.

[27] The acrostic form of Lamentations means that in most chapters each new pair of lines starts with the next letter of the alphabet—although it is not that straightforward, as Koosed explains.

[28] Koosed, "Psalms, Lamentations," 201.

hand the "brace" of the acrostic form, going back to the author's "ABC," helps the writer to start putting things back together: "Stripped down to nothing, the writer begins by simply repeating the letters over and over again, hoping that they will later reorder into words and thus reorder the world."[29] On the other hand, even this fails, as the acrostic form is not upheld throughout the book and in three poems there is a glitch in the order of letters. "One begins to make meaning by simply reciting the alphabet but meaning falters even at this foundational level because ultimately there is no clear and straightforward sense to be made out of such tragedies."[30] Also within the strophes, the lines are not equal but follow a *qinah* meter, a 3+2 rhythm. "The poem skips a stress; even with their brace, the words walk with a limp."[31] Lamentations limps.

Imagining a new future with the vision of a prophet starts with a visionary and honest analysis of the current situation and compassionate grief, Brueggemann contends. Does the church have liturgies that limp? Does the church have liturgies that enter so deeply into the grief that alternative realities can be imagined in destroyed places, in relationships beyond repair, in cold bureaucracy that leaves people destitute? Does the church have liturgies that are broken and speechless, like the book of Lamentations, which is the book of "Ah!" (as a cry of despair)?[32] Lamentations teaches the church to grief, to limp, to express the pain in liturgical form. Paradoxically, it is in this way that new hope can be found, eventually. It is by attending to brokenness, to that which is considered in the eyes of the surrounding culture to be weak and meaningless, that God's strength, love, hope, and joy become visible. Redescribing reality starts where there is seemingly no reason to hope. Underlying such prophetic imagination is a belief in a faithful, living God.

[29] Koosed, "Psalms, Lamentations," 202.

[30] Koosed, "Psalms, Lamentations," 202.

[31] Koosed, "Psalms, Lamentations," 201.

[32] The title and the first word of chapters 1, 2, and 4 are a cry of despair. Katongole, *Born from Lament*, 50.

Liturgy and the Life of the Community

Is the prophetic imagination enough to redescribe the centre-and-margins dynamic in churches? Is reimagining reality by entering the grief and forging hope going to bring those at the margins into the centre, and those in power down from their thrones? This message has been preached from the times of the prophets, and even before, until this very day, and yet the examples of exclusion mentioned in the introduction are all taken from contemporary church life. The church does not seem to get it, even after thousands of years, songs, and sermons. Well-crafted liturgies have not changed the fact that some are still pushed to the margins and others hold the centre. One should be forgiven for being sceptical. Saliers is correct when he writes: "Beautiful and theologically 'correct' texts may too easily be surrounded by means of communication in the liturgy that contradict the very teachings and stories about God's mercy, justice, and love that are ingredient in the Scriptures read and prayers prayed."[33] However, he also offers a key to move beyond the sceptical questions above. Commenting on the formative aspect of the nonverbal elements of the liturgy, he argues that "primary affections such as awe in the presence of God, delight in the created order, gratitude for life, and compassion for neighbour require a human ethos of respect, care, hospitality, inclusion, and the like."[34] Liturgy can be conducive to such primary affections, but it cannot properly evoke them when the ethos of the gospel is absent. In other words, liturgy presupposes, as well as informs, ethics.[35]

Gordon Lathrop's concept of juxtaposition—one thing gains meaning in light of the other—is useful in this regard.[36] Liturgy gains

[33] Don E. Saliers, "Afterword," in E. Byron Anderson and Bruce T. Morrill, eds., *Liturgy and the Moral Self: Humanity at Full Stretch Before God* (Collegeville, MN: Liturgical Press, 2002), 209–24, 215.

[34] Saliers, "Afterword," 215.

[35] For more on the relationship between liturgy and ethics, see, e.g., the collections of essays in E. Byron Anderson and Bruce T. Morrill, eds., *Liturgy and the Moral Self: Humanity at Full Stretch Before God* (Collegeville, MN: Liturgical Press, 2002); and Pieter Vos, ed., *Liturgy and Ethics: New Contributions from Reformed Perspectives*, Studies in Reformed Theology 33 (Boston: Brill, 2018).

[36] Gordon W. Lathrop, *Holy Things: A Liturgical Theology* (Minneapolis: Fortress Press, 1993).

meaning when it comes before and after a life informed by gospel ethics. It is worthwhile quoting Saliers at length:

> Participation in the symbolic action requires more than participation in the phenomena of worship; it requires participation as a living community engaged in the struggle to show in life what is implied in the gathering. Opening up the ethical levels of meaning in the shared meal in the name of one who creates and redeems a world from itself transforms not simply the interior life of feeling and desire but the social relationships that make us human in the sight of God.[37]

Saliers leaves no doubt: liturgy is transformative of life in all its relationships, not just the inner life. We might wonder when liturgy gets stuck in unhealthy dynamics of centre-and-margins whether life is seen apart from liturgy rather than juxtaposed by it. The texts of traditional liturgies—even if one is critical of some aspects, for example unhelpful gendered language and images—are profound in meaning. If the worshippers would let their lives be transformed by the liturgy (both the verbal and the non-verbal aspects of it), we may wonder whether (at least parts of) the liturgy would help the community change and move beyond a centre-and-margins dynamic. In other words, another liturgical revision will not change anything if the life of the community remains unaffected. At the same time, liturgy should be affected by what happens in the community and the world. Why should community life be affected by the liturgy if the liturgy remains unaffected by the community? Only when liturgy creates space for the dreams and hopes, joys and grief, leaping and limping of the community will it be able to redescribe reality with prophetic imagination, and only then will the juxtaposition of liturgy and life be meaningful.

Conclusion

Reimagining the centre-and-margin dynamic does not mean reversing the centre and margins. This would reverse the roles of those involved but perpetuate the same dynamic. Moreover, given the multilayeredness and complexity of exclusion and marginalisation,

[37] Saliers, "Afterword," 224.

such a reversal would not be as straightforward as it sounds. Someone might even be at the centre in their liturgical role and simultaneously feel marginalised because of, for example, a disability. It is important to realise that centre-and-margins is a metaphor. Reimagining this metaphor requires that we move beyond getting the metaphor "right." Revised or new metaphors will always fail, because any metaphor or analogy goes only so far. It is the reality behind it that needs to be dealt with. The reality that is referred to in this chapter is that some people feel excluded by the liturgy and the liturgical community. Examples were given in the introduction and can be multiplied endlessly. Following Brueggemann, the concept of reimagining reality points to entering the reality of those who grieve. With Saliers, this reality can be thought of as the reality of those who are victims of injustice. As this chapter has shown, injustice can happen within liturgical communities themselves, whenever and for whatever reason people are excluded. Scripture might sometimes be seen as part of the problem, but it also constructively offers metaphors that describe another reality. That reality is described as invisible yeast or as a small mustard seed. At stake is not simply a reversal of centre and margins. Reimagination of exclusionary and power dynamics means a reordering of value systems, a reimagination of what is important, strong, and wise. The biblical yardstick for such reimagination is the double command of loving God and neighbour.

Jeremiah, Amos, Jesus, Paul, James, and others all criticise liturgical practices in light of God's call to justice. Perhaps this is why Brueggemann can claim that the prophetic imagination starts with grief. When communities and individuals enter the grief and exclusion of fellow human beings (and all of creation, cf. Rom 8:19-22), they will learn about injustice and possibly their own role in it. Seeing injustice and everything else that diminishes God's good creation leads to grief, and from there to new visions for the world. These griefs and hopes in turn should inform the liturgy, just as the rich texts and gestures of the liturgy lead to lament over that which diminishes and hope for God's reign. This process is neither smooth nor linear, nor will every tear be wiped away in this world (Rev 21:4). However, liturgical revision that dares to redescribe the centre and margins with prophetic imagination presupposes belief in a God who is alive and faithful. This belief is the ground to join the poet of Lamentations in grief and hope: we are limping with a living God.

Chapter 11

A World Made New in Christ

Christopher Irvine

Introduction

The liturgy is the primary context in which the Bible is performed and received as the Word of God, and the most obvious occasions are those when the Bible is read in the celebration of daily prayer, the celebration of the Eucharist, and the pastoral services. Echoes of Scripture are also sounded in the prayer texts of the liturgy. Indeed, many of these texts, even if not directly drawn from biblical texts, allude to them and strike the ear as sounding biblical. The texts of the Bible simply stand behind the voicing of the church's prayer and praise. But what place has the natural environment in the varied range of biblical literature?

In relatively recent times it was common to denote what earlier generations called "the Bible story" as a grand narrative, an overarching story. This metanarrative, to use a term borrowed from literary criticism, was taken to be the story of salvation, stretching from the creation and fall of humankind, through the election of God's people, to the birth of Jesus, his messianic destiny, and the consequences of his fate in dying and rising in the creation of a new Israel, the church. This all-encompassing narrative came to be viewed with suspicion by post-modern critics. However, an appreciation of a "storyline" through the diverse books of Scripture stretches back to the earliest discussions of which texts should be included in the canon.

Telling the biblical story was also a recommended pedagogical strategy to excite the interest of enquirers to the faith. When a deacon from Carthage wrote to Bishop Augustine of Hippo (354–430) asking how he might effectively convey a sense of the living God in human history and experience to those enquiring about Christian faith, Augustine responded in a short treatise called *De Catechizandis Rudibus* (AD 405). In this unique text, Augustine says that the initial instruction should be cast in terms of a story, a *narratio*, outlining the full sweep of the biblical story, beginning with creation. By necessity, this was to be a selective story, focusing on the cardinal points in the history of God's dealings with God's people. And this, although episodic, was to be presented as a unified narrative. Beginning with an account of God's purpose in creation, the narrative was to lead to the present experience of enquirers, and, most significantly, to open up for them the divine drama that has yet to unfold. As Augustine said, it was to be the story of God's love for the world, and one that can awaken hope and love in the hearts of enquirers as they come to discern their place and calling in God's world.[1]

However, the way in which the biblical story has been told has generally been narrowly, if not exclusively anthropocentric, focusing on the creation, fall, and redemption of humankind. In this way of telling the story, the natural world has simply been presented as the hinterland, or the stage on which the divine drama of the salvation of humankind is acted out. In this perspective the environment appears quite peripheral, if not marginal, to the Christian enterprise. But the assumptions behind this way of seeing and telling the story should be questioned and subjected to further scrutiny, and indeed, they already have been. It was well over forty years ago that the systematic theologian Jürgen Moltmann observed that apart from the passage about the lilies in the Sermon on the Mount (Matt 6:25-34, Luke 12:22-32), the environment seemed to be an absent theme in the New Testament. And yet, he argued, the natural world was embedded in the Christian doctrines of the resurrection (the new creation) and eschatology (God's ultimate purpose).[2] In addition, one should also reckon with what came to be referred to, from the third century onwards, as the second book, the book of nature, placing what may

[1] Augustine of Hippo, *De Catechizandis Rudibus*, chap. 4, PL 40 coll. 314–15.

[2] Jürgen Moltmann, *The Future of Creation* (London: SCM Press, 1979), 123.

at first seem to be on the margins of the Christian story at the very centre. Antony the Great (ca. 251–358), who withdrew into the wild places to give himself wholeheartedly to the pursuit of God, spoke metaphorically of the created world as the book that was always with him. Similarly, Athanasius, bishop of Alexandria (ca. 296–373), opined in one theological treaty that one pathway to knowing God was through reading creation, an idea that was later developed by Augustine of Hippo (354–430), who argued that nature was the universally accessible "book" through which one could read God's work and will and purpose.[3] There were then two books, nature and Scripture, and perhaps it was the theological poet, Ephrem the Syrian (ca. 306–73), who most succinctly caught the relationship between these two witnesses to the Creator when he wrote about how nature and Scripture were yoked together in their witness to the One who is both the Lord of nature and Lord of Scripture.[4]

Far from being a flight of Christian imagination, the view that the natural world speaks of God is arguably anchored in Scripture itself and is biblically validated in the letter to the Romans, where Paul writes of how the order of creation speaks to us of the power and nature of the deity (Rom 1:19, 20; cf. Acts 14:15-17). The implication here is that the very existence of the world can draw the attentive observer of nature to consider God as the Creator, (cf. Job 38:4ff.), and this is the point that is nuanced by Augustine when he says that in eliciting wonder, the natural world can lead to the offering of praise to God the Creator.[5] In this expanded vision, the natural environment may well be seen as being, to a large extent, the cause, the medium, and the theatre of praise in equal measure.

[3] Augustine of Hippo, *Enarrationes in Psalmos* 47:7, PL 36 col. 516; cf. *Confessions* XIII.15,17. Augustine's disciple Eucharius, Bishop of Lyons (d. 460), set out in a short tract how the things of nature could be read spiritually, a typology in which an element in the natural world was correlated to specific scriptural images and meanings. See Eucharius, *The Formula for Understanding Things Spiritually* PL 50 coll. 701–832.

[4] Ephrem the Syrian, *Hymns Against Heresies* 28:11, and *On Paradise* 5. *St Ephrem the Syrian: Hymns on Paradise*, trans. Sebastian Brock (Crestwood, NY: St. Vladimir's Seminary Press, 1990); E. Beck, *Des Heiligen Ephraem des Syrers Hymnen Contra Haereses* (Corpus Scriptorum Christianorum Orientalium vol. 169 [text] and vol. 170 [translation], Scriptores Syri Tomus 76–77, Louvain 1957).

[5] Augustine of Hippo, *Confessions*, I.

Beginnings and Ends

Reading back to the beginning, to the earliest creation narratives in the book of Genesis, we find that the making of humankind is literally grounded in the stuff of the earth, as the etymology of the words "humanity" and "humus" testify. So far from being peripheral, even those who are created in the divine image and likeness have an affinity with the earth, and therefore have an organic link with the environment. But these creation narratives also hold a real difficulty for the environmentally aware reader. What is especially problematic is the reading of the creation hymn in Genesis 1, which emphasises the "dominion" over the rest of creation that is apparently given to humankind (Gen 1:28; cf. Ps 8:4-6). This sense of dominion over nature was exaggerated during the so-called Enlightenment, most famously by René Descartes, and has led to the rapacious attitude that sees the natural world as being entirely at the disposal of human beings to plunder, exhaust, and then discard at will.

This attitude has had a devasting effect on the environment and the natural life it is able to sustain, and it urgently needs to be corrected. This may be achieved by first recognising the underlying logic of the context of the term "dominion," and by reading it intertextually, that is, alongside other creation writings in the Bible. The first point to emerge from doing so is that the term "dominion" is embedded in a priestly source, and as such, belongs to the language of priestly offering, a discourse that sees even the land and all that it sustains in terms of a divine gift. As the book of Leviticus makes plain, the land *belongs* to God and is not entirely at the disposal of human beings. Indeed, it needs from time to time to lie fallow so that nature may replenish itself (Lev 25:23). So whatever language is used to speak of the priestly act of offering and sacrifice, the logic is that of gift. This sense of gift is clearly stated in another, and probably more familiar priestly source text in 1 Chronicles. In this passage, King David muses on his role, and the role of the whole people of God, and concludes that the archetypal priestly act of offering is inevitably an offering back to God of what has been received: "For all things come from you, and of your own have we given you" (1 Chr 29:14b).

So, in the context of this wider Old Testament priestly tradition, we may rightly see humankind as being a part of nature, rather than apart from nature, and construe the role of humanity in relation to the rest of creation as that of "priests of creation." This is to say that integral to the special dignity of those created in the *imago dei* is the responsibility placed upon us to live in the natural world in ways that show it to be God's gratuitous creation. Furthermore, and this is to see God's gift in its wider perspective, human beings should acknowledge the fact that there are other creatures in God's good creation that have a value in themselves, apart from any human control or utility.[6] Job 39:9-12 and Psalm 104:26 provide further evidence.

Again, the sense of human beings having dominion over the natural world is qualified when the narrative of Genesis 1 is read alongside Genesis 2, which communicates the clear sense that humankind is placed in the garden "to till it and keep it" (Gen 2:15b). The pictorial language here is generally taken to refer to stewardship. And although this term is not quite as problematic as the term "dominion," it is also one that is contested.[7] The objection to the word "stewardship" is that the term suggests that all God makes and holds in being is placed at our disposal to be used for our own interests, comfort, and purposes. Alternative terms such as "management" or "tenant" suggest themselves, but this simply shifts the terms of the discussion. The substance of the matter is to see what it is that both terms point to, which is the proper ordering of the natural world and the role of humankind in positively valuing and actively caring for the environment as the common home of all God's creatures. In this light, it could be said that in relation to God's purposes, humankind and the wider environment need to be seen together, even to the point of being inextricably bound up together in a shared destiny from beginning to end. In this regard we may invoke the Hebrew prophet's promise that the coming redemption would be accompanied by the burgeoning of life in the natural world (see Isa 35:1), and recall

[6] David Ford, *Christian Wisdom: Desiring God and Learning in Love* (Cambridge: Cambridge University Press, 2007), 113–14.

[7] See John D. Zizioulas, *The Eucharistic Communion and the World*, ed. Luke Ben Tallow (London: T&T Clark, 2011), chap. 7; *In the Image and Likeness of God: The Buffalo Statement* (London: Anglican Consultative Council, 2015), sec. 9 and 16; Kevin Irwin, "Sacramental Theology After *Laudato Si'*," in *Full of Your Glory: Liturgy, Cosmos, Creation*, ed. Teresa Berger, 267–83 (Collegeville, MN: Liturgical Press, 2019).

John Milton's recognition that Christ, God's creative Word, was the "Author and the end of all things."[8]

In the Bible God's work as Creator is figured in terms of Word and Wisdom. As Word, God calls and sustains all things in being (Ps 33:6a, 9), and as Wisdom, God is involved in and permeates all things (Wis 7:24-25, 8:1). Both senses coalesce in the prologue of John's Gospel, in which Christ is presented as the source of all things (John 1:3), and underlies the mystery theology of the later Pauline epistles that celebrates how all things will find their ultimate cohesion and meaning in Christ, thus making Christ both the source and fulfilment of creation (see Eph 1:9ff.; Col 1:16-17). This same conviction is echoed in some contemporary liturgical texts that were first associated with the feast of the Ascension. One collect prayer, for instance, looks forward to the time when all creation will worship at Christ's feet.[9] But the impression is given that somehow the fate of the natural environment is tied up with the choices and actions that human beings make. A stark and strange warning is sounded in the book of Revelation, suggesting that those who are intent on wrecking the planet are themselves on a path to self- destruction (Rev 11:18-19). On the other hand, and more positively, the Christian vocation is a call to work with Christ, to be a co-worker with Christ, and one may reasonably apply this to the act of praying for, and actively caring for the natural environment, and in protecting and promoting the well-being of all creatures.

The sense that the fate of the order of creation is related to the unfolding of the drama of salvation is vividly portrayed in a key text in Paul's letter to the Romans. In Romans 8:18-22, Paul speaks of how creation itself is in bondage to decay and looks for the revealing of the children of God for its liberation and fulfilment. A catena of texts

[8] John Milton, *Paradise Lost*, ed. John Leonard (London: Penguin, 2000 [1667]), VII, line 591, 165.

[9] Martin Dudley, *The Collect in Anglican Liturgy* (Collegeville, MN: Liturgical Press, 1994), Collect 524.215. The source was the South African [Anglican] *Modern Collects* of 1972 provision for Ascension Day. It appears in the *ASB* and the Church of Ireland *Alternative Prayer Book* of 1984 for Pentecost 21, and in *A Prayer Book for Australia* (1995) for Ascension Day. It includes the phrase "and bring the whole created order to worship at his feet." The Anglican Church of Canada's *Book of Alternative Services* has it for Ascension Day with the version "and bring the whole of creation to worship at his feet."

corroborates and add to the meaning of our *locus classicus*, most notably, Romans 11:36: "from him and through him and to him are all things," and a text from Colossians: "[Christ] is before all things, and in him all things hold together" (Col 1:17). These passages assert that Christ is both the source and the ultimate fulfilment of the material creation, a conviction that may well be echoed in the climactic doxology, the ascription of praise at the end of the eucharistic prayer: "by whom, and with whom, and in whom," asserting first, the destination of the worshipping assembly's praise, and secondly, implying that the material elements of the Eucharist themselves, the bread and the wine over which thanksgiving has been made, find their fulfilment in being divinized to become the means of communion with God. This sense is highlighted if the words of the doxology are accompanied by an elevation of the elements in a ritual gesture of offering at the conclusion of the prayer.

Recognising that the Earth Belongs to the Lord

Much attention has recently been given to the materiality of Christian sacramental worship, especially of the elements of water, oil, bread, and wine.[10] And by referring these "things" to the redemptive and sanctifying work of Christ and the Holy Spirit in the Prayer of Thanksgiving, they themselves are redeemed to become effective signs pointing to the goal of creation. As such, the sacramental elements anticipate "the omega point," as it was styled by the pioneering priest and mystic palaeontologist, Teilhard de Chardin (1881–1955), when God will be "all in all" (1 Cor 15:28).[11] Sacraments, in other words, are not only grounded in creation but also show its fulfilment, for they point both backwards and forwards, back to the source of all things, and forward to their fulfilment as vehicles of God's transformation as God seeks to make all things new in Christ, through the operation of the Holy Spirit. This brings us to a fuller trinitarian perspective, but even in the loftiest theological rhetoric, the materiality of worship is far from being diminished. In every sacramental act

[10] See David Grummett, *Material Eucharist* (Oxford: Oxford University Press, 2016), and Christopher Irvine "Liturgy and Creation," in the forthcoming *Handbook of the Doctrine of Creation* (London: T&T Clark, 2021).

[11] Pierre Teilhard de Chardin, *The Phenomenon of Man* (New York: Harper Collins, 2008 [1959]).

we are ultimately reconnected to nature and to those human skills of taking the natural materials to make flour and bread, wine and oil, the very things that become the divinely appointed means by which Christians are united with Christ, strengthened and healed by the anointing Spirit, and nourished in life eternal.

The emphasis on the materiality of the Eucharist not only highlights our connection to the natural world, but also throws into relief our care for the environment. A particular instance of this is seen in how we handle what remains of the eucharistic bread and cup after the administration of Communion. Most denominations provide guidance to the presider of the Eucharist on what to do with the remaining elements if it is not to be reserved for the absent sick. These directions vary, but a good example is the rubrical direction in the Communion service of the Church of England's 1662 *Book of Common Prayer*, which directs the minister to "reverently eat and drink" what remains of the consecrated elements after the administration of Communion.[12] This direction may betoken a sense that the consecrated elements are no longer "ordinary food and drink," as one of our earliest accounts of the Christian Eucharist insists, but also resonates with a New Testament text that has more than a tangential bearing on the meaning of the Eucharist, and one that impacts on how we should respond to one of the biggest environmental issues in the affluent West today. The text in question is the direction Jesus gave to the disciples after the incident of the feeding of the multitude: "Gather up the fragments that nothing remains" (John 6:12). The environmental issue in view here is that of waste. It is a singular abuse of stewardship to dispose of nearly a third of all the foodstuffs that are produced. At its worst, the glut of the rich is at the expense of the global poor, and to produce more than is required is to accelerate the degradation of fertile soil. And so, it is in the light of these considerations that we can see that how the worshipping community handles and cares for its spiritual food and drink, particularly in what remains and is left over from the eucharistic feast, is indicative of its attitude to the wider social and natural environment.[13]

[12] Bryan Cummings, *The Book of Common Prayer: The Texts of 1549, 1559, and 1662* (Oxford: Oxford University Press, 2011), 406.

[13] Frank Senn, "The Care of the Earth as a Paradigm for the Treatment of the Eucharistic Elements," in *Creation and Liturgy*, ed. Ralph N. McMichael (Washington, DC: The Pastoral Press, 1993), 235–50.

Praying for the Environment

The logic dictates that if our worshipping and sacramental life is so grounded in the natural world, then the subject of our prayer, both individual and corporate, should extend to the environment. But how are we to pray, especially in this time of ecological crisis, and how might these prayers be framed? We have already hinted that the best-sounding liturgical texts are those that either voice or resonate with biblical texts, but the real challenge in looking for ways of praying for the environment is to find a register of language that is sufficiently robust and versatile to speak to the unprecedented situation of the global ecological crises that we find ourselves in. What is required, especially at this time, is a language of prayer that rings true, conveying a passionate care for the natural world without slipping into sentimentality or that kind of theological sloppiness that blurs the distinction between creation and the Creator, a distinction that was so well drawn by the poet-priest George Herbert (1593–1633) in "The Pulley," in which he spoke of "nature and the God of nature."[14] So, again, we turn to Scripture.

In his *Laws of Ecclesiastical Polity*, the Elizabethan apologist Richard Hooker (ca. 1554–1600) set out in considerable detail the multiple functions of Scripture in a liturgical church. The public performance of Scripture was both doxological as well as didactic. And although Hooker was fully aware of the different genres of writing in the Bible, he regarded both Old and New Testaments as presenting a single story (Book 1.xiv.4). However, in his polemic against a fundamentalist reading, Hooker asserted that not every line of Scripture carried an equal freight of meaning, and perhaps more surprisingly, suggested that the contemporary reader would not find all their questions and concerns directly addressed in the Bible.[15] One could easily feel that this is the case as we look for biblical words to express our concern and care for the environment. Our prayer for the care of the environment is complicated further when we recognise the different forms of liturgical prayer: there are prayers of thanksgiving, of penitence,

[14] George Herbert, "The Pulley," in Louis L. Martz, ed., *George Herbert and Henry Vaughan* (Oxford: Oxford University Press, 1986), 144–45.

[15] Richard Hooker, *Laws of Ecclesiastical Polity*, Book I.268.25–26, in *The Works of That Learned and Judicious Divine Mr. Richard Hooker with an Account of His Life and Death by Isaac Walton*; arranged by Rev. John Keble, MA, 7th ed., rev. Very Rev. R. W. Church and Rev. F. Paget (Oxford: Clarendon Press, 1888); 3 vols., vol. 1.

and intercession, for instance, each having their distinctive forms and theological grammar. Of these different forms of prayer, prayers of thanksgiving may well be the easiest prayers to craft, as there is a variety of texts across the biblical canon—stories, songs, and poetic compositions—that evoke the theme of creation.

Faced with a crisis of the magnitude of our present environmental crisis, however, individual and congregational prayers of penitence seem to be especially apposite. Indeed, the urgency of the situation has been acknowledged not only by the frequent calls to prayer by Pope Francis, but also in a resolution of the seventeenth Anglican Consultative Council meeting in Hong Kong in 2019 to promote a day of public repentance during Creationtide (September 1 to October 4, the feast of Francis of Assisi), for our wanton failure to care for creation.[16] Finding a literary and liturgical form to carry and convey the weight of corporate penitence is a real challenge, but there is one element that may assist us, and that is the biblical genre of lament. This genre serves to express individual and corporate expression of grief and sorrow, and in its biblical forms has its characteristic structure and rhythmic pattern.

It is particularly striking, in this light, that in the various expressions of lament in the writings of the prophets and in the psalms, there is not a single text that explicitly addresses the matter of environmental degradation, the depletion of the soil, deforestation, extreme weather conditions, and pollution of seas, lakes, and rivers. It may be possible to bypass the difficulty by saying that unprecedented situations require entirely fresh compositions, and to some extent this may be true. But as with all compositions, in language as well as in music, there are conventional forms, and these forms give weight to what it is that we want to express. Furthermore, as stated at the outset, the liturgical texts that have stood the test of time are those bibliophonic texts that bear repetition and are performed aloud as words addressed to God by the worshipping assembly. As Cally Hammond has demonstrated, the first test of any liturgical writing is how it sounds.[17] Liturgical language needs to have a strong metre,

[16] For the season of Creation-tide, see the ecumenically supported website https://seasonofcreation.org.

[17] See Cally Hammond, *The Sound of the Liturgy: How Words Work in Worship* (London: SPCK, 2015).

and, like the words of Scripture itself, is written to be read aloud and heard.[18]

Finding the Language

And so to recap, in seeking to find the language to pray for the environment, three points suggest themselves. The first, and probably the most significant factor driving us to pray, is the global scale and urgency of the environmental crisis. The second is the need to identify those biblical passages which in some way resonate with this pressing situation. Finally, the prayer must be cast in a language that is sufficiently robust and specific in its reference to the present calamity. As to the genre of the prayer, this must take account of the very seriousness of the situation, and the realisation that human actions have at least compounded the climate and environmental crisis. In that light, the most immediate need is not only to have prayers of confession acknowledging our own individual and corporate culpability, but also to find a form to express our sorrow for the crisis that is close to the biblical form of a lament in the writings of the prophets and in the psalms.

An attempt to compose a public lament at a time of environmental and climate crisis for a recent publication of liturgical resources produced a medley of phrases, rather than lifting a single piece of continuous biblical poetic prose or psalmody. The basis on which these biblical verses were selected was their reference to the natural world and their resonance with a sense of an impending calamity, and they were interspersed with newly forged lines that explicitly name some of the critical situations and challenges that are being experienced around the world. The specificity of these newly composed lines gives the lament a sense of immediacy, and it is given gravity by being woven into the weft of biblical words and phrases. The whole composition has a biblical-sounding refrain at the beginning and ending of the lament: "The land cries out to you, O Lord." The biblical verses deployed in the lament are drawn from both prophetic writing and psalmody. For example, there is the line from Hosea warning that

[18] Consider, for instance, the formula of prophetic utterance: "Thus says the Lord," and more explicitly: "Blessed is the one who reads aloud the words of this prophecy, and blessed are those who hear . . ." (Rev 1:3).

the beasts of the field, the birds of the air, and the fish in the sea languish (Hos 4:3), and another that adapts the language of Psalm 63: "the water springs are silent and the streams run dry: the green places are a dry land." Between these two passages are words that evoke the realities of the current crisis, the increasingly frequent and destructive wildfires: "the earth is scorched: the air polluted," and the rising sea levels: "the waters surge, and floods devastate the land." As in a psalm of lament, what follows the heartfelt cry describing the feared situation is a direct appeal to God. This confident appeal to God leads to the final section expressing an element of resolution, in this case, two lines drawn from Isaiah: "the desert shall rejoice and blossom" (Isa 35:1) and "the mountains and hills shall break into singing" (Isa 55:12b).[19]

Equally challenging is the composition of the prayers of intercession, and a number of these are available in both printed and digital form as a resource. What is required in this form of prayer are direct, arresting petitions, or biddings for prayer that voice both an appreciation of the variety of life in all forms and colour on earth, and the particular and pressing needs of the natural world such as habitat loss, or pollution. The vocabulary and syntax of biblical prayer moves from thanksgiving and praise to petition, and at its best, intercessory prayer should also follow this pattern of prayer. It should move, for instance, from a general expression of joy in creation, echoing the biblical verdict: "Behold, it is very good," to the articulation of specific and current needs, such as those suffering from the effects of flooding or wildfires, to those, like farmers, who manage the landscape and those working to develop and harness renewable energy and green technology. The aim of such a broad spectrum of voiced concerns is to make our prayer more immediate, and for it to sound more like a faithful expression of hope than a catalogue of environmental disasters.

Concerns for the environment stretch back before the heightened present climate crisis, and mention should be made of the well-crafted prayer resources, touching a variety of scenarios ranging from the blessing of farm animals to forest and forestry, which are provided

[19] Archbishops' Council of the Church of England, *A Time for Creation: Liturgical Resources for Creation and the Environment* (London: Church House Publishing, 2020), 44–45.

by the Anglican Church of Canada. These resources, that include biblical readings, canticles, and *berakah* prayers were probably composed and compiled by Paul Gibson nearly thirty years ago and are still available on the website of the Anglican Church of Canada. In its original published form this resource included a set of guidance notes on praying for the environment.[20] These notes present the creation as God's gift and express the view that what should speak and reflect something of God's glory is degraded and destroyed by our exploitation and misuse of the natural world. Alongside this pioneering work, mention should also be made of another Anglican source, a supplementary prayer book from Kenya that includes a Litany for the Preservation of the Environment. This prayer resource also includes six short gobbets of Scripture from the book of the prophet Isaiah. The notes printed before the litany say that it may be used in church, or interestingly, "near a threatened environmental site."[21]

The provision of biblical readings in these and similar resources is inevitably selective, and they are drawn predominantly from the Old Testament, because the figurative language in which they are cast dramatically evokes the natural world. Wider questions of the reception of biblical texts in the compilation and use of lectionaries are dealt with elsewhere in this volume, but some specific observations could be made here regarding the performance of Scripture in relation to our care for the environment. The first is the note in the Canadian resource that prayer for the environment should regularly feature in the liturgy of the local church, and that it should not be restricted to those Sundays in the three-year Common Lectionary that contain readings that make reference or allude to the natural world. Second, it should be noted that although the Church of England abandoned the thematic approach to lectionary construction and use that was deployed in the *Alternative Service Book* of 1980 and adopted the Revised Common Lectionary in 2000, one of the two themes that was carried over to the new lectionary provision was the theme of creation allocated to the second Sunday before Lent.

[20] General Synod of the Anglican Church of Canada, *Occasional Celebrations of the Anglican Church of Canada* (Toronto: Anglican Book Centre Publications, 1992) 181–83, https://www.anglican.ca/wp-content/uploads/OccasionalCelebrations.pdf.

[21] Anglican Church of Kenya, *Our Modern Services* (Nairobi: Umzima Publishing House, 2014), 224.

But what of the readings themselves? As previously mentioned, apart from Genesis 1 and 2, biblical passages that are taken as being scriptural references to creation and the natural world are largely incidental, figurative or, at best, oblique references. But on further and closer reading, the number of these passages exceeds our initial expectations. Comparatively recent liturgical revision illustrates the point. The two-year lectionary for the Eucharist in the Church of England's *Alternative Service Book 1980* for the Ninth Sunday before Christmas provided a set of six readings, plus appropriate psalmody. The new Church of England provision provides no less than thirteen separate readings, plus selected psalmody, and the most recent commended resource lists twenty-seven Old Testament Scripture readings, three readings from the Apocrypha, and fourteen from the New Testament that are reckoned to touch the themes of the creation, the environment, harvest, and other agricultural festivals. The reference here to agricultural festivals is a sufficient nudge to move to the next section of this exploration.

Stepping Out

Most readers would probably agree that the first act of worship is that of gathering, the coming together of worshippers around the Word and around the table of the Eucharist, a coming together in one place, the "still centre" in which the prayers of the assembly are offered. But this is not the full story. Since Christianity became a legal and public religion, processional liturgy has been a significant expression of worship, even if the practice has waxed and waned through the centuries of Christian corporate prayer.[22] Most of these processions have taken the worshipping assembly beyond the walls of the church and into the surrounding built and natural environment. These processions claimed that the world beyond the physical building of the church also belonged to the Lord and came within the ambit of God's kingdom.

[22] Processional liturgy has been a constant preoccupation of John Baldovin, SJ, who throughout his distinguished scholarly career has addressed this topic, from *The Urban Character of Christian Worship: The Origins, Development and Meaning of Stational Liturgy* (Rome: Oriental Institute Press, 1987) to his recent entry on "Processions" in the *Reallexicon für Antike und Christentum*, vol. 28 (Stuttgart: Anton Hiersemann Verlag, 2018).

Among these processional liturgies, and one that has survived the vicissitudes of church history, is the Rogationtide procession. The origins of Rogation days are hazy, but as the name suggests (from the Latin *rogo, rogare,* "to plead") they are associated with "asking," specifically asking for divine favour and advantage. Originally, in Roman civilisation, this meant asking the gods for victory over one's enemies, and for their blessing on the crops in the surrounding gardens and fields, so that they would be free of disease and be sufficient to feed the population. Appropriated in a Christian context, this asking for blessing was combined with an urgent appeal to God that the petitioners might be spared disaster and disease. What remained a defining feature was the corporate stepping out into the surrounding environment. The days for these religious perambulations came to be written into liturgical calendars as days for prayer and fasting. The discipline of fasting added an urgency to the prayer, and the form of prayer adopted for these processions was the litany, a series of petitions for divine favour and assistance.[23] The annual custom of the Rogation processions, observed on the three days before the feast of the Ascension, began in Gaul, was adopted in Rome, and then spread more widely by the time of Pope Leo III (795–816). In England Rogation processions were widely established in the Anglo-Saxon Church. The calendrical placing of these days was significant, and may indicate a theological conviction that in Christ, the things of the earth are caught up with things heavenly. And although the prayers on these occasions had a largely penitential tone, they also included forms for the blessing of crops. As the clergy and the people walked through the parish, there were frequent stops at key geographical boundary points, as well as at shrines and chapels for readings and prayers.[24] Psalms were also included, and, as we gather from one Anglo-Saxon Rogationtide homily, the procession culminated in the singing of the final verse of Psalm 67: "God will bless us: and all the ends of the earth shall fear him."

[23] The litany as a form of prayer stretches back well before Gregory the Great (ca. 540–604), who referred to the Great Litany being of great antiquity.

[24] M. Bradford Bedingfield, *The Dramatic Liturgy of Anglo-Saxon England* (Woodbridge: The Boydell Press, 2002), 191–200.

In the later Middle Ages, the Rogation processions became noisy and popular occasions, generally led by a processional cross.[25] Some of the people carried handbells, others held green branches, while the clergy carried relics of the saints, thereby extending the realm of the sacred into the surrounding countryside. These processions came to be proscribed in England at the Reformation, and all outdoor processions were suppressed in 1547. However, Rogation perambulations were encouraged by a Royal Injunction issued by Queen Elizabeth I. Rogation days were reinstated in the Kalendar of the 1559 *Book of Common Prayer*, and two homilies were provided for the clergy in the second *Book of Homilies*. One of these opens with the invitation to consider the marvellous creation of the world and goes on to speak of God's working in and through everything and every creature: "in the earth to give fruit . . . in our bread and drink to give nourishment."[26]

Suspicion that these practices had pagan origins was voiced from time to time, and yet the practice of rogation walks was certainly encouraged by many influential English religious writers. George Herbert defended the practice in *The Country Parson* on the grounds that it promoted local social cohesion and encouraged parishioners to live more generously in providing for the poor. Included in Herbert's strenuous affirmation of what he considered to be the old and popular custom of Rogation walks was the blessing of God for the fruits of the field. This element was stated in even stronger terms by Thomas Traherne (ca. 1637–74). His extensive and eloquent treatment of the Rogation procession included an explicit statement about imploring God's blessing upon the fruits of the earth, and a clear sense that such walks demonstrated that the natural world was also the domain of God. The glory of the God who was worshipped in church was physically seen, he said, by those who walk through the countryside. Moreover, by so walking through the countryside, those who

[25] Eamon Duffy, *The Stripping of the Altars* (New Haven: Yale University Press, 1992), 136.

[26] "Homily for the Days of Rogation Week," in *The Second Book of Homilies* (Oxford: Oxford University Press, 1832), 432.

do so can come to recognise that the fields and "all the world [is] the House of God."[27]

More recent liturgical provision for Rogationtide has referred to creation and included prayers for the natural environment. The 1995 prayer book of the Anglican Church of Australia, for instance, notes that prayers of thanksgiving may be offered for the whole created order.[28] In the Church of England's provision, petitions in the Litany (the traditional liturgical form for the Rogation procession) are provided in *Times and Seasons* (2006), and these directly touch on environmental concerns. This set of petitions is provided in both contemporary and traditional language, and is included in a new Litany specifically composed for the Rogationtide Procession.[29] The central petition articulates a prayer for all who "care for the earth, the water, and the air," and asks that "the riches of [God's] creation may abound from age to age."[30] In a Rogation procession, the prayer is expressed as much in the physical action of walking along lanes and footpaths, as in the words that are spoken and heard along the way. In this sense it could be said that this form of prayer is as integral to the natural environment as the land art of Richard Long.[31] For the Rogationtide procession is a direct engagement with the environment; it not only brings the environment into our prayer, but also physically demonstrates the biblical conviction that the whole universe is God's creation, and that the earth is the Lord's (Ps 24; cf. 1 Chr 29:11).

Lex Orandi, Lex Vivendi

Recent years have seen various calls for prayer and practical action in response to the environmental crisis, both from church leaders and ecumenical bodies around the world, from the call of the third Ecu-

[27] Cited by Denise Inge, *Happiness and Holiness: Thomas Traherne and His Writings* (Norwich: The Canterbury Press, 2008), 257.

[28] *A Prayer Book for Australia* (Alexandria, NSW: Broughton Books, 1995), 451.

[29] Archbishops' Council of the Church of England, *Common Worship: Times and Seasons*, (London: Church House Publishing, 2006), 614.

[30] *Common Worship: Times and Seasons*, 615. The petition was adopted from material for the Rogation procession provided in a resource volume published by the Episcopal Church of the United States of America, *The Book of Occasional Services*, 2nd ed. (New York: Church Hymnal Corporation, 2003), 103.

[31] William Malpas, *The Art of Richard Long* (Maidstone: Crescent Moon Publishing, 2011). See also http://www.richardlong.org/.

menical European Assembly that asked for a dedicated season in which Christians of all denominations should pray for the protection of the natural world and the promotion of sustainable lives,[32] to a more recent meeting of Anglican bishops, women leaders, and youth representatives from fourteen different African countries in September 2018.[33]

The year 2015 saw the publication of two highly significant documents: the encyclical of Pope Francis, *Laudato Si'*, and the so-called Buffalo Statement agreed by the International Commission for Anglican-Orthodox Theological Dialogue, *In the Image and Likeness of God: A Hope-Filled Anthropology*.[34] These two documents set out the severity of the environmental and climate crisis and recognize that this crisis is inseparable from the call to practise social justice. For it is inevitably the poor of the world, and other species of creatures and their habitats, that are most vulnerable and are most severely affected by the climate and environmental crises. The clarion call sounded in the Anglican-Orthodox Statement could not be more urgent: "Whole ecological systems have been destroyed . . . and climate change on a global scale now appears all but irreversible."[35] In his encyclical, Pope Francis expresses his desire to address every human being living on the planet, and he delivers the same uncompromising message: "Doomsday predictions can no longer be met with irony or disdain."[36] We are not left with this gloomy verdict, however. The following chapter of the encyclical outlines the kind of actions that can mitigate, if not totally avert, ecological and social catastrophe, and the authors of the Anglican-Orthodox Statement promise a further publication

[32] The tenth resolution of the Third European Ecumenical Assembly in Sibiu, Romania, proposed a time for creation (September 1 to October 4) in which Christians were to be encouraged to protect creation, promote sustainable lifestyles, and reverse their contribution to climate change.

[33] Meeting at the Good Shepherd Retreat Centre, Hartebeespoort, South Africa, September 2018.

[34] Pope Francis also called for September 1 to be observed as a World Day of Prayer for the care of creation.

[35] International Commission for Anglican-Orthodox Theological Dialogue, *In the Image and Likeness of God: A Hope-filled Anthropology* (London: The Anglican Consultative Council, 2015), 30.

[36] Pope Francis, *Laudato Si'* 161. For a critique see Peter McGrail, "*Laudato Si'*—The Ecological Imperative of the Liturgy," in Dennis O'Hara et al., *Integral Ecology for a More Sustainable World: Dialogues with Laudato Si'* (New York: Lexington Books, 2019).

on practical ways in which we, "the priesthood of creation," may care for the planet. In this sense, our prayer for the environment needs to flow into action, so that there is no dissonance between what is voiced in the liturgy and the choices we make and the ways in which daily lives are lived on this "fragile planet earth."

For this reason, there needs to be a liturgical form to express our commitment to care for creation. An attempt to do this is set out in a short "Act of Commitment" that is included in *A Time for Creation* (2020). This liturgical unit, based on a reading of the biblical notion of covenant, was written with the intention that it should be used as part of the dismissal in either the Eucharist, or a Service of the Word. The introductory sentence echoes the passage in Paul's letter to the Romans of a groaning creation looking to be liberated at the revelation of redeemed humanity, and then members of the assembly are asked to pledge themselves to care for creation, reduce their waste, value the diversity of life, and to live sustainably as far as they can. And as with all Christian endeavours, the petitioners ask for God's assistance to do this. As God's wisdom has created and permeates all things, so wisdom is invoked here, that life in all its forms may flourish, and that those who pledge themselves to care for creation may continue to be inspired to join creation in voicing praise to God the Creator.[37] For in the final analysis, God is the Creator, and the privilege and responsibility of God's priestly people is to acknowledge and join in creation's praise of the Creator, as the *Te Deum Laudamus* jubilantly asserts: "All creation worships you, the Father everlasting."[38] Implicit in this doxological text is a key element in the doctrine of creation, namely that by its very existence, creation praises the Creator and that this praise is anterior to the swell of praise expressed in Christian worship. This conviction has been poetically caught in a contemporary psalm prayer for Psalm 98, a prayer which asks that worshippers may tune the song of their hearts to the music

[37] Archbishops' Council of the Church of England, *A Time for Creation: Liturgical Resources for Creation and the Environment* (London: Church House Publishing, 2020), 48.

[38] The *Te Deum* is a trinitarian canticle that developed over time from the fifth century. Initially a canticle in monastic prayer to herald the dawn of the new day on Sundays, it was then adopted more generally for use at Morning Prayer on Sundays and feast days.

of creation.[39] For this to happen, perhaps one could add that worshippers may need to be more alert and aware of the natural world around them.

This theological perspective opens a horizon of hope that impacts on the quotidian. At one level there is the hope that individuals, communities, and indeed nations will take practical steps to ameliorate and reduce the effects of the current environmental crisis. But there is a deeper and sustaining hope, a hope that can guard us from sliding into that parody of biblical apocalypticism that sees the ecosystems of the world moving inexorably to extinction, and this is the hope that is grounded in the conviction that as Creator, God has a purpose for creation. This hope issues from the authentic apocalyptic vision of "a new heaven and a new earth" (Rev 21:1), of a world made new in Christ through the action of the renewing Spirit. And it is this same Holy Spirit who can also inspire and work in and through the children of God, to whom the earth looks for its liberation from the despoliation of natural resources and suffocating pollution of the air, soil, seas, and waterways.

[39] Archbishops' Council of the Church of England, *Common Worship: Daily Prayer* (London: Church House Publishing, 2005), 794.

Chapter 12

Children Are Church

Ann Loades

My overall perspective in theology is shaped by connecting "sacramentality" with "spirituality," and with some attention to children.[1] For the benefit of any reader of this present essay, however, so far as I can tell, few writers of theology or liturgy, let alone liturgical theology, have found children to deserve their attention, notwithstanding the central importance of children in any and every human society,[2] their well-being[3] and in the practice of religion.[4] My deficiencies may, I hope, provoke others to attend to the importance of the issues I

[1] Ann Loades, "Sacramentality and Christian Spirituality," in *The Blackwell Companion to Christian Spirituality*, ed. Arthur Holder, 254–68 (Oxford: Blackwell, 2005).

[2] Noteworthy are the complications of social and political shifts which have made possible, e.g., the separation of "procreation" from "heterosexual marriage," "assisted" pregnancy, the variant family formations which may result from anti-discrimination legislation, consequences for inter-generational grandparenting, together with the possibilities of serial monogamy, polyamory. Any of these will require unequivocal support for children negotiating their lives with adults and their relationship with churches and their liturgy. Cf. Joe Rollins, *Legally Straight: Sexuality, Childhood, and the Cultural Value of Marriage* (New York: New York University Press, 2018); Rickie Solinger, *Pregnancy and Power: A History of Reproductive Politics in the United States* (New York: New York University Press, 2019).

[3] See, for example, the British Academy's Childhood Programme, thebritishacademy/ac.uk/childhood/, and further important articles sponsored by the British Academy, https://medium.com/reframing-childhood-past-and-present.

[4] Possibilities include Susan Ridgely, ed., *The Study of Children in Religions* (New York: New York University Press, 2011).

raise. This will certainly alert us to the range of non-theological resources on which we must draw in paying attention to children.

On Becoming Liturgical Entrepreneurs

Everyone engaged in nourishing children in liturgy, that is, in an ecclesial group in which the worship of God is a priority, needs to sustain those ordained to take responsibility for liturgy as public service/worship, but not simply to leave them to it. The responsibility for worship is a matter to be shared by all those involved, of whatever age. Moreover, there is no necessary connection between ordination and having a secure and perceptive understanding of children, nor can this be easily acquired in the course of preparation for ordination. Not everyone needs to know everything—how could they? But there is much that can be shared and much that can be learned from children themselves. Congregations thus perhaps need to organise continuous and sustained group work, each group including someone who will find out what will be offered to others at regular meetings, as is the case with professionals in many spheres who need to update their perspective on their work. Local libraries may be helpful, together with a congregation's own investment in resources—meaning not just word but music and the arts very broadly construed. Learning and sharing is a way forward; no one person becomes an isolated authority for all. Everyone has something to contribute, and any congregation hopefully includes people concerned with children in all their variety at different stages of their life, eager to ensure good experiences for generations following their own.

Beginning: Finding a Starter Kit

We all need to recognise that the Bible is indeed the Christian Church's collection of texts authorised for use in worship, but that neither Bible nor liturgy dropped into existence ready-made.[5] It can

[5] John Barton, *A History of the Bible: The Book and Its Faiths* (London: Penguin, 2020); David C. Parker, *Textual Scholarship and the Making of the New Testament* (Oxford: Oxford University Press, 2012). Of primary importance also are Douglas A. Knight and Amy-Jill Levine, *The Meaning of the Bible: What the Jewish Scriptures and Christian Old Testament Can Teach Us* (New York: Harper Collins, 2011).

be illuminating to compare the Bibles of different ecclesial groups which may have different collections of texts, possibly in a different order, and very likely in different translations, and it is the language of the Bible which could and should infuse the ritual of worship. This may require attention to vestments and furnishings, actions, choral speech as well as singing, prayers, the practice of silence, reading, and reading "out loud," intercessions (needing special care), collections for charity, preaching, music-making—whatever.[6] Much can be learned to enrich the study of the Bible as well as liturgy by comparing and studying one with another, and by the occasional discussion of a sermon![7] So we proceed from the recognition that the foundation of theology is in liturgy, liturgical theology, whatever other forms of theology may, as it were, co-exist with it or be developed from it. The language matters, and liturgy is best served by biblical and poetic languages which bring it alive, make connections between "then" and "now," by metaphors (speaking of one thing in relation to another, as in bread and wine—body and blood; and symbolism, one thing signifying another, as in the previous example), modes of language alive and action familiar in Orthodox liturgy and in much need of recovery in many Western churches.[8]

[6] See Steven R. Guthrie, "Temples of the Spirit: Worship as Embodied Performance," in *Faithful Performance: Enacting Christian Worship*, ed. Trevor Hart and Steven R. Guthrie, 91–107 (Aldershot, UK: Ashgate, 2007). For "sacrament" as both words of commitment and relish for sacramental signs of divine presence, see Ann Loades, "Sacrament," in Adrian Hastings, Alistair Mason, and Hugh Pyper, eds., *The Oxford Companion to Christian Thought: Intellectual, Spiritual and Moral Horizons of Christianity* (Oxford: Oxford University Press, 2000), 634–37.

[7] See, e.g., Christoph Schwöbel, "Read-pray-trust: One Theologian's Encounters with Scripture," in *Theologians on Scripture*, ed. Angus Paddison, 161–79 (London: Bloomsbury T&T Clark, 2016); Bridget Nichols, "Highways to Zion: Rediscovering Scripture through Liturgical Prayer," *Anaphora* 12, nos. 1–2 (2018): 35–66.

[8] Nicholas Wolterstorff, *Acting Liturgically: Philosophical Reflections on Religious Practice* (Oxford: Oxford University Press, 2018), 9 and 121–47, and his *The God We Worship: An Exploration of Liturgical Theology* (Grand Rapids, MI: Eerdmans, 2015). See also Gail Ramshaw, *Reviving Sacred Speech: The Meaning of Liturgical Language; Second Thoughts on Christ in Sacred Speech* (Akron, OH: OSL Publications, 2000); and her *Pray, Praise, and Give Thanks: A Collection of Litanies, Laments and Thanksgivings at Font and Table* (Minneapolis: Augsburg Fortress, 2017).

Treasures in Waiting

Especially given resources for the unpredictability of life to be found in the psalms as well as language for the praise of God, it is essential that the psalms become familiar to those within a worshipping community and made accessible to children. There are centuries-long practices of rewriting the psalms into versions which do not require chant and are singable and sayable in church by children, and memorised and prayed at home and school—if a church-related school. One source well worth exploring is the Church of Scotland's *Hymnary*, with psalms themselves and their paraphrases, as well as some short songs, doxologies and amens.[9] Even very small children can sing and understand such words, (doxology: glory-song) and we all learn by singing along with one another. "Alleluia" ("Praise God") and "Amen" ("So let it be") from Hebrew also remind us that we are indebted to both testaments of the Bible. We need to attend also to the fact that the biblical character of the liturgy and its performance has had a profound influence on life beyond church in many ways, some of them barely given attention by theologians, but in and by which everyone, not the least children, may well be nourished. In fact, liturgy may now be made accessible via its being online in ways until recently inconceivable, and well worth exploring.[10]

Children's Caregivers Finding Words for a Sense of Divine Presence

We turn now to children themselves, as in Hugh S. Pyper's brief essay on children. This helpfully indicates the problems facing writers in theology relying on divergent attitudes to children in the past (as "unspoiled" or "prerational" or "prey to original sin"),[11] together

[9] Church of Scotland, *Church Hymnary*, 4th ed. (Norwich: Canterbury Press, 2015). For a version of the psalms by a poet professionally concerned with education in primary schools, see Gordon Jackson, *The Lincoln Psalter: Versions of the Psalms* (Manchester: Carcanet, 1997), 12.

[10] One example is the set of e-books by David Stancliffe, *The Gospels in Art, Music and Literature: The Story of Salvation in Three Media* (London: SPCK, 2014–15), each reading introduced by an artwork. Also noteworthy is Gordon Giles, *O Clap Your Hands: A Musical Tour of Sacred Choral Works* (London: SPCK, 2008).

[11] Hugh S. Pyper, "Children," in Hastings et al., *Oxford Companion to Christian Thought*, 110.

with ambivalence about the desirability of procreation/having children at all to begin with, through to consideration of childhood as a distinctive stage of life to cherish. He acknowledges that it is now vital to attend to new disciplines understanding child development.[12] A quite different direction (though again minus explicit attention to new disciplines) has been taken by Herbert Anderson in his exploration of "childness"—invaluable characteristics of children which are not limited to childhood.[13] His basic recommendation is that a child is fully human, though much of what is present in a child is yet to be realised. "Teaching" is not a one-way activity, for children may teach adults to listen to them and thus learn empathy for them, as well as offering children unconditional hospitality and shelter, the wisdom of dependency and neediness, and lifelong and inescapable vulnerability and interdependence (as with the elderly and fragile). Children need to be respected and honoured, protected indeed but "let go" as they mature, living as clear-eyed as children can, growing up embodying compassion, a sense of responsibility both for what lies within a "family" network and, to extend Anderson's perspective a little, the practice of courage and of hope. For while much can be changed, not everything can be "fixed" in every political and social culture.

We might note, however, that apart from theology undertaken by pastoral theologians such as Anderson and some of his colleagues, thinking about children does not seem to command nearly enough attention from theologians, even indirectly through consideration of children's parents or "caregivers," except at most in the terms indicated above. Neither is explicit attention given to how children's lives may be construed, expressed, and found in liturgy. Yet from such fundamental human experiences as being "mother" and "father" or "the one who cares" or is "given care" are derived language for God, notwithstanding a basic rule that any and every way of referring to God is both "Yes" and "No," both sayable and unsayable. So far as "mother" is concerned, resources may well be found in biblical tradi-

[12] A much needed example is Doris M. Kieser, *Catholic Sexual Theology and Adolescent Girls: Embodied Flourishing* (Waterloo, ON: Wilfred Laurier University Press, 2015).

[13] Herbert Anderson and Susan B. W. Johnson, *A New Respect for Children and Families* (Louisville, KY: Westminster John Knox Press, 1994), 9–28; Herbert Anderson, "Sense and Nonsense in the Wisdom of Dr. Seuss," *New Theology Review* 14 no. 3 (2001): 37–50. A key phrase is "going at the pace of the children" (Gen 33:12-14).

tion, as, for instance, where traces of texts from Isaiah, are given a place in liturgical texts.[14] What is involved here is certainly a significant issue for those concerned with children, whatever the circumstances of their own conception and birth and upbringing. For as Margaret Hebblethwaite suggests (both in connection with Mary the mother of Jesus and, we may add, in many appallingly difficult situations[15]), motherhood may be seen as "a reflection of God's own nature" in that it is connected with "innovative creativity, because human life originates in the mother's body; with powerful protection, because the womb is the safest of environments; with painful transformation, because the mother gives birth through labour; and with life-giving love because the mother feeds the child on herself at the breast. Thus women themselves, together with men, may then rightly discover 'the dignity of being made in the image of God.'"[16] Further, as Bonnie J. Miller-McLemore comments, "caring for children requires deep reserves of energy, extended periods of patience, and a heightened intellectual activity that seldom has been recognised as such"—recognised and affirmed within everyday life.[17] The words attributed

[14] See, e.g., Canticle 38, "A Song of Jerusalem Our Mother" (Isa 66:10, 11a, 12a, 12c, 13a, 14a, b), in Archbishops' Council of the Church of England, *Common Worship: Daily Prayer* (London: Church House Publishing, 2005), 589.

[15] See Grace Thomas, "Everywoman Eve," in Hannah Malcolm, ed., *Words for a Dying World: Stories of Grief and Courage from the Global Church* (London: SCM Press, 2020); Elaine Storkey, *Women in a Patriarchal World: Twenty-five Empowering Stories from the Bible* (London: SPCK, 2020); Debbie Blue, *Consider the Women: A Provocative Guide to Three Matriarchs of the Bible* (Grand Rapids, MI: Eerdmans, 2019).

[16] Margaret Hebblethwaite, "Motherhood," in Hastings et al., *Oxford Companion to Christian Thought*, 453–54, 454. Mary's receptivity to the Holy Spirit is central to the work of Sir James MacMillan, including his "Quickening" (on reverence for life), in collaboration with poet Michael Symmons Roberts, and his Choral Symphony No.5, with its alternative title, "Le Grand Inconnu"—the mystery of the Holy Spirit.

[17] Bonnie J. Miller-McLemore, *Also a Mother: Work and Family as Theological Dilemma* (Nashville: Abingdon Press, 1994), 158. On the importance of "the visceral, bodily connection" with a tiny baby, see Janet Morley, *Love Set You Going: Poems of the Heart* (London: SPCK, 2019), 21, commenting on Rowan Williams's poem, "Our Lady of Vladimir." On seeing how "paying close attention to babies can help us see long-standing philosophical problems in a new light," being "interpersonal and social creatures before we can be anything else," see Liz McKinnell, "Philosophical Plumbing in the Twenty-First Century," *Centenary Celebration: Anscombe, Foot, Midgley, and Murdoch*, Royal Institute of Philosophy Supplements 87 (2020): 221–33, 230–31. See also Mary Midgley, *Beasts and Man: The Roots of Human Nature* (Hassocks, UK: Harvester Press, 1978), on our inherited emotional constitution in biological thinking;

to Mary, the mother of Jesus in Luke's Gospel also remind us that women need to be both courageous and tough (Luke 2:34-35)! It is indeed possible to address God as "Mother" with the same confidence (and degree of hesitation) as God is addressed as "Father." Images of both are found in the first chapters of the Gospels according to Matthew and Luke.

A particular point can be developed from thinking about Joseph and human "fatherhood," rendering "father" as a metaphor for God as Trinity, not necessarily as problematic as some have found it to be.[18] We may thus affirm the truth of "God the Father above us, God the Son with us, and God the Holy Spirit within us," its practical meaning being that "God is on our side."[19] Young and old learn this language for God as they say, sing, and pray the *Gloria*, with Trinity Sunday celebrated as a major feast. Trusting that God is indeed on our side may focus our attention on the figure of Joseph in the Gospel of Matthew, a workman who also has to grow food for his family, whose life highlights the vital importance of the men who work towards saving and providing resources for children, as Joseph does for the child to whom Joseph has committed himself.[20] Any visitors from the surrounding countryside—shepherds, for instance—would know how important it was to bring food for the family, to ensure that Mary is well enough nourished to be able to breastfeed her child. But Joseph, the Magi, and later saints have a vital role to play here.[21] For a "migrant reading" of the role of the second group (whether as Magi or kings) may well generate a different perception of their im-

---

Mary Midgley, *Wickedness: A Philosophical Essay* (London: Routledge, 1984), 88–92, on children's play and aggression; Rowan Williams, "Children and Choice," in *Lost Icons: Reflections on Cultural Bereavement* (London: T&T Clark, 2001), 13–63.

[18] See Janet Martin Soskice, "Calling God Father," in *The Kindness of God: Metaphor, Gender, and Religious Language* (Oxford: Oxford University Press, 2008), 66–83.

[19] Helen Oppenheimer, *Finding and Following: Talking with Children about God* (London: SCM Press, 1994), 167–68. See the *Church Hymnary* arranged in a Trinitarian pattern including "Doxologies" 806–8, recalling also the *Gloria patri* which concludes each psalm—well within the range of children to learn and to say, sing, and pray.

[20] See "The Role of Joseph" in Sarah Drummond, *Divine Conception: The Art of the Annunciation* (London: Unicorn, 2018), 40–51.

[21] Saint Nicholas (who is not the Santa Claus of much popular culture) needs to be identified and celebrated for children as a successor of the Magi in his provision of money and gifts for near-destitute children. And the Christingle service has its place here, with the symbolism of its oranges, ribbons, and candles readily understood by children.

portance and their generosity at Epiphany, by making possible a flight to life in a new country, as is the case with many seekers of asylum in our own time. In adopting a child as yet unborn and then undertaking to bring the baby to safety with his mother, Joseph may then be seen as someone who represents "a positive and transformative masculinity." That is, he reminds us of "the many fathers who risk their lives for the sake of their children and die trying to protect them by taking them and their children on hazardous journeys in search of life and a future." They denounce terror by fleeing, and their flight is "an act of courage as much as it is a quest for life."[22] Many First Testament texts clearly reflect a world in which people had to move around for safety and to find resources for a new life, so it must now be a priority to continue to honour those who do what they can to meet the needs of desperate family groups whoever and wherever they may be. Street children among the homeless need particular attention and should be brought in to share in liturgy.[23] It must also be a priority to find homes for children outside "institutions" wherever possible and practicable, and to put time, energy, and resources into clubs and organisations which foster the skills and abilities of all kinds, which may initially be unknown to the children themselves. Once able to return to his own part of Galilee, Joseph would have been able to find shelter, grow food, and with Mary, support his whole family group, as migrant families hope for themselves.

One of Us: The Son of Mary and Joseph

We know very little about the childhood of Jesus and can at best make only some possible suggestions which are recognisable by children. A primary task is to make it clear to children that he was born as they are born, that he was one of them. The Hebrew of Psalm

[22] Monica Jyotsna Melanchthon, "The Flight to Egypt: A Migrant Reading—Implications for a Lutheran Understanding of Salvation," in Kenneth Mtata and Craig Koester, eds., *Lutheran Hermeneutics and the Gospel of Matthew* (Leipzig: Lutheran World Federation/Evangelische Verlangsanstalt, 2015), 153–68, 163; Seforosa Carroll, "Reimagining Home: Migration and Identity in a Changing Culture," in Jione Havea, *Theological and Hermeneutical Explorations from Australia* (Lanham, MD: Lexington Books, 2021), 167–79.

[23] Ethna Regan, "Catholic Social Teaching and Homelessness: The World Tribe of the Dispossessed," *Journal of Vincentian Social Action* 4, no. 1 (2019): 24–32, at https://scholar.stjohns.edu/jovsa/vol4/iss1/8.

40:6 translates, "Ears thou hast dug for me/ mine ears thou hast opened," that is, as bodily creatures we have ears—like many other creatures, even if not so acute![24] For if all goes well, from an unborn child's very first moments, before knowing that she or he is a person formed by and made to interrelate with others, a child hears its own heartbeat and that of its mother. There are many more sounds to hear, sort out, interpret, connect up or distinguish, respond to in fear or delight or puzzlement, whilst all unbeknownst to an unborn baby, within its fragile skull the miracle of the inner ear is being formed. At birth, Jesus experienced being face to face with his mother when being fed, being smiled at and smiling back, mother or father just in focus, being talked to, sung to, listening, trying to respond. He may well have learned to sing when very young, banging and thumping things, discovering the miracle of thumbs and fingers, perhaps sometimes able to watch travelling musicians interacting with one another. If blind or not fully sighted a child may still be able to sing and develop exceptionally sensitive hearing. If not able to hear clearly a child nevertheless may experience rhythm and sound bodily in ways most of us may never explore. Jesus would have been miserable when teething or if he fell over learning to walk, survived some ailments, and sometimes have been argumentative and impossible to please. Given the number of things that needed doing to keep his family fed, as soon as he was able to help, he would have had to tackle whatever was within his reach. From his parents he could have learned some psalm texts to sing, and most importantly the Shema as in Deuteronomy 6:4-5, as well as discovering how to celebrate the Sabbath, Passover, and other major feasts.

Beyond a childhood recognisable to children, we have no idea how Jesus became the extraordinary person recorded in the gospels, though we know a good deal about life in Galilee and the farming community in which his family was based.[25] It has been suggested that he may possibly have attended something like a synagogue school for boys. From a very young age they would attend to learn their letters, read and chant texts out loud, learn an extraordinary

[24] Paul Haupt, "Mine Ears Hast Thou Opened," *Journal of Biblical Literature* 38, nos. 3 and 4 (1919): 183–85, 185.

[25] Jean-Pierre Isbouts, *Young Jesus: Restoring the "Lost Years" of a Social Activist and Religious Dissident* (New York: Sterling, 2008), 67–76.

amount by heart, and even become what came to be known in later Judaism as "living texts."[26] Whether any such school existed, however, let alone in Nazareth, is as yet problematic in the absence of relevant archaeological and textual evidence. A quite different resource for learning how to worship was available from time to time, however, for it is clear from the Fourth Gospel that Jesus as an adult attended the great feasts celebrated in Jerusalem, where his family had some relatives. Recalling Mary's visit to Elizabeth, the wife of Zechariah, it is worth exploring how he may have learned from his relatives, committed to the worship of the magnificently rebuilt temple in Jerusalem. To them a much-longed-for son had been born, named John by his father. Attending the Passover feast each year in Jerusalem, Jesus' parents surely visited their kin there. When Jesus went missing on their return from one such visit, they began looking for him among their kin and acquaintances. They eventually located him in the temple learning from the teachers available there, quizzing them about what they had to say. It is at least possible that Jesus learned a great deal about the worship of the temple from John and his family.

How and why Jesus recovered from years of labour beyond the age when he lost his father, returned home, and focussed on the miseries of Galilee in his time is a further story, but he can at the very least be appreciated by children as a most provocative storyteller.[27] In addition, there is no way of avoiding the fact that at some point he must have found that he had an extraordinary gift for exorcism, like some other men of his times. He may have been shocked into discovery of that particular gift by those who recognised it in him before he did, in confrontations with some desperately disturbed people. Finding gifts of exorcism and healing exhaustingly burdensome may explain why he so often needed to head off into the hills by himself, given the demands on him to heal bodies, restore minds, preach the "turn around" of repentance, forgive sins all connected

[26] See Michael O'Connor, "The Singing of Jesus," in *Resonant Witness: Conversations between Music and Theology*, ed. Jeremy S. Begbie and Steven Guthrie, 434–53 (Grand Rapids, MI: Eerdmans, 2011).

[27] The best book available on the parables is arguably Amy-Jill Levine, *Short Stories by Jesus: The Enigmatic Parables of a Controversial Rabbi* (San Francisco: Harper Collins, 2014). See also Paula Gooder, *The Parables* (Norwich: Canterbury Press, 2020).

in the Lord's Prayer, and preach blessings for the vulnerable and prayer even for one's actual or supposed enemies. So far as children are concerned, however, what needs to be established is Jesus' trust in God, no matter what might become of him, beyond even the worst that the eventual collusion between Herod and Pilate could achieve. It could well be helpful if churches recovered the crucifixes which eventually appeared in the first millennium, that is, those which were empty of a body, beautifully decorated as for a festival, or which displayed Jesus transfigured in glory. Images of torture and the Way of the Cross have their place, but not in the imagination and emotions of children.

Of first importance also are the narratives of Jesus transforming the grief of parents of sick and dying children, notwithstanding the texts which make it easy to suppose that, because of what became his footloose life, he had little concern for friends and families. Yet he clearly depended on a network of support for himself and his companions and relied on their hospitality; he had to free himself from the anxieties of his family group, quite possibly fearful of drawing attention to themselves as the source of the man who sometimes provoked disturbances. If he had ever been married, as one would expect Joseph to have arranged for him, it is just possible that he had lost a young wife and a baby himself, which could also account in part for his footloose life. That apart, there are texts which need to be grouped together for children to know, which show how important the lives of the children he met were for Jesus. He was known as someone who would touch children—perhaps a hug of blessing for those whose eagerness to be with him became a reminder of how to be eager for the reign of God. The accounts of Matthew 19:13-15, Mark 10:13-16, and Luke 18:15-17 have exercised immense affective power on the Christian imagining of Jesus' attitude to children. He went so far as to identify himself with children (Luke 9:47-48), and he knew what it was like to be a generous father (Luke 11:11-13). The gospels offer at least a framework for children to realise that Jesus of Nazareth would have them in his heart.

Thus, I am suggesting that what we need to do is focus attention on what happens to children and those who are desperate for their well-being prompted by the narratives of all sorts of people in both Testaments, both named or unnamed, and for children themselves, with an especial focus on Jesus of Nazareth. Then we may go on to see that since "human creatures could not survive their long childhood without continuing devoted support, children need to make unbounded demands upon their parents and depend upon them for tireless comfort," parental love is therefore fit to be an image of God's love.[28] Thence we learn fidelity in interdependence on one another in order to become truly ourselves, capable of happiness, learning the "grace of courtesy" to one another, saying "Please" and "Thank you," not least at meals together. Thus "to receive blessings, whether human or divine with gratitude," indeed becomes life-enhancing.[29] So too may thinking kindly about unattractive people, God loving each and every one differently with unfailing particular partiality, responding to one another when in the wrong by saying "Sorry," and offering and receiving forgiveness, whatever that may mean in different circumstances. Being human and in the divine image also requires human persons to support the exercise of justice and mercy beyond the network of family, given that the gospel discerns God's justice in bearing the brunt of what human life is like or can be like.[30] Trust in God and not terror of God are what faith hopes to find and sustain, symbolised at the very least by the rainbow of Genesis 9:13-14, which has become such an important image (a sacramental sign) in the crisis of the recent pandemic, children themselves painting and decorating it in so many different ways. Apart from anything else, the rainbow may remind us that gifts and graces take many forms as children find a sense of their own identity: so ask, suggest, praise, celebrate, rage at wrongs, refuse, accept, regret, and grieve, and trust to God to transform the hazards of life.

Grief, Lament, and Celebration

In the very midst of the celebration of a child safely born to his mother (who had the courage to risk the hazards of pregnancy and childbirth) comes the lament of "Holy Innocents," both much neglected and much needed.[31] It seems extraordinary that there are

[28] Helen Oppenheimer, *Christian Faith for Handing On* (Eugene, OR: Cascade, 2013), 136. See also Michael Sadgrove, *Lost Sons: God's Long Search for Humanity* (London: SPCK, 2012); Benjamin Britten's *The Prodigal Son* (1968), one of many artworks on the parable.

[29] Oppenheimer, *Christian Faith*, 136–38.

[30] Oppenheimer, *Christian Faith*, drawing on observations made, 136–51.

[31] See the lack of resources identified in Bridget Nichols, "The Feast of the Holy Innocents and Anglican Remembering," *Anaphora* 13, no. 1 (2019): 1–28.

many whose lament needs to be heard and for whom liturgy seems to make so little provision.[32] There are longing-to-be-parents for whom medically assisted reproduction may or may not be a success in the sense of a baby safely born, and born healthy; there are others who suffer "multiple reproductive losses,"[33] whether being unable ever to establish a pregnancy or to avoid miscarriage, or having to face a decision to have an induced abortion of an unborn child grievously handicapped.[34] Children die despite the desperate efforts of their parents, relatives, grandparents, and siblings expecting them to be safe in disasters, accidents, and school shootings. Rachel weeps both for the slaughtered young as well as for children grown or growing into adulthood (Jer 31:15-16; Matt 2:18), through street violence, domestic abuse, drug addiction, alcoholism, suicide, and military combat in its many forms.[35]

In this light, the prospect of Mothering Sunday becoming "emotional hell" must be avoided at all costs. It needs to be a "special effort day," and reconsidered not only in part as a form of commemoration for "lost" children, but now involving siblings grieving for lost family members (including their own siblings), for friends, for grandparents,

[32] A father will not forget the experience of carrying the coffin of a stillborn child, born too early to survive, or born with a condition which will mean heartbreaking early death. Linda L. Layne, "'True Gifts from God': Paradoxes of Motherhood, Sacrifice and Enrichment," in *Motherhood Lost: A Feminist Account of Pregnancy Loss in America* (London: Routledge, 2003), attends to the suffering of both parents; Santiago Piñón, "Losing a Child: A Father's Methodological Plight," in *Feminist Trauma Theologies: Body, Scripture and Church in Critical Perspective*, ed. Karen O'Donnell and Katie Cross, 248–65 (London: SCM Press, 2020); Sue Morton, "Graven on the Heart," *Church Times* (11 October 2019): 19; Margaret Pritchard Houston, "Pray You, Love, Remember," *Church Times* (11 October 2019): 20–21.

[33] See Karen O'Donnell, *Broken Bodies: The Eucharist, Mary and the Body in Trauma Theology* (London: SCM Press, 2018), with pages on the Annunciation-Incarnation as trauma and Mary's recovery when seeking safety with Elizabeth (167–69, 175–81). Karen O'Donnell finds the possibility of recovery from knowing that she held "a place of death" within herself in the reformation of the Eucharist as "generative and life-giving ritual, focussed on nourishment and life," 126, and the revelation the Spirit already present, 91.

[34] There is also the grief and struggle of parents of a child born with "developmental disabilities"; see Edward Foley, ed., *Developmental Disabilities and Sacramental Access: New Paradigms for Sacramental Encounters* (Eugene, OR: Wipf and Stock, 2020).

[35] Paul M. Joyce and Diana Lipton, *Lamentations through the Centuries* (Chichester: Wiley-Blackwell, 2013), 88–92, not least in the twentieth century; Nicholas Wolterstorff, *Lament for a Son* (Grand Rapids, MI: Eerdmans, 1987).

and much-loved "others," including the pets and companion animals integral to family well-being.[36] After commemoration, however, in part it could then become a celebration for all, and one of the days on which considerable effort is made to make it possible for families to get to church, preferably arriving to an "Agape." Some of them may be in desperate need of hot food and drinks and needing also a "bring and share" gathering at the end of the liturgy. Given its present location in the early part of the year, but well after Holy Innocents, the second half of a renamed and re-thought special Sunday celebrating families of whatever form would be an opportunity to celebrate the return of spring and new life in nature, on which we all so much depend. (In particular, given that children today are well familiar with the natural world and its non-human inhabitants, the day could be one of those on which such texts are read as Job 38–41, Psalm 104, the so-called Hymn of Creation from the Septuagint version of Daniel (the *Benedicite*, or blessing of God sung from out of the burning fiery furnace), said by alternating voices, verse by verse and not forgetting Isaiah 6:1-3. Such texts can further remind us to celebrate the autumnal feast of St. Michael and All Angels (the extraordinary "company of heaven" so conspicuous in interacting with human creatures in biblical texts). We need reminders and readings of those narratives, and they prompt a great opportunity for children to bring and share their own "makings" of angelic presence, or to find them in their own churches.

Joining Up for Life with Others and with God

The feast of St. Michael and All Angels precedes the feast of St. Francis of Assisi in the autumn and helps to make sense of his

[36] See Froma Walsh, "Human-Animal Bonds I: The Relational Significance of Companion Animals," *Family Process* 48, no. 4 (2009): 462–80; and "Human-Animal Bonds II: The Role of Pets in Family Systems and Family Therapy," *Family Process* 48, no. 4 (2009): 481–499. Helen Waddell's *Beast and Saints* (London: Cassell, 1934) would be another source worth exploring throughout the year, together with the importance of animals both for company and assistance, of wide social interest and importance beyond immediate family. Elizabeth A. Johnson, *Ask the Beasts: Darwin and the God of Love* (London: Bloomsbury, 2014), writes on the "community of creation," ecology, and the love of God. The importance of C. S. Lewis's Narnia series should not be overlooked!

vision. Singing William Draper's "All creatures of our God and King" could lead into familiarity with its inspiration, Francis's own "Canticle of the Creatures," which can be said verse by verse. It should also be recognised that there are many other good stories to be told, as indicated by a church calendar and its list of those to be commemorated and honoured. Those commemorated on All Saints' include more than St. Francis, and more than those deemed to be "saints" in all their variety, past and present, including the local ones. The saints in a biblical sense include the unsung, as well as those given some sort of officially proved status.[37]

This brings us to the importance of baptism, the celebration of new life which is a gift to the human community. Baptized "beginners" are being invited to become members of the communion of saints, beyond whatever is "family" for them. The phrase and its importance is easily overlooked and forgotten in its place at the end of the Apostles' Creed (which traditionally gives us an outline of the faith of Jesus' earliest disciples, those he sent out), short enough for everyone to learn. The Apostles' Creed tends to be eclipsed, however, owing to the fact that the Nicene Creed (or another authorised profession of faith) is used at the only Sunday service available for people to attend.[38] Under these circumstances, the Nicene Creed inevitably becomes more familiar than the Apostles' Creed. It is easy then to forget the significance of the third part of the latter, with its placing of the "communion of saints" together with the Spirit, the church, and possibility of forgiveness. There is more to it, however, than simply that reminder of the saints, for in the Latin of the Creed, the phrase *communio sanctorum* is helpfully ambiguous in that it can both mean "saintly persons" and "sacred things," that is, sacraments, of which the foundational one is baptism. Its importance is then to associate the two. The Apostles' Creed is easily memorisable by a growing child, and marks the initial stage of recognition that "without the creed to guide me I should know neither how to call upon God, nor

[37] Elizabeth A. Johnson, *Friends of God and Prophets: A Feminist Theological Reading of the Community of Saints* (New York: Continuum, 1998), is an ecumenical theology of the "saints."

[38] In contexts where a number of parishes are grouped under the care of one priest, there may not be a service in every church each Sunday, and the forms of service most likely to be offered are the Eucharist, and the "Service of the Word", which allows much discretion to local co-ordinators of liturgy and worship.

on what God to call."[39] A problem arises, however, if a baptism is located in a Eucharist. Although the declaration of faith required of both the regular congregation and the baptismal candidates and their supporters is an interrogative form of the Apostles' Creed, it may not be familiar to either group. Equally, it may well be that members of the baptismal group do not know the Nicene Creed either if they are making some tentative steps into a church community. It is thus not surprising that baptismal groups may, on occasion, take the opportunity to leave the church during the sign of peace, the one moment up to that point when a congregation is able to shuffle around out of its confinement in fixed pews. A better way to communicate the importance of the baptism would be to rethink its place, making it central to a non-eucharistic service. It must of course be assumed that there will always be somewhere warm and comfortable to feed and change a child and provide support for parents and godparents both before and throughout the liturgy and beyond it, from which therefore no one is excluded.[40] While a welcoming social gathering might be offered by the regular congregation to the baptismal candidates and their supporters afterwards, it is common for families to arrange a celebration at home or at a restaurant.

Some consequences follow which have wider implications. That is, whatever the value of the symbolism of placing a fixed font and its decoration towards the back of a church, likely to be one of the coldest spots in the building, that may have the consequence of both a regular congregation and a baptismal group supposing that the latter's place is near the font, that is, behind the rest of the congregation. Such an arrangement can easily produce a sense of the marginality of the baptism to the life of the whole community, rather than the transition into the life of the baptized. A baptism might therefore be shifted up to the front of the congregation, where children and parents who are regular worshippers should as a matter of course be most welcoming, able to delight in the presence of a baptismal party, with

[39] Austin Farrer, *Lord I Believe: Suggestions for Turning the Creed into Prayer* (London: Faith Press, 1958), 14.

[40] On being a godparent, see Stanley Hauerwas, *The Character of Virtue: Letters to a Godson* (Grand Rapids, MI: Eerdmans, 2018), with an introduction by Samuel Wells, the child's father. Perhaps having the godparent write an annual letter to the godchild would be a helpful practice in reinforcing of the role of godparenting.

children ready and eager to play their distinctive part in worship and of which they are perfectly capable.

Building Confidence

If a programme of parallel activities is needed for children, this should be in an attractive, warm space easily and quickly accessible, but not the "new normal" of an "all ages, shapes, and sizes" liturgy. Churches cannot exist by fostering the habits of "geriatric assemblies," quite possibly behaving as they were themselves expected to behave as children, tidily organised into fixed seating from which mobility was difficult if not impossible. The once frequent repetition of the question, "When are you going to get rid of the children from the church?" and the movement from "children should be seen but not heard" to "children should be neither seen nor heard" is heard much less frequently in contemporary worship. Where it persists, it represents disaster for a community.[41] Nor should anyone suppose that they are welcome primarily as possible sources of income and legacies, but rather for the wisdom which may have grown across a lifetime, for which no one ever asks or which is ignored as and when offered. It becomes easier to give up. On enquiry, it may be found that members of a "geriatric assembly" also need to be honoured, and indeed may welcome some involvement with children in liturgy, perhaps as honorary godparents for the service, and beyond it.

Sociable weekday buggy (stroller) visits to a church hall are invaluable, and it could well be that these might include some of the excellent instruction and activities originally devised for occasions when children are taken out of a liturgy (sometimes referred to as children's Liturgy of the Word), but which have a place on these visits.[42] It should also be possible to arrange for churches to be open for regular "exchange" visits, so that children can explore the building for themselves and find out what and why its contents are as they are. Older members of a church community could be present to make that pos-

[41] Stephen Burns, "Faithfulness or Betrayal? Tradition in 'Geriatric Assemblies,'" in *Theological and Hermeneutical Explorations from Australia: Horizons of Contextuality*, ed. Jione Havea, 95–109 (Lanham, MD: Lexington Books/Fortress Academic, 2020).

[42] See the three-volume set devised by Sarah Lenton, *Creative Ideas for Children's Worship* (Norwich: Canterbury Press, 2011).

sible. For them, too, the buildings and its furnishings and decoration speak in different ways to any and all of which human persons, older and younger, will respond differently, and from which much will be learned in an informal but invaluable way. What is planned for children but open for adults may be a revelation as much for the latter as for the former.

That apart, the first necessity in a church in which children will both be welcome and expect to participate actively in a service is to clear most if not all the pews, and to furnish a nave with seating which can be stacked on trolleys to be moved out of the way, or easily moved about into different formations. (In church jurisdictions with their own rules on fabric and accountability to heritage organisations, such rearrangement may not be possible.) Those who have difficulty in seeing and hearing must be given pride of place, but with the proviso both that the church will be honouring their presence, but also that of the "present and future" church, that is, children and their caregivers. In some places, for example, where there is a church school (from nursery up to school-leaving age) it may be practical to hold an Agape or even a Eucharist in a school chapel or a hall, together with staff and caregivers, in which the children especially have well-planned roles to play. For the very young this may become a Eucharist including activities designed around the needs of child participants, with carefully prepared prayers and intercessions read by older children or adults if need be. The Messy Church movement, which now has an international presence, has developed exemplary materials.[43] Wherever possible, however, children need to be part of the gathered congregation. There, they can read aloud or take turns saying prayers with coaching. They also need to hear biblical texts, whilst sermon-time might be a breakout point for them to exit and return at a later point in the liturgy, having been given some interesting things to do at home which they might return and share the following week. The wisdom of Orthodox tradition reveals the importance of "feeding" the very young at their baptisms and allowing them to share in the antidoron (unconsecrated bread) thereafter. Like baptism, this is a gift to the children, and its significance is sustained for them by the adults present. The significance of a blessing hardly makes sense if

[43] https://www.messychurch.org.uk/resource/holy-communion-messy-church

it is deemed to be some sort of substitute for communion, and a Eucharist involving the very young—as it must—is problematical unless this is clear. One advantage of not having a set liturgy, or indeed being "church" on at least some occasions is to expect that children themselves may respond in unpredictable ways to hearing a reading of whatever kind. For instance, in response to the reading of John 13—Jesus' washing of his disciples' feet—in a parish hall that was set up with a few chairs, pitchers of water, basins, and towels, the first to sit to have his feet washed was a recently baptized two-year-old who was quickly accompanied by other younger members present. With assistance, the two-year-old boy then washed his mother's feet, which had a profound effect on her, given all that she had done and would continue to do to nurture a baby-becoming-boy.[44]

Children Are Church!

Much needed, therefore, is a pattern of opportunities for all to comprehend what liturgy signifies, whatever one's age. As Gail Ramshaw has so percipiently pointed out, "[t]he baptized child grows up in the life of the Church, participating emotionally, through symbols, years before the child's cognitive responses are like those of adults. To be baptized is to worship God, to assemble weekly, and slowly, slowly, to grow deeper into that baptized life of grace." So it is not "instruction about God through graded materials," but most certainly requires a specific emphasis on the work of the Holy Spirit at every point of a life in faith.[45] Furthermore, "The participation of people with developmental disabilities in the worship life of the Christian community is a powerful source of support for their families" when they too find a role or are found a role with other children in liturgy, other than by simply being present.[46]

Somewhat strangely there is little to suggest what could well be an obvious way into liturgy for children, and that is their participation in a choir for worship. Some churches and cathedrals with re-

[44] Bryan Cones, *This Assembly of Believers: The Gift of Difference in the Church at Prayer* (London: SCM Press, 2020), 198.

[45] Ramshaw, *Reviving Sacred Speech*, 146–47.

[46] Herbert Anderson, "Pastoral Epilogue," in Foley, *Developmental Disabilities*, 131–40, 138. See http://herbertanderson.org.

sources to fund those who can teach children to sing offer both Saturday singing schools from early years on, from which children in appropriate age groups can be grouped into choirs. The same church or cathedral may also have a more specialised group of children in a school whose timetable is arranged specifically so that they can both practice and sing a daily eventide service as well as Sunday services. Not all, however, will necessarily seize the opportunity to have the children of such a choir offered the opportunity to become participants in a liturgy other than in the choir. A choir's front row view of the liturgy could be especially of interest to boys with breaking voices, but all might well be able to read out loud both biblical texts and prayers, given their voice training, as well as undertaking roles in a service. Whatever else, the singing of children will likely enliven the "geriatric assemblies" which might well be transformed both by their presence and by that of their relatives who accompany them.

The Roman Catholic Diocese of Leeds, UK, has pioneered a transformative programme of music for children, though without explicitly linking it to any other form of liturgy for them so far as its website publicity reveals. St Anne's Cathedral in Leeds, serving a multilingual city in which children speak both a mother tongue and English, is the core of an enterprise which extends to over fifty state schools, reaching four thousand, five hundred children weekly from ages five through eighteen to twenty-one. Its one hundred choral groups, six of which are especially attached to the cathedral and who sing in Latin and other languages, plainsong and other musical styles, include children who are offered tuition for lessons on the accordion as well as piano and organ, if suitable. There is also a vital link with a local Roman Catholic primary school in which every child from nursery on has lessons on singing in groups, which prepares them for choir life if able to choose or be chosen for a role. In addition, it is in the primary school that children receive the kind of religious education that in other churches or cathedrals is supposedly possible by removing children from part of a liturgy. Of crucial importance, the new education in music programme in the United Kingdom may help restore the sense of the vital connection of music for children, and thus a way of their being able to participate in liturgy.[47]

At some point, however, there could well be the possibility of one particular liturgy which could become more conspicuously a children's feast than is commonly the case, and that is confirmation. Shifting patterns, notably the trend in parts of the Anglican Communion to admit children to communion before confirmation, and the provision for parish priests to confirm on behalf of the bishop in Roman Catholic communities, require a flexible approach to preparation. This may well include religious education or re-education for parents, depending on the theological literacy shared by the whole community of which they are a part, and baptism itself, and its primary significance, may need to be a prior stage of commitment. One way or another, a celebration of the stage of life—at about twelve years of age—most carefully associated with the change in Jesus' life in which he would have been expected to join his father in his work, might become a feast for families of whatever configuration with a quite specific focus on a stage of Jesus' own life, but located well in advance of the challenges and threats of adulthood and its responsibilities. Another celebration at the age of maturity—a variable age, eighteen in the UK and twenty-one in the US—might then take place as a further service of transition and renewed trust in God for present and future life.[48] Both on the verge of adolescence and adulthood children could be enabled to continue to participate in liturgy, assuming that they have already been enabled to do so. They are unlikely to be found in congregations unless that is made possible for them; their absence would be a loss for everyone. In this matter, we must seize the day.

[47] See the report of the UK Government's Department of Education, "The Importance of Music: A National Plan for Music Education," https://assets.publishing.service.gov.uk/government/uploads/system/uploads/attachment_data/file/180973/DFE-00086-2011.pdf. From the US online forum for teachers and parents, The Inspired Classroom, see https://theinspiredclassroom.com2017/05.

[48] See Paul de Clerck, "The Confirmation of Baptism: A Historico-Theological Interpretation Towards a Renewed Pastoral Approach," *Studia Liturgica* 42 (2012): 190–96.

Chapter 13

Liturgy, Gender, and Identity

Stephen Burns

Preface

At the outset of this discussion it may be helpful to recall that the very word "Bible" is plural: *ta biblia*, the books[1]—books held across a range of Christian conviction as books with much to say, that are "long . . . for our short lives" as one contemporary liturgical theologian memorably put it.[2] Compiled for use in assemblies, these books not only give insight into the diversity of—including disagreements in—the assemblies that they are in part about, but in widely practised habits of reading they are heard by assemblies in ways that bring forward their diversity as well as ways they merge. Lectionary patterns of reading Hebrew Scripture/Older Testament, psalms, New Testament, gospels—and then one of several found side-by-side—

[1] See Gordon W. Lathrop, *Holy People: A Liturgical Ecclesiology* (Minneapolis: Fortress Press, 1999), 25, who goes on to contend, "When I take a Bible in my hands, even when I am alone, I take up the whole community of voices that addresses me there as well as all the people with whom I read these books in a continuing community of interpretation. The very fact of the books being gathered together as one book is a *liturgical* fact" (26).

[2] Gail Ramshaw, *Treasures Old and New: Images in the Lectionary* (Minneapolis: Fortress Press, 2002), 12. In another place, *Word of God, Word of Life: Understanding the Three-Year Lectionaries* (Minneapolis: Augsburg Press, 2019), Ramshaw writes of what we may note is a singular designation, "the word of God," as "a door that opens to the faithful a crowded dining room filled with conversation about divine mystery" (8).

starts to make evident a certain plurality even before any further study of the "stories, poetry, prophecy, law, proverbs, letters and other genres" which comprise these books.[3] At the same time, these books (and these books above other books) are also key to common prayer in various possible forms—not only forms of common prayer which have been dictated by "acts of uniformity," to use Anglican terms for dynamics with analogues across plenty of other traditions. Liturgy, often itself a kind of composite of bits of the books—and whatever the lections may be on any given occasion—has long been and remains a prime way by which different kinds of Christians may learn that "there are many ways of being in accord with the Bible other than doing direct interpretation of it,"[4] a point that admittedly may be harder to learn and affirm in some ecclesial contexts than in others, for a variety of reasons. Yet even where nothing like an Act of Uniformity is in play, other liturgical dynamics may work against diversity in certain ways, and depending on where one goes to church, some-to-much liturgy might seem to be highly preoccupied if not with conformity, then with a measure of singularity, notions of "one": among examples that could easily be multiplied, one unrepeatable baptism; two "becoming one" in marriage; on some accounts at any rate only one gender able to represent what is deemed to be needed for ministry understood in particular ways, all of which may be related to readings of bits of the books, whatever other sources are or are not deemed relevant to understanding.

Approaching gender issues, the least that may be said is that one way of beginning to think about such issues in relation to Bible and liturgy is in terms of challenges to any tendency to tilt towards oneness at the expense of diversity, which in their own way *ta biblia* might themselves be held to manifest and model to liturgical assemblies.

Contexts

The year 1963 was when "sexual intercourse began," or so Philip Larkin's satirical "Annus Mirabilis" has it, 1963 being, he notes, be-

[3] David F. Ford, "Faith in the Cities: Corinth and the Modern City," in *On Being the Church: Essays on the Christian Community*, ed. Daniel W. Hardy and Colin Gunton, 225–54, 226 (Edinburgh: T&T Clark, 1989).

[4] Ford, "Faith in the Cities," 225.

tween "the Chatterley ban" and the Beatles' first album.[5] We may set alongside Larkin's cultural markers a number of ecclesial developments that begin to sketch the context for considering gender issues as they have come to present in liturgy through recent decades.

In 1961, in Britain, Australia, and other countries, the oral contraceptive pill had become widely available (if at first only to married women). Just a few years earlier the 1958 Lambeth Conference of Anglican bishops and a 1959 World Council of Churches' report on sexual ethics had both relaxed teaching about contraception commonplace in church communities. The former was non-prescriptive about how responsible parenthood should be achieved, and the latter asserted a view of there being "no moral difference" between different types of contraception, including drugs. When in 1968 the Roman Catholic Church produced *Humanae Vitae*, it received different kinds of readings—even by national conferences of Catholic bishops—and has remained a significant marker of the erosion of churches' authority to pronounce in matters of sexual ethics, as the document's reception revealed that quite evidently Roman Catholics were acting on their conscience in order to use artificial contraception as readily as many others.[6] As for 1963 itself, a Quaker report, *Towards a Quaker View of Sex*, became the first among the churches to begin to affirm homosexual relationships, several years after the Wolfenden Report recommended decriminalization of homosexual behaviour in Britain, in 1957. As things turned out, homosexuality, gay and lesbian, and queer sexuality (to employ just some of the shifting nomenclature over time) was by the turn of the millennium to engulf if not the Quakers, then various other ecclesial communions in sometimes acid controversy, the successive Lambeth Conferences of the Anglican Communion from 1988 to 2008 being a very high-profile case in point. Many other examples could be added of cultural, medical, and ecclesial shifts from the 1960s as to presumed norms about sexual relationships and roles within them, and to roles in both domestic and social life more generally. Yet a basic, salient observation to draw together

[5] Philip Larkin, *The Complete Poems*, ed. Archie Burnett (London: Faber & Faber, 2014), 121.

[6] See John Mahoney, *The Making of Moral Theology: A Study of the Roman Catholic Tradition* (Oxford: Clarendon Press, 1989).

from whatever examples is that, as Robert Song says, "the churches are still reeling."[7]

Not least because of the Second Vatican Council—issuing as its first document a Constitution on the Sacred Liturgy in 1963—liturgical reform has also been a mark of recent decades, albeit not always directly engaging change brought about by the so-called sexual revolution. This essay will focus mainly on (1) feminist impact on Christian liturgy; but will also consider, in two shorter final sections, (2) the emergence of rites for same-sex marriage, its analogues or alternatives; and (3) growing awareness of transgender identity, not least as it may fuel wider efforts to "queer the liturgy," and Christian theology at large. Taken together, these three themes provoke recognition of the considerable and sometimes trenchant resistance that exists within the churches to contemporary perspectives on and expressions of gender, as well as some small-scale change. For there is in fact a notable range of response—from welcome to pushback—around the instability of categories by which "new" issues have sometimes been able to be brought into focus in ecclesial discussion that encircles liturgical revision and renewal. It must be acknowledged, though, that whatever churches make of the situation, how gender might be understood, questions of how many genders there may be, and what kinds of (what has come commonly to be termed) "performance" of gender exist in social life and in sexual relationships is in some significant flux. Inherited understandings—either held fast or yielded by the churches—that might have long linked sex and gender, not least with notions of "nature" and the "natural," are more widely giving way to views that see gender as socially constructed, and crucially have to do not just with appreciation of difference but with "signifying power."[8] To enquire about gender issues and the liturgy entails wide-ranging "gender-attentiveness,"[9] though what capacity the churches will sustain for the undertaking remains moot, given divergent trajectories of welcome and pushback to wider contempo-

[7] Robert Song, *Covenant and Calling: Towards a Theology of Same-Sex Relationships* (London: SCM Press, 2014), 93.

[8] See the highly influential Joan W. Scott, "Gender: A Useful Category of Historical Analysis," *American Historical Review* 91 (1986): 1053–75.

[9] To adopt a phrase from Teresa Berger, *Gender Differences and the Making of Liturgical History: Lifting a Veil on Liturgy's Past* (Aldershot, UK: Ashgate, 2011), 17.

rary perspectives: perspectives in which gender may refer "to all gendered identities—women, men, eunuchs, lesbians, hermaphrodites, syneisactics, transgendered people, and others—precisely in their gendered particularities."[10] As Teresa Berger asserts, gender is a "web of oppositions and relations," and furthermore "unstable and context specific,"[11] which at the very least means that as a category it (to echo Judith Butler's classic *Gender Trouble*[12]) troubles any suggestion of "generic, non-sexed humans."

Before moving to my foci, some ancillary points are relevant in relation to examples of cultural and ecclesial change already cited: First, that according to at least some secularization (and/or, as they are sometimes reframed, pluralization) theories, the widespread retreat of women from the churches since the 1960s—whatever the reasons—is pivotal in some accounts of church decline,[13] and in any case it now seems that at least the Church of England has seen its last generation of active lay women.[14] This may also be, or at any rate become, a pattern for others. Then, an erosion of ecclesial authority with respect to sexual ethics is now very broadly and deeply embedded. For example, the Archbishop of Canterbury, Justin Welby, noted in the early 2010s that younger people (he said under-35s) see some churches' resistance to gay marriage as not only "incomprehensible" but "wicked."[15] And by the mid-2010s, an ecumenical Australian report could suggest that "the majority of young people look at the churches with some suspicion and even disdain. Many see them as irrelevant and out of date. They see them as exclusive and intolerant,

[10] Teresa Berger, "Femininity and Sanctity: Where Gender Constructions and Hagiography Meet," in *A Cloud of Witnesses: The Cult of Saints in Past and Present*, ed. Marcel Barnard, Paul Post, and Els Rose, 63–78, 63 (Leuven: Peeters, 2005).

[11] Berger, "Femininity and Sanctity," 63.

[12] Judith Butler, *Gender Trouble: Feminism and the Subversion of Identity* (Abingdon: Routledge, 1990), a highly influential text in gender studies across a wide range of disciplines.

[13] Notably Callum G. Brown, *The Death of Christian Britain: Understanding Secularization, 1800–2000* (Abingdon: Routledge, 2009).

[14] Abby Day, *The Religious Lives of Older Laywomen: The Last Active Anglican Generation* (Oxford: Oxford University Press, 2017).

[15] Press Association, "Young People Think Opposition to Gay Marriage Is Wicked, Says Archbishop," *The Guardian*, 28 August, 2013, https://www.theguardian.com/uk-news/2013/aug/28/gay-marriage-opposition-wicked-archbishop.

even repressive, particularly in relation to different expressions of sexuality."[16]

The struggle of churches to speak (in welcome or pushback) about matters of sex and gender—or to be met with disdain when they might try to do so—is related to another site of scandal, that is, clerical abuse of the vulnerable young, not to say ecclesiastical cover-up and in some instances, continued confusion around safeguards that would better enable the recognition of abuse or dynamics that make ways for it.[17] While child sexual abuse has increasingly and rightly become a concern of at least some theologians, the wider task of developing a theology of children's flourishing—best-case scenarios to put alongside important preoccupation with worst-case scenarios—remains largely unbegun, neglecting clues like children as "epiphanies" to, or the "living prayer" of the parents and communities in whose care they may be raised.[18] While such fecund ideas wait for attention, they are potentially promising because they start to set Christian perspectives on sex and gender in a much wider context, adjusting inherited foci in Christian ethics that largely ignore children bar in prenatal life (i.e., the question of abortion) and adolescent sexual expression on its way to "marriage," with all that these ethical foci may presume about the particular responsibilities for two sexes, "women" and "men," right or wrong. The loss of elders, disdain of the young, and growing disengagement—sometimes active disassociation either from nominal affiliation or one that involves worship—also raise challenges in terms of liturgical tradition, around how whatever practices are cherished are to be, or indeed, can be handed over if there are fewer and fewer to hand them to.[19] For as long as ecclesial

[16] Philip Hughes, Stephen Reid, and Margaret Fraser, *A Vision for Effective Youth Ministry: Insights from Australian Research* (Nunawading, VIC: Christian Research Association, 2015), v.

[17] Stephen Burns, "Liturgy after the Abuse," in *Resilience and Vulnerability: Body and Liberating Theologies*, ed. Jione Havea, 173–86 (Lanham, MD: Lexington Books, 2020); Stephen Burns, "Ordination Services, After the Abuse," *Liturgy* 34, no. 2 (2019): 41–49.

[18] Epiphanies: Helen Oppenheimer, "Blessing," in *The Weight of Glory: The Future of Liberal Theology*, ed. Daniel W. Hardy and Peter Sedgwick, 221–30 (Edinburgh: T&T Clark, 1989); Living Prayer: Ann Loades, "Death and Disvalue: Some Reflections on 'Sick' Children," *Hospital Chaplain* 93 (1985): 2–7, 4.

[19] Stephen Burns, "Faithfulness or Betrayal? Tradition in 'Geriatric Assemblies,'" in *Theological and Hermeneutical Explorations from Australia: Horizons of Contextuality*, ed. Jione Havea, 95–110 (Lanham, MD: Lexington Books/Fortress Academic, 2020).

cultures which still enjoy larger churchgoing numbers[20] feel no need to address such questions with urgency, they may be sleepwalking towards a rude awakening that reflects the experience of worshipping communities now hugely depleted in some countries and contexts.[21] At the same time, questions about who might participate in Christian assembly impinge in specific ways upon the liturgical foci to be perused below, as it would be easy to follow much of the extant discussion by targeting questions about feminism and liturgy at the struggle for women's ordination, questions around gay marriage on its availability or otherwise to the ordained,[22] and challenges from trans experience in terms of how this might relate to presidency.

All of this is important, yet it is where the weight of much reflection (where it has begun at all) has rested. But a too narrow focus on leaders, presiders, the howsoever ordained and their roles, can harmfully occlude questions about the "full, conscious and active participation" of assemblies in their diversity.[23] It can also forget vital enquiry as to who is supposed to constitute the assembly, given that many liturgical futures are already marked by loss of elders, disdain of the young, and growing disengagement, with people sometimes disengaged for good reasons: if not snapping at churches' pushback to contemporary perspectives on gender, then recoiling from the legacy of the churches' sometimes ambiguous commitments to tackling abuse. This last observation points to another problem concerning power, with which gender in contemporary perspectives has much to do.

[20] Here we may recall Philip Larkin's "Church Going" (1955), and the discoveries it enabled, despite the fact that according to the poem he waited until he was sure the building was empty—no liturgy!—before entering.

[21] Compare, for example, rates of attendance, across traditions, in the US and Australia.

[22] The Church of England's infamous report *Issues in Human Sexuality* (1987) admits certain same-sex relationships, but not for the clergy.

[23] See, in general, Stephen Burns and Bryan Cones, eds., *Liturgy with a Difference: Beyond Inclusion in Christian Assembly* (London: SCM Press, 2019), and in particular, Stephen Burns, "No Participation, No Liturgy," in *Fully Conscious, Fully Active: Essays in Honor of Gabe Huck*, ed. Bryan Cones and Stephen Burns, 2–11 (Chicago: Liturgy Training Publications, 2019). Also in *Liturgy (SCM Studyguide)*, 2nd ed. (London: SCM Press, 2018), I try to encourage liturgical enquiry from three angles—the presider's chair, pew (that is, the midst of the assembly in its diversity), and door (alert to questions of who is absent, and how they might enter)—as I see little point in much liturgical discussion conducted from only the first of these categories.

Feminist Liturgy

A 1960 essay on sin by Jewish scholar of religion Valerie Saiving is sometimes regarded as a key point of origin for what has developed as "second-wave" feminist theology,[24] though important precursors should not be forgotten, including *The Women's Bible* of 1895[25]—more or less contemporary with suffragette struggle, and the like of wartime assertion of the worth of women's work by Dorothy L. Sayers—given that women's work was then necessary (as it was in Sayers's own case) for women marrying divorcees responsible for children yet also themselves the mother of children born "out of wedlock," to whose care no man was committed.[26] Sayers's particular experience is one pointer towards the statistic that, just before World War II, 30 percent of mothers were pregnant on getting married,[27] a situation not the same but similar to Sayers's own, but indicating that whatever may have changed in the 1960s or later was in part a culture that enabled freer naming and discussion of lived experience.

Changing Language

By the 1970s some specifically feminist work in liturgy was beginning to thrive in the first throes of second-wave feminism. It did so along two main lines: one being pressure to revise liturgical language about human beings, the other in movement towards the ordination of women. With respect to the former of these, biblical translation was in a period of some upheaval. The Revised Standard Version, compiled (and in the case of the New Testament, also revised) between 1952 and 1971, was shifting some sensibilities. While retaining "Thou" in address for God, it adopted "you" with respect to human beings, so fuelling common parlance about the latter in devotional

[24] "The Human Situation: A Feminine View," *Journal of Religion* 40, no. 2 (1960): 100–112. This seminal essay has been much anthologized, e.g., Carol P. Christ and Judith Plaskow, eds., *Womenspirit Rising: A Feminist Reader in Religion* (San Francisco: Harper & Row, 1979), 25–42; David Ford and Mike Higton with Simeon Zahl, eds., *The Modern Theologians Reader* (Chichester: Wiley-Blackwell, 2012), 261–66.

[25] Ann Loades, "Elizabeth Cady Stanton's *The Women's Bible*," *The Oxford Handbook of the Reception History of the Bible*, ed. Michael Lieb et al., 307–22 (Oxford: Oxford University Press, 2011).

[26] Ann Loades, *Feminist Theology: Voices from the Past* (Oxford: Polity, 2000), 169–92.

[27] See Song, *Covenant*, 93.

and liturgical arenas. The use of man/men for the human community progressively receded from common parlance, being reserved instead for male humans. Subsequent biblical translations then started to reflect this, as by the time of the New Revised Standard Version of 1989. Liturgical revisions followed from amendments in biblical translations and selections for lectionaries,[28] with resources from the 1980s onwards tending to adopt alternatives to what was increasingly becoming considered androcentric language. A relatively uncontroversial example would be the adjustment of a line in a general confession like "we have sinned against you and against our fellow men" to "against our neighbour."[29]

Parallel work on hymnody presented special challenges, not least because the affective pull of hymns was/is greater for many than even beloved spoken texts. The "inclusive" turning of words in step with beats and melodies and their shaping in sense lines found a kind of apex with the 1995 *New Century Hymnal*, loved and loathed by those with opposing views of it, yet with an introduction with a sense of clarity about the problems it perceives with inherited hymnody (including some considered in later parts of this essay) and confident intent about how it addresses them.[30] Liturgical revision involving translation of creeds stumbled against some major points of difference, not only with respect to wording the cooperation of Mary and the Holy Spirit in the incarnation. The depiction of the orthodox claim that Christ Jesus became man/truly human has been a matter manifesting some intransigence.[31] The ongoing storm centre, however, has proved to be the question of women in orders, and especially readings

[28] See Gail Ramshaw, *Word of God, Word of Life: Understanding the Three-Year Lectionaries* (Minneapolis: Augsburg Fortress, 2019), for the best currently available introduction to the Revised Common Lectionary. Note also the all-too-brief principles of emendation of the New Revised Standard Version of the Bible in the three-part (Years A, B, and C in turn) lectionary collection, Gordon Lathrop and Gail Ramshaw, eds., *Readings for the Assembly* (Minneapolis: Fortress Press, 1996, 1997, 1998), vii–viii in each volume.

[29] As the shift from the Church of England's *Alternative Service Book* (1980) to *Common Worship* (2000).

[30] *New Century Hymnal* (Cleveland, OH: Pilgrim Press, 1995), and on subsequent hymnal revision, the excellent study by Becca Whitla, *Liberation, (De)Coloniality, and Liturgical Practices: Flipping the Song Bird* (New York: Palgrave Macmillan, 2020).

[31] See Ann Loades, "Regarding Mary and the Trinity," in *Grace Is Not Faceless: Reflections on Mary* (London: DLT, 2021), 49–61.

of the requirements of "priesthood" understood in certain ways, ways that are of course not unrelated to tussles over translating key creedal phrases.

Ordination of Women

Women have been ordained in some traditions since the mid-nineteenth century: 1853 for Antoinette L. Brown in the US, and then 1917 for Constance Coltman in the UK and 1927 for Winifred Kiek in Australia, all in the Congregational Church.[32] Accounts of early Pentecostalism also suggest welcome for the leadership of women, whether or not they were ordained. Yet it was not until the 1970s that bumpy Anglican reception of women into priesthood became the focus of very public controversy, with the irregular ordination of the so-called Philadelphia Eleven in 1974.[33] This act represented a countermove to another notable liturgical action in the Northeast United States less than three years earlier, when Mary Daly (formerly a Roman Catholic, on her way to becoming defiantly post-Christian) became the first woman ever to preach at Harvard University Memorial Chapel, in/famously calling in her sermon for others to follow her out of the building and leave the church, in "exodus." Contrary to Daly's action, the Philadelphia Eleven represent as it were a raid on the church, a storming and occupation of ecclesial structures. As the preacher on the occasion suggested, "as blacks refused to participate in their own oppression by going to the back of the bus in 1955 in Montgomery, women are refusing to cooperate in their own oppression by remaining on the periphery of full participation in the Church."[34] Both acts—exodus and occupation—were proposed as responses to patriarchy.

[32] See Julia Pitman, "A History of the Presidency of Women: Snapshots from the Movement for Women's Ordination in America, Britain and Australia," in *Presiding Like a Woman*, ed. Nicola Slee and Stephen Burns, 66–76 (London: SPCK, 2010).

[33] For background and context, see Stephen Burns and Bryan Cones, "Carter Heyward (1945–)," in *Twentieth-Century Anglican Theologians: From Evelyn Underhill to Esther Mombo*, ed. Stephen Burns, Bryan Cones, and James Tengatenga, 175–84 (Chichester: Wiley Blackwell, 2020).

[34] David Hein and Gardiner H. Shattuck, eds., *The Episcopalians* (New York: Church Publishing, 2004), 178.

In 1989, the first woman was then ordained bishop in the Anglican Communion, again in the Northeast US. This was Barbara Harris, whose recent memoir makes clear at least some of her struggle, not only on account of her gender but also her skin colour. Her account includes opposition early in her adulthood even to women serving on the vestry (council) of her parish, and before that, being faced at her own confirmation by an "aging white bishop, who wore white cotton gloves when he visited Black congregations so that he did not ever have to touch our heads."[35]

One of the Philadelphia Eleven, Reneé Alla Bozarth, later wrote an astonishing poem, "Mary—Proto-priest of the New Covenant," which brings forward some insights into sacramentality, intentionally gendered and focused on Mary and Eucharist: for just as Jesus' mother came before him, and just as before whatever the Upper Room meal was on the eve of Jesus' death, there was some kind of barnyard breakfast around his birth. Only because of Mary's body and blood is it possible to receive the body and blood of Christ.[36] This line of thinking is an opening pursued by Karen O'Donnell's recent work in *Broken Bodies*, on what she dubs the "Annunciation-Incarnation" event, Mary being the first to "offer up the bodily elements that will become the flesh and blood of Christ," so providing the model for priesthood.[37] Tina Beattie[38] is a proponent of allied arguments from her own Roman Catholic perspective, just as were Tissa Balasuriya

[35] See Barbara Harris with Kelly Brown Douglas, *Hallelujah Anyhow! A Memoir* (New York: Church Publishing, 2020), p. 21 for vestry, p. xvi for confirmation, and on p. 75 a miniature about an unusual liturgical ministry at her own episcopal ordination, during voicing of opposition: "Suddenly I was aware that someone was standing beside me. It was, in fact, my mother. She took my wrist in her hand, looked me straight into the face and said quietly to me, 'Have no fear. God is on our side. . . .' Then she stared into my eyes and said, 'This is your momma,' . . . and went back to her seat."

[36] The poem is cited in Burns and Cones, "Carter Heyward," 178.

[37] Karen O'Donnell, *Broken Bodies: The Eucharist, Mary and the Body in Trauma* (London: SCM Press, 2018), 90.

[38] Tina Beattie, *God's Mother, Eve's Advocate: A Marian Narrative of Women's Salvation* (London: Continuum, 2002). See also Tina Beattie, "Vision and Vulnerability: The Significance of Sacramentality and the Woman Priest for Feminist Theology," in *Exchanges of Grace: Essays in Honour of Ann Loades*, ed. Natalie K. Watson and Stephen Burns, 235–39 (London: SCM Press, 2008).

and Leonardo Boff before,[39] the latter two, both themselves priests, subject to sanctions for their ideas. Fifty years of second-wave feminist consciousness has brought some but by no means widespread fully humanly inclusive liturgical leadership.

Feminist Gesture

In some contexts, Roman Catholic most obviously, there has been near to no movement on women's ordination to priesthood, and this is also the case across considerable parts of the Anglican Communion.[40] In the Catholic case, Susan Ross's conundrum is revealing: "How many sacraments are there?" "Seven for boys, and six for girls."[41] Yet even where women have begun to be received into presbyteral and episcopal orders, much work remains to be done in agitating for more than the achievement of having "women priests" towards celebrating consistent with a "feminist ecclesiology."[42] In the first place, the leadership of women may all too easily result in what is little more than the "adoption as unisex"[43] of patriarchal patterns. In addition, many feminist proposals about revision of liturgy seem to stop at adjusting language, crucial as that is, without also thinking about space and symbol, movement and gesture, as feminist issues. To make that good, more clues will need to follow from the like of Rosemary Radford Reuther's classic *Women-Church*, which lifted up the value of a "celebration center" with a "conversation

[39] Tissa Balasuriya, *Mary and Human Liberation: The Story and the Text* (Valley Forge, PA: Trinity Press International, 1997); Leonardo Boff, *The Maternal Face of God: The Feminine and Its Religious Expressions* (London: Collins, 1989), with—it should be noted—feminist theologians tending to put some distance between views in both of these books and their own perspectives.

[40] A point that may be more obvious from, e.g., Australia, than, e.g., the UK. In Australia, Sydney, the largest diocese, and one able to gain majority in General Synod, is trenchantly opposed to women priests, fosters trinitarian-subordination teaching related to this stance, and is a major influence on the conservative evangelical Global Anglican Future Conference (GAFCON) movement across the Anglican Communion.

[41] Susan Ross, *Extravagant Affections: A Feminist Sacramental Theology* (New York: Continuum, 2001), 21–22.

[42] Stephen Burns, "From Women Priests to Feminist Ecclesiology?," in *Looking Forward, Looking Backward: Forty Years of Women's Ordination*, ed. Fredrica Harris Thompsett, 99–110 (New York: Seabury, 2014).

[43] This phrase is Gail Ramshaw's.

circle" as well as intentional "communalization" of roles in the assembly, and Letty Russell's *Church in the Round* which valorised leadership that stands with, not over, others around a "round table" with no special places of privilege.[44]

As yet, relatively little feminist liturgical work has attended to ceremonial scenes and ritual pictures in which whatever words, texts, or scripts are used. Yet as Nicola Slee asserts, "space is a feminist issue," and feminists have tended to favour liturgical space that allows celebration to take place "face to face" and "on the level" as well as "in the round."[45]

Proposals about feminist styles of presidency[46] have, amongst other things, drawn attention to aspects of communalization that await retrieval from the tradition,[47] though a crux remains presidential posture and manual acts in making Eucharist, with feminists tending to advocate the decentring of the *in persona Christi* tradition with gesture that suggests not just *in persona Christae/Christx* but that locates that presence with the whole assembly, and in its diversity.[48] In feminist perspective, the assembly is to be one in which, in Nicola Slee's words, "all are honoured," the only etiquette is "the performance of grace," the single dress code is "the garments of honesty,"

[44] See Rosemary Radford Ruether, *Women-Church: Theology and Practice* (San Francisco: Harper, 1985), Letty M. Russell, *Church in the Round: Feminist Interpretation of Church* (Louisville, KY: Westminster John Knox Press, 1993), and for further discussion of juxtaposition of the two, Stephen Burns, "Four in a Vestment? Feminist Gesture for Christian Assembly," Slee and Burns, *Presiding Like a Woman*, 9–19.

[45] Nicola Slee, *Fragments for Fractured Times: What Feminist Practical Theology Brings to the Table* (London: SCM Press, 2020), 60–78.

[46] Burns, "Four in a Vestment"; Bryan Cones, "Evoking the Other: Towards Feminist Gesture for Any Assembly," *Feminist Theology* 28 (2020): 198–215.

[47] A good case in point is John K. Leonard and Nathan D. Mitchell, *The Postures of the Assembly During the Eucharistic Prayer* (Chicago: Liturgy Training Publications, 1994), with its argument that the *orans* posture was long a congregational posture, retrieval of which was popularized, without feminist intent, by Richard Giles, *Creating Uncommon Worship: Transforming the Liturgy of the Eucharist* (Norwich: Canterbury Press, 2004).

[48] Bryan Cones, *This Assembly of Believers: The Gift of Difference in the Church at Prayer* (London: SCM Press, 2020), a superb study of much relevance to many aspects of gender issues in liturgy. For proposals towards communalizing rubrics, see especially Bryan Cones, "Looking for the Body's Language," in Stephen Burns and Robert Gribben, eds., *When We Pray: The Future of Common Prayer* (Melbourne, VIC: Coventry Press, 2020), 257–76.

and the "fine cuisine" shared is no less than the "the bread of justice,"[49] with these being the measures by which Christ's presence is discerned and affirmed.

Expansive Language

To return to language matters: while, up to a point, "inclusive" language with respect to human persons may have been received in many places, albeit while others go backwards, "expansive" language—diverse metaphors employed in "naming towards God"[50]—has gained much less traction.[51] For example, a review of all the "authorized rites of the Anglican Communion" for Eucharist reveals that only one reference is anywhere made to God as "mother."[52] Expanding gendered language may be part of but not the whole agenda of expansive language, though tackling the overwhelming prevalence of male-gendered language associated with God is close to the heart of feminist concern. As hymn writer Brian Wren has memorably observed, the Bible has funded a skein of images—he suggests, idols—of the divine in terms of "KINGAFAP—the King-G-d-Almighty-Father-Protector."[53] His own hymns have offered among the most lively alternatives, at least in terms of the churches' song: a "gambler" God, "spinning the wheel of creation," "giving it randomness," "taking a million chances," among many memorable suggestions.[54] Gail Ramshaw's work on text for prayer, "keeping it metaphoric, making

[49] Nicola Slee, "At the Table of Christa," in Slee and Burns, *Presiding Like a Woman*, 178, and Slee, *Seeking the Risen Christa* (London: SPCK, 2011), 56.

[50] This phrase is from Catherine Vincie, *Celebrating Divine Presence: A Primer in Liturgical Theology* (Collegeville, MN: Liturgical Press, 2009).

[51] Marjorie Procter Smith, *Praying with Our Eyes Open: Engendering Feminist Prayer* (Nashville: Abingdon Press, 1995) remains an excellent and challenging text on such matters, situating categories of inclusive and expansive language in relation to "non-sexist" forms.

[52] Gail Ramshaw, "A New Look at Anglican Eucharistic Prayers," *Worship* 86 (2012): 161–67, a review of Colin Buchanan, *Anglican Eucharistic Liturgies, 1985–2010: The Authorized Rites of the Anglican Communion* (Norwich: Canterbury Press, 2012).

[53] Brian Wren, *What Language Shall I Borrow? God-talk in Worship: A Male Response to Feminist Theology* (London: SCM Press, 1989), 119 and chap. 5.

[54] Wren, *What Language?*, 139.

it inclusive,"[55] is also highly significant, discerning what she labels the "myth of the crown" (akin to figures in Wren's acronym) and expressing discontent because "it is as if despite Jesus' revolutionary witness against the status quo, the myth of the crown, so powerful in imagination and pervasive in speech, shaped the proclamation of the gospel with its ancient values, its pyramidical assumptions, and its triumphalist tone."[56] Yet Ramshaw holds that—contra some other feminist theologians who want to abandon it (she cites Sallie McFague's *Models of God*[57] on God as "mother, lover, and friend")—the myth of the crown can be re-rendered: "the gospel can teach the church both to speak and to break the myth. If God as the crown of the universe chose to be born in a stable, the myth of the crown has to be radically revised. The crown is now on the serving maid." For starters, she thinks that "to the extent that the myth sanctifies male supremacy, it must yield to the baptismal equality between the sexes,"[58] though pervasive change is required: "What if the church were to proclaim the crown by boldly, in all its affairs, crowning the poor and the dispossessed?"[59]

i. *Trinity*

Biblical resources for expansive language are abundant. The trinitarian God, Ramshaw avers, is "a God of comfort, compassion, consolation, glory, goodness, grace, holiness, justice, light, love, mercy, mystery, peace, power, providence, splendor, truth, wisdom. Our God might be called (1) the Ship of Salvation, (2) Rainbow of promise, (3) Mighty Fortress, (4) Everlasting Arms, (5) Healer of our every ill, Castle, Creator, Fire, Friend, Guardian, Guide, Haven, Homeland, Hope, Judge, Light, Lover, Maker, Mother, Protector, Redeemer, Refuge, Rock, Ruler, Savior, Shield, Sovereign, Strength, Teacher,

[55] Gail Ramshaw, *Liturgical Language: Keeping It Metaphoric, Making It Inclusive* (Collegeville, MN: Liturgical Press, 1998).

[56] Ramshaw, *God Beyond Gender*, 64.

[57] Sallie McFague, *Models of God: Theology for an Ecological, Nuclear Age* (Philadelphia: Fortress Press, 1987).

[58] Ramshaw, *God Beyond Gender*, 68.

[59] Ramshaw, *God Beyond Gender*, 70.

Temple, Treasure, Tree of Life, Whirlwind."[60] In some places in her work a plethora of images is employed in the form of an "abecedary,"[61] a convention which seems to have some roots in certain Jewish practice given that her *Saints on Sundays* explores the *Ashamnu* from the Yom Kippur service: "We abuse, we betray, we are cruel," with each letter of the alphabet furnishing a vice to be confessed.[62]

Her strategies for reducing male-gendered liturgical language parallel her work on presentation of the Revised Common Lectionary,[63] so for example "LORD/Lord" may be cast as "Living One" and "kingdom" becomes "dominion." Her encouragement of expansive language involves not least working with a trinitarian mood so to speak: with triplets—a conscious development of Reformation era use of doublets[64]—of which her eucharistic prayer for Trinity Sunday, "Triple Praise," is an outstanding example: "Holy God, Holy One, Holy Three!" with the prayer making threefold petitions: "Transfigure our minds, ignite your church, nourish the life of the earth," and "Make us, while many, united. Make us, though broken, whole. Make us, despite death, alive." The prayer ends in triple praise: now, tomorrow, forever.[65] The prayer is also replete with images for divine mystery juxtaposed alongside one another, always in threes. Sometimes Ramshaw's triplets of images are explicitly given their biblical roots, as in a set of Eastertide collects appearing in US Methodist resources: light, beauty, rest; bread, milk, honey; shepherd, lamb, gate; grove, lover, well; sovereign, banquet, crown; holy one, altar, cloud—the first set of triplets ("O God, our light, our beauty, our rest") alluding

[60] Gail Ramshaw, *Praying for the Whole World: A Handbook for Intercessors* (Minneapolis: Augsburg, 2006), 42, drawing here on both biblical allusion and metaphor in well-worn hymnody, the latter of course often alluding to the former.

[61] See Gail Ramshaw, *A Metaphorical God: An Abecedary of Images for God* (Chicago: Liturgy Training Publications, 1995).

[62] Gail Ramshaw, *Saints on Sundays: Voices from Our Past Enlivening Our Worship* (Collegeville, MN: Liturgical Press, 2018), 38.

[63] A practical suggestion is that the *Sanctus* might be rendered "Holy, holy, holy, Living God of power and might." See Ramshaw, *God Beyond Gender*, 56.

[64] Ramshaw, *Saints on Sunday*, chap. 21 (on Thomas Cranmer).

[65] The centrepiece of Gail Ramshaw, *Pray, Praise and Give Thanks*, first included in United Church of Canada, *Celebrate God's Presence* (Etibicoke, ONT: United Church Publishing House, 2000), 256–58.

to Psalm 27:11, Psalm 27:4, and Matthew 11:29, the others drawing on other scriptural portions.[66]

Ramshaw's work deserves wide attention because at least some aspects of it have had more influence on official liturgical resources across an ecumenical range than that of other feminists engaged in the crafting of language.[67] It also represents some impeccably orthodox possibilities at great remove from the kind of feminism only (by their own account) tangentially related to the Christian tradition, perhaps more focused on "woma/en" as their central subject than they are on a divine other.[68] It is perhaps because feminist publishing has often presented these more and less orthodox options alongside each other[69] that the more orthodox possibilities have been neglected.

ii. *Christ*

Contending with the figure of Christ Jesus has involved a range of feminist suggestions, with considerable weight given to an argument that Sophia, woman-wisdom, is ripe for revival because eminent in Scripture. In her biblical and patristic studies, Sally Douglas unambiguously connects this figure from both Hebrew Scripture and the Apocrypha to Jesus, concluding that "it is Jesus-Woman Wisdom who is the giver of the feast, and who lives and dies and is raised in radiance, and it is the paradoxical face of Jesus-Woman Wisdom who can both challenge *and* comfort, with a fresh yet ancient, expression of christology," Wisdom 6:12, 7:26 and 29, 2 Corinthians 4:4-6, 1 Clement 36:2, Wisdom 7:27, 8:17-18, and John 1:15 being just some of her

[66] *United Methodist Book of Worship* (Nashville: United Methodist Publishing House, 1992), 399–400, having earlier appeared in Gabe Huck, Gordon Lathrop, and Gail Ramshaw, eds., *Easter: A Sourcebook* (Chicago: Liturgy Training Publications, 1988), 163–64.

[67] Her work is included in at least official Anglican, Methodist, Presbyterian, United, as well as her own Lutheran (Evangelical Lutheran Church in America), churches' resources, and also various publications of the World Council of Churches.

[68] Diann L. Neu, *Stirring Waters: Feminist Liturgies for Justice* (Collegeville, MN: Liturgical Press, 2019), is an example of the latter, at least in Ramshaw's opinion. See Gail Ramshaw, "Wording Prayer," in Stephen Burns and Katharine Massam, eds., *The SCM Companion to Feminist Theologies* (London: SCM Press, forthcoming [2022]).

[69] This important observation is made by Anita Monro, "A Kaleidoscopic Vessel Sailing a Kyriarchal Ocean: The Third Wave Feminist Theologies of Women-Church (1987–2007)," Havea, *Theological and Hermeneutical Explorations*, 25–43.

clues.[70] An adjacent and intriguing possibility has also emerged in relation to "Christa"—Christ as female as depicted in some notable pieces of 1970s art on crucifixion, promoted in the writing of Carter Heyward and others, and receiving a more expansive treatment—in terms not just of her suffering but "risen forms"—in the remarkable work of Nicola Slee[71]: for example, a prayer opening "Christa, our sister / come spread your table in our midst" asks that Christa would break the bread of freedom, pour the wine of jouissance, dance, and delight, "banqueting among us / at the tables of the poor."[72] So far as I know, Christa awaits adoption by any official liturgical resource, though for some Christian communities it could well turn out to be crucial in the testing and expression of claims about incarnation.

Engaging Tradition

One of the important points that Slee makes about Christa is that she has precedents in the tradition, just as Douglas is meticulous in her searching of ancient texts from the Bible and beyond. These dynamics reflect priorities in at least some forms of feminist liturgy, and are illustratively represented in Teresa Berger's approach, at least latterly. Berger's earlier work, *Dissident Daughters: Feminist Liturgies in Global Context* (2001) is important as a collection of narratives about feminist liturgical experiments, often on the edges of denominations, sometimes about communities of women who had separated from their ecclesial traditions. Yet it ends with a quotation from Kathryn Tanner that asserts that feminist theology is "strengthened" to the extent that it can "wrestle[ ] with claims that have traditionally been important in Christian theology." Indeed, Tanner continues, "the

[70] Sally Douglas, *Early Church Understandings of Jesus as the Female Divine: The* Scandal *of the Scandal of Particularity* (London: Bloomsbury, 2016), 169. Other readings develop alternative proposals around such texts and images, with Margaret Barker's *Mother of the Lord: Volume 1: The Lady in the Temple* (London: Bloomsbury, 2012), of special note not only for its contentions about the origins of Marian devotion but on the excision of a female form of divinity from memory of the first temple.

[71] Nicola Slee, *Seeking the Risen Christa*; Slee, *Fragments for Fractured Times*, 219–59. For discussion of Slee on Christa and earlier expressions in art and theology, see Stephen Burns, "Deterrence," in *Feminist Theologies: Interstices and Fractures*, ed. Rebekah Pryor and Stephen Burns (Lanham, MD: Fortress Academic Press, forthcoming [2021]).

[72] Slee, *Risen Christa*, 149.

more traditional the material with which it works, the greater the influence of feminist theology." Berger takes up this conviction to talk in her own voice of "tradition-friendliness" that on the one hand claims neglected elements of the tradition while on the other hand "reconfigur[es] what is authorized as 'Tradition'."[73]

In her work a decade later, *Gender Differences and the Making of Liturgical History* (2011), Berger neither mentions *Dissident Daughters* nor invokes "feminism" as a keyword. Rather, she attends to "gender separations in liturgical space," showing how early shifts from household gatherings to "public sanctuaries" were gendered developments, while pilgrimages mediated between the differences allowing women a larger role than in more stable public space. She also takes on what she calls "gender on and under the table," looking at early examples of "breast milk as eucharistic metaphor" and re-evaluating early documents which explicitly indicate that a woman could "eucharistise" bread with words closely akin to *The Apostolic Constitutions*. And she explores male and female "bodily flows"—menstruation, ejaculation, birth-giving—and their influence on what she names "liturgical anxieties," and how such flows have impacted women's participation and women's presidency. So, in these and other ways, the later Berger examines the "gender-troubled" business of liturgical leadership, giving particular attention to Mary's "priestly womb and priestly breast" to which the tradition attests, albeit marginally as compared with other eucharistic tropes. Berger's "history of gender trouble" is intent on unsettling supposed norms as her retrievals enact a similar kind of strategy to what Ann Loades, herself echoing a scriptural parable (Luke 15:8-10), calls "searching for lost coins."[74] Yet depending on where and with whom one worships, precious little of these feminist perspectives may be likely to surface in church.

Coda: Same-Sex Marriage

Recent decades have seen numerous experimental rites for blessing of same-sex relationships, with scholarship suggestive of earlier precedents even in ancient sources, aside from readings of biblical

[73] Teresa Berger, *Dissident Daughters: Feminist Liturgies in Global Context* (Louisville, KY: Westminster John Knox Press, 2001), 229–30.

[74] Ann Loades, *Searching for Lost Coins: Explorations in Christianity and Feminism* (London: SPCK, 1987).

material to animate such rites, including from more conservative quarters.[75] Frank Senn's account of changing his mind on the question of same-sex marriage is just one powerful testimony to re-reading Scripture and coming to different kinds of conclusions about it from views he held earlier, having previously been a spokesperson for a somewhat conservative group of Lutherans.[76] The rite Senn constructed for the marriage of one of his two gay sons is close to models of marriage in inherited ritual books, in his case forms from the Episcopal Church (in which recent official change to the church's doctrine of marriage may prove to be an important trigger for wider liturgical reform). Even though in Senn's case he found himself unable to offer a nuptial blessing, he did exchange the blessing he deemed appropriate for a mixed-gender wedding for a warm prayer that the couple be "enfolded in God's grace—his (sic) unearned lovingkindness."[77]

At the moment, outside denominationally endorsed resources much bolder models are also emerging in relation to the blessing of different kinds of queer unions, including those of a polyamorous nature, where declarations of consent, exchange of symbols, and so on are "repeated as needed."[78] It remains to be seen whether any churches will take this further step of dismantling the exclusivity that official liturgies have presented as central to marriage, however patchy exclusivity looks in much biblical material depicting (what would now be termed heterosexual) polygamous arrangements, quite apart from the prevalence of polygamous arrangements in global Christian contexts today. That being as it is, what unofficial rites tend to stress is their presumed "witness to the wide and wonderful

[75] Jim Cotter, *The Service of My Love: The Celebration and Blessing of Civil Partnerships* (Sheffield: Cairns Publications, 2007), as an early example for same-sex unions; Michael Vasey, *Strangers and Friends: A New Exploration of Homosexuality and the Bible* (London: Hodder and Stoughton, 1995), as an example of a quite conservative reading of Scripture, not least by a notable liturgist.

[76] Frank Senn, "I Had to Do It For My Son," in *Liturgy With a Difference: Beyond Inclusion in Christian Assembly*, ed. Stephen Burns and Bryan Cones, 79–97 (London: SCM Press, 2019). Other conservatives remain so; another Australian example would be the Diocese of Sydney donating a million dollars to the "No" campaign resisting equal marriage: https://www.theguardian.com/australia-news/2017/oct/10/sydney-anglican-diocese-donates-1m-to-no-campaign-for-same-sex-marriage-vote.

[77] Senn, "I Had to Do It," 92.

[78] See Scott Haldeman, "The Queer Body in the Wedding," in Burns and Cones, *Liturgy With a Difference*, 61–76, and 166, 169, for rubrics of such a rite.

diversity of God's creation," declaring that "all are welcome" even though "the church has not always been a place where we have been able to gather and hear the blessing of God." Such rites may "celebrate" determination to "welcome[ ] everyone regardless of whom we love," giving thanks to God that "God moves us, and the whole world, into deeper and wider patterns of love."[79]

It may be that the first major old-line denominational ritual book to include any kind of same-sex marriage rite is the 2018 *Book of Common Worship* (*BCW*) of the Presbyterian Church (US). Its texts elide reference to specific genders in a single rite of marriage (that is, the same rite is used for partnerships of any composition of two). While the introduction notes that "Marriage involves a unique commitment between two people, traditionally a man and woman,"[80] after that it speaks only about the like of "both members of the couple" and "the two people marrying." Yet part of the groundwork for the *BCW* rites, in the *BCW* co-editor's *Inclusive Marriage Rituals* just a few years earlier, does speak about the like of "both genders,"[81] so while its own observation that change with respect to same-sex marriage rites has been rapid is quite correct,[82] its lingering binaries invite attention to another focus of rapid change—transgender identities.

Coda: Transgender Identity and Queer Liturgy

Transgendered experience especially challenges any persistent prescriptive associations between sex and gender. At least up until 1973 transpersons might have been considered "homosexual,"[83] and only in very recent decades have wider cultural mores about trans-identity shifted somewhat. Subsequently, transpersons are increasingly visible in churches, and some churches have offered public

[79] Kimberley Bracken Long and David Maxwell, eds., *Inclusive Marriage Services: A Wedding Sourcebook* (Louisville, KY: Westminster John Knox Press, 2015), 193. See also Kimberley Bracken Long, *From This Day Forward: Rethinking the Christian Wedding* (Louisville, KY: Westminster John Knox Press, 2016).

[80] Presbyterian Church of the USA, *Book of Common Worship* (Louisville, KY: Westminster John Knox Press, 2018), 687.

[81] Long and Maxwell, *Inclusive Marriage Services*, 199.

[82] Long and Maxwell, *Inclusive Marriage Services*, 10.

[83] Marcella Althaus-Reid and Lisa Isherwood, eds., *Trans/formations* (London: SCM Press, 2009), 11.

welcome to them, albeit amidst considerable pushback from some quarters.[84] Arguably, though, (in the good company of Christa) transpersons have many precedents in Christian tradition, and this is something apologists have been keen to stress, in part stemming from conviction that "the Bible is transgender friendly."[85] Virginia Ramsey Mollenkott encourages churches to explore "gifts" that transpersons bear in their persons and suggests seven "lessons" congregations can learn together with transgendered people, with her sense of transgender-friendly Scripture being the first in the skein. Among the others are that transpersons "can help to heal religious addictions to certainty" and that they "incarnate the concept that just as all races are 'one blood,' all genders and sexualities are 'one continuum.'"[86] According to Mollenkott, they may also be "specially gifted at building bridges between the seen and the unseen."[87] Testimony from transpresiders adds depth to the latter contention, as in Rachel Mann's discussion of pressures to "pass" and "go stealth" in her role as a priest and transwoman, while she also emphasises an iconoclastic dimension (Mollenkott might say gift) of transgender presence: "work[ing] in the midst of the community as critique of the church's pernicious love of kyriarchical power."[88]

Whether or not that tall order can be met, transgender experience certainly troubles much second-wave feminist liturgical work over several decades now, insofar as shunting liturgy into more inclusive modes has involved preoccupation with decentring "man," "he," and male-gendered metaphors. Hence, feminist alternatives, where

[84] Harriet Sherwood, "Church of England Plan for Welcoming Trans People Under Fire," *The Guardian*, 29 January 2019, https://www.theguardian.com/world/2019/jan/29/church-england-plan-welcoming-trans-people-under-fire-clergy-lay-members-bishops-withdraw-guidance.

[85] See Althaus-Reid and Isherwood, *Trans/formations*, 8, 47, 49.

[86] Virginia Ramsey Mollenkott, "We Come Bearing Gifts: Seven Lessons Religious Congregations Can Learn from Transpeople," in Althaus-Reid and Isherwood, *Trans/formations*, 46–58, 47.

[87] Mollenkott, "We Come Bearing Gifts," 47.

[88] Rachel Mann, "The Performance of Queerness: Trans Priesthood as Gesture Towards a Queered Liturgical Assembly," in Burns and Cones, *Liturgy With a Difference*, 35–46, 44. See also Rachel Mann, "Presiding From the Broken Middle," in Slee and Burns, *Presiding Like a Woman*, 133–39, with her trans experience set in context of attention to very specific bodiliness in Rachel Mann, *Love's Mysteries: The Body, Grief, Precariousness and God* (Norwich: Canterbury Press, 2020), e.g., 22–30.

they have emerged at all, now stand in question: "men and women," "he or she," naming towards God as "mother and father," and so on may still occlude the diversity of an assembly. So in light of lessons learned with transgendered persons, much feminist liturgical work needs to be rethought, and gains perhaps let go, in favour of new searching for language and ritual forms more fully humanly inclusive. A "third wave" of feminist theology, at interstices with queer theology, is already alert to this agenda, but is yet to surface in churches' official liturgical resources.[89] Yet if "there is a 'trans' core to this incarnational religion"[90] it needs to come forth, and not in stealth. Emphasising "the counter-cultural importance of Christianity's focus on being human, rather than male or female"[91] could prove to be more "traditional" than some Christians yet imagine, given that Susannah Cornwall connects "the 'kenotic hymn' of Philippians 2:5-11 [which] counsels that humans emulate Jesus, who did not consider equality with God something to be grasped" with the view that "to exploit, to cling, or to grasp at equality with God is what is happening when humans decide that a single . . . reading of gender tells the whole story of God."[92]

To Conclude

In shifting and unstable terrain, exploration of gender issues and liturgy and Bible might well rest as best it can on two aphorisms. First, from Augustine: "If you are comprehending what you are saying, you are not talking about God,"[93] which might encourage at least some who have not yet listened for wisdom sought in second- and

[89] Introductions include Patrick Cheng, *Radical Love: An Introduction to Queer Theology* (New York: Seabury Press, 2007), and Linn Tonstad, *Queer Theology* (Eugene, OR: Cascade, 2018), the latter majoring on the corpus of work by the highly significant Marcella Althaus-Reid.

[90] Althaus-Reid and Isherwood, *Trans/formations*, 1.

[91] Michelle O'Brien and Christina Beardsley, *This Is My Body: Hearing the Voices of Transgender Christians* (London: Darton, Longman & Todd, 2016), 31.

[92] Susannah Cornwall, "The *Kenosis* of Unambiguous Sex in the Body of Christ: Intersex, Theology and Existing 'For the Other,'" *Theology and Sexuality* 14 (2008): 181–99, 189.

[93] Augustine, "Sermons on New Testament Lessons," cited in Ramshaw, *God Beyond Gender*, 7.

third-wave feminism eventually to do so. The other comes from Stanley Hauerwas, to be remembered not least by churches when they attempt to relate their doctrine and liturgy to elders in retreat, disdainful young, and concerning disengagement on many sides: "the demand to be normal can be tyrannical unless we understand that the normal condition of our being together is that we are all different."[94]

[94] Stanley Hauerwas, *Suffering Presence: Theological Reflections on Medicine, the Mentally Handicapped, and the Church* (Notre Dame, IN: University of Notre Dame Press, 1986), 214.

Conclusion

Reading the Bible through the Liturgy

Gordon Jeanes

There is an easy assumption that the work of liturgy is simply to apply to modern worship the content and meaning of the Bible. This could be taken for granted as broadly the consensus underlying the dispute among reformers of the sixteenth and seventeenth centuries, whether a church could be ordered only by what was positively prescribed by Scripture (as was held by more radical reformers) or whether a church had the liberty to order itself in any way that was not directly contrary to Scripture (as was held, for example, by the leadership of the Church of England). Both sides would be uncomfortable with the modern situation in which there is an acute scholarly awareness of the historical development of Christian thought and practice, and also wide diversity of contemporary practice. For example, Catherine Reid notes the fact that that the modern Church of England marriage service promotes the sense of the equality of the partners in marriage despite the fact that "nowhere in Scripture . . . is equality in marriage urged" [Note 12]. Indeed, it can be claimed that perhaps above all in the marriage of divorcees liturgical practice goes directly contrary to the words of Christ and the command of Scripture. One response to this might be simply to condemn such a custom as a falling away from biblical teaching.

However, any such definition of orthodoxy as being defined only by a literal sense of texts in the Bible will quickly come up against much more important problems, the doctrine of the Trinity for one. Not only is the word not found in the Bible, but the development of the doctrine was a long, contested process over centuries. R. P. C. Hanson described the whole long and difficult Arian crisis as essentially the problem, "How can an unyielding monotheism accommodate the worship of Jesus Christ as divine?"[1] The early Christian practice highlighted contradictions in the Biblical writings which had to be harmonised somehow, but the end result was by no means clear at the time. The issue became, and remains, one not just of the Bible itself but of the Bible rightly interpreted.

In *A History of the Bible*, John Barton introduces the chapter entitled "The Theme of the Bible" with the King's College Cambridge service of Nine Lessons and Carols, and describes how the readings set out a scheme of Fall and Redemption which is traditional to Christianity but, as he then explains, completely foreign to a Jewish understanding of the Bible.[2] Nine Lessons and Carols is a service barely a hundred years old so it can hardly have made a massive mark in the history of Christianity. But its great popularity will have cast its message far and wide across the population in England and beyond, that that is what the Bible "means." David Kennedy explores the richness of the theme in a wide variety of uses.

The liturgy here is by no means the progenitor of such a reading, leaning as it does on Paul, particularly in Romans. Paul interprets the sin of Adam as introducing death in a manner which is broadly paralleled in inter-testamental literature, above all in Wisdom 2:23-24, but not in Genesis or the Hebrew Bible itself.[3] (Nor is it cited much by the other writers of the New Testament.) But from at least the second century CE it has become the dominant narrative in Christianity, especially in the West. Christopher Irvine shows that this idea of a story, a *narratio*, was consciously adopted by prominent early Christians as a tool for education and conversion. And in this respect one could say that the liturgy has been principally the messenger of the Bible and theology, from the *felix culpa* of the Exsultet to Nine Lessons and Carols.

[1] *The Search for the Christian Doctrine of God* (Edinburgh: T&T Clark, 1988), 874. And see, e.g., Frances Young, *The Making of the Creeds* (London: SCM Press, 1991), 33–34.

[2] John Barton, *A History of the Bible: The Book and Its Faiths* (London: Allen Lane, 2019), 311ff.

[3] See James D. G. Dunn, *The Theology of Paul the Apostle* (London: T&T Clark, 2003), 82–90.

The Tradition and the Rule of Faith

There has been much study of the development of the canon of the biblical books. But when we deal with the question of a canon, John Barton points out that in early Christianity the Canon or Rule of Faith was more spoken of than the canon of Scripture.[4] Starting with summaries which can be found in the books of the New Testament but which would have pre-existed them, formulae developed and stabilised into a fairly standard pattern which we find from Irenaeus on.[5] The texts were broadly similar to the early creeds with their emphasis on God the Creator and Father of Jesus Christ, and on the birth, death, and resurrection of Christ, and today would be taken by a modern worshipper as a paraphrase of the Apostles' or Nicene Creed.[6] This was not a matter of tradition as "extra information" in addition to that in Scripture but rather a tradition of how Scripture is to be interpreted. (The Gnostic idea that God is not interested in creation is firmly ruled out in Irenaeus's versions of the Rule.) This was "Scripture rightly interpreted." For worshippers today the recital of the Creed on a Sunday may well feel a tedious exercise in jargon (which many may not even understand or agree with), but more fundamentally it functions as a template which gives the Bible a shape, a single story through which a diverse group of texts can be understood. It is what those who have come as strangers into a church hear as the overall story which embraces the readings and sermon of that occasion; it is what a child brought up in the faith is formed by as much as anything else they may absorb.

Specifically, the Creed (and here I consider particularly the Nicene Creed) concentrates on a number of salient points which are central to the Christian tradition and its interpretation of the Bible. We may start with its overall trinitarian shape, with Jesus Christ and the Holy Spirit named, their divine status affirmed, and their relation to God the Father described. The role of God in creation is asserted—this was of great significance in countering Gnostic ideas and perhaps it

[4] John Barton, *People of the Book? The Authority of the Bible in Christianity* (London: SPCK, 1998), 30.

[5] *Adversus Haereses* 1.2; 3.4.1; 4.53.1. For these and the Rule of Faith in other writers see R. P. C. Hanson, *Tradition in the Early Church* (London: SCM Press, 1962), 75–129.

[6] The relation of the Rule of Faith to the early creeds is not straightforward. See, e.g., J. N. D. Kelly, *Early Christian Creeds*, 3rd ed. (Harlow, UK: Longman, 1972).

should be noted more in these days of ecological crisis. But then we move in the story of the divine economy directly to a narrative of the conception and birth, and then the death and resurrection, ascension, and glorification of Jesus, the Son of God. These events are the focus of the great seasonal cycles of Christmas and Easter, but in Ordinary Time the congregation, hearing readings from the gospels of the life and teaching of Jesus, can imaginatively insert them into the overall narrative. The activity of the Holy Spirit in the Creed mirrors that of the Son, with a share in the work of creation as the "giver of life" and then as the inspirer of "the prophets"; and then the narrative segues into church, salvation, and the final consummation. So it is that the Creed summarises the narrative in the Christian tradition as creation-redemption-consummation along with the affirmation of the trinitarian God.

It may be noticed that the Old Testament is referred to twice in the Nicene Creed (though not at all in the Apostles' Creed). The first time is when the resurrection of Christ is stated to be "in accordance with the Scriptures." Many people may understand that as referring to the New Testament accounts of the first Easter Day, but its origin was a claim that the events of Christ's death and resurrection were in fulfilment of God's promises set out in the Old Testament. And this, together with the Holy Spirit being described as the one who "has spoken through the prophets" presupposes rather than argues the *raison d'être* of the Old Testament to be first and foremost a prophetic book looking to Jesus as the coming Messiah, the Son of God. It sets out the story of God and the world of creation and fall in which the coming of Jesus is both a culmination and a solution. As such, the subordination of the Old Testament to the New is built into the Creed itself.

Barton wonders whether his point about the Rule of Faith might be described as "a Catholic theory of biblical authority" and emphasises the role of Scripture as the judge of the Rule of Faith.[7] But his central point is one held by scholars who would not be described as "Catholic." Neville Clark of the Baptist tradition supports a similar account:

[7] Barton, *People of the Book?*, 32.

> The whole concept of a fixed canon of sacred writings is not native to the Christian community in its formative years. Its inheritance from Judaism was the Tradition of Israel, embodied in Law, Prophets, and an open and changing collection of other writings. . . . Prior to the final years of the first century A.D. there was no Jewish canon to inherit. . . .
>
> The very existence of the Christian community, however, meant that alongside the Tradition of Israel a new Tradition was coming to birth. Comparatively early, it began to find literary expression.[8]

Clark describes the Bible first as the "bearer of a Tradition constantly reforged, reformed, reapplied in each new critical situation, each successive age" and then as "the authoritative Tradition of the People of God." In both its acquisition of such a status and its application he sees worship as central:

> The formation of the canon involved not only the recognition of the customary usage of such scriptures within the liturgical assembly but also the judgement that these writings should, by their continued liturgical use, supremely form and mould the Christian community of the future. . . . The Bible . . . belongs essentially at the heart of Christian worship, for it is above all a proclamation to be heard. It is not a handbook of doctrine or ethics. Only in a very indirect way does it provide the controlling context within which the basic decisions of faith and life can and must be made.[9]

In her chapter, Cally Hammond demonstrates how the subordination of the Old Testament to the New is expressed ritually, and likewise in many churches the supremacy of the gospel books. The status of the Bible is established by being read in public worship, and a hierarchy of books within the whole.This hierarchy reflects the way that they relate to a greater revelation, not words on a page but a person: Jesus Christ himself who is proclaimed by the Christian Scriptures (and this includes the Christian Old Testament) as the Messiah, the Son and Word of God. It was the life, death, and resurrection of

[8] Neville Clark, "Scripture in Liturgical Perspective," in *The Word in Season: The Use of the Bible in Liturgy*, ed. Donald Gray, 19–20 (Joint Liturgical Group; Norwich: Canterbury Press, 1988).

[9] Clark, "Scripture in Liturgical Perspective," 23.

Jesus that his followers had to make sense of. In order to do so they searched the books of the Hebrew Bible for evidence that he was truly God's anointed; and by doing so they established a new way of reading and understanding the Scriptures which thereby were transfigured as the Old Testament. (It goes without saying that this reading was not shared by rabbinic Judaism. Hence, the full title of Barton's book: *A History of the Bible: The Book and its Faiths*. Two faiths shared a single Scripture with a contested meaning.) And so, in the Christian tradition, the Old Testament speaks of Jesus who is to come, the New Testament bears witness to his impact, and the Gospels speak with his very words. And through his words Christ is held to be present in the worshipping assembly.

The early history of Christianity still involved contested interpretation, most acutely in Gnosticism and beliefs that rejected the identity of God, the Father of Jesus Christ with God the Creator to whom the Hebrew Scriptures bear witness. Clearly, as in the instance of Marcion, such an extreme position was possible only by a re-editing of the works of the New Testament as well as a rejection of the Old.

Liturgy Ignoring Scripture?

Any study of this kind might suggest something like a conversation between liturgy and the Bible rather than a simple reading by one of the other. However, it is a sobering thought that, very often, we see through these essays not so much a conversation as a communication gap between the two. What is described here is not so much what liturgy *should* do as what it does do.

Thomas O'Loughlin suggests that readings from Scripture were largely tokenistic in many traditional churches, the lectionary plans were haphazard, and the passages badly selected, and many clergy ill-equipped to cope with the introduction of the modern lectionaries. Modern reforms have courageously tried to overcome this deficit, and, as Normand Bonneau points out, the Roman Catholic lectionary was careful to avoid a thematic approach to the readings in Ordinary Time. Let Scripture be Scripture! But even while the Sunday lectionary may be more expansive and its treatment more central in preaching, Lizette Larson-Miller portrays the Bible as less dominant in modern funeral liturgies, and Catherine Reid shows how allusions and motifs from Scripture have been elided in the marriage service.

At those moments of wonder and at times of greatest need, Scripture's voice is muted. This problem seems to run right across the ecumenical spectrum: anecdotal evidence suggests that in many charismatic churches Scripture readings are often of little priority. If traditional lessons from Scripture are felt no longer to be applicable in today's society, what do we need to hear? Very often that may be simply riches that we are overlooking. On the one hand, many of the challenges our societies face today are there within the pages of Scripture: the abuses of wealth, the plight of the migrant, and the refugee. Christopher Irvine explores attempts to include environmental issues into a biblical liturgy. As we become more conscious of the abuse of power in sexual relations, do we need to reflect on the story of David and his family?[10] And if marriage is an "honourable estate" what praise is there of celibacy which follows the example of St. Paul and of Christ himself? On the other hand Anne McGowan asks how the celebration of the Easter season may be given attention equal to Lent and Holy Week. And Ann Loades proposes the rediscovery of the narrative tradition in the Bible with regard to Jesus, as something of great benefit to children, though that can hardly be exclusive to them. But we are caught between the Scylla of simplistic biblical use and the Charybdis of demanding sophistication. The *Common Worship* baptism service set out to achieve as wide a coverage of Bible themes relating to baptism as possible, but the service was judged to be difficult for many to apprehend.[11] As John Baldovin comments, biblical education is necessary for its riches to be apprehended.

Léon van Ommen complains about the liturgical neglect of lament, which only serves to reinforce the "centre" against the marginalised.

[10] Robin Green acknowledges the way in which the revised Church of England marriage liturgies celebrate sexual union but complains that "which the new liturgy has sacrificed is an honest recognition of the ambiguity of human sexuality. Although the 1662 Anglican liturgy was at fault in many ways, it did show a more realistic grasp of the destructive, as well as creative, power of sexuality." *Only Connect: Worship and Liturgy from the Perspective of Pastoral Care* (London: Darton, Longman & Todd, 1987), 101. Probably such a sceptical approach would be difficult to maintain within the marriage service itself, but are there other settings within which it could be explored?

[11] *Common Worship: Christian Initiation* (London: Church House Publishing, 2006), 306–7, 322–24; Simon Jones, *Celebrating Christian Initiation* (London: SPCK, 2016), xviii–xix, 57–58.

As a parish priest, I understand his point and indeed would expand it; from my own experience it can be very difficult to challenge any dominant worldview in an act of worship. I have often wondered if people in church expect above all to be affirmed, and any attempt to present a wider viewpoint has to be carefully gauged so as not to meet with instant rejection. We all have countless strategies by which we evade a true encounter with God, and we can invoke liturgy or the Bible itself to do so.

Barton speaks of the liturgy as constructing "something like what the structural anthropologists call *bricolage*: taking something from here, something from there . . . and forging them into a new unity."[12] I often think of the liturgist's task as that of the scribe trained for the kingdom of heaven who brings out of his treasure what is new and what is old (Matt 13:52). But given the observations above, we may wonder when *bricolage* becomes mere cherry-picking. An authentic act of liturgical craftsmanship has to engage in the exercise of exploring the question: What have the Bible and the tradition to say to us here and now?

Liturgy Interpreting Scripture?

Bridget Nichols has shown how broad and pervasive the Bible is in liturgical language and practice, and how it gives substance both to our vision of God and also our response to him. But as for specific examples where the liturgy has been said to have an authoritative influence on the interpretation of the Bible and doctrine, a few examples have been cited in history but they are not easy to sustain. For example, Origen claimed that infant baptism was a practice inherited from the apostles, but that is now not taken seriously as evidence for more than a generation before that theologian, let alone as authority for the custom.[13]

Perhaps the most famous instance for students of the early church is the development of the doctrine of the divinity of the Holy Spirit, where Basil of Caesarea, among others, appealed to the baptismal formula in the church's liturgy as evidence for the divinity of the

[12] Barton, *People of the Book?*, 76.

[13] *Commentary on Romans* 5.9.11; Everett Ferguson, *Baptism in the Early Church* (Grand Rapids, MI: Eerdmans, 2009), 368–70.

Spirit with the Father and the Son. But it would be wrong to claim from this point that the liturgy is a separate source of doctrine from Scripture. As Anthony Meredith points out, other writers of the time have quoted Matthew 28:19 without making any connection between liturgical custom and doctrine.[14] Certainly the use of the text in the baptismal formula of the church gave it a prominence that cannot be ignored, but overall the issue is best described as one where theologians have reflected on the Bible and practice together. As A.N. Williams puts it: "The position that came ultimately to prevail was not simply that of a community or that expressed in sacred texts or oral traditions or practices of worship, but of a community reasoning about the relation of all these."[15]

Liturgy Undergirding Scripture?

We are brought back instead to the most basic data of early Christianity: the use of Scripture in its worship from at latest the second century, and the worship of Jesus as God, picking up and reinforcing the general terms used in the New Testament narratives. The custom has seen different expressions and uses in the tradition and conceivably could have been steered away from the Trinitarian form which prevailed.[16] But any other course, both radical and counter-factual, ultimately is simply to admit the logical possibility that the Tradition could have developed in an alternative course. And non-Trinitarian versions of Christianity, far from overturning "tradition," have merely created their own traditions of the interpretation of the Bible.

The worshipping practice of the church cannot be said to provide data or rules about specifics. It is more basic than that. Aidan Kavanagh rightly says that the "law of belief" shapes the "law of worship," "but the latter *constitutes* or *founds* the former."[17]

[14] Anthony Meredith, *The Cappadocians* (London: Geoffrey Chapman, 1995), 32.

[15] A. N. Williams, *The Architecture of Theology: Structure, System and Ratio* (Oxford: Oxford University Press, 2011), 87.

[16] See, e.g., Bryan D. Spinks, ed., *The Place of Christ in Liturgical Prayer: Trinity, Christology, and Liturgical Theology* (Collegeville, MN: Liturgical Press, 2008); Rowan Williams, "Angels Unawares: Heavenly Liturgy and Earthly Theology in Alexandria," *Studia Patristica* 30 (1997): 350–63.

[17] Aidan Kavanagh, SJ, *On Liturgical Theology* (New York: Pueblo, 1984), 92.

Geoffrey Wainwright speaks of liturgy as "a hermeneutic continuum," where it has been and remains today as the prime situation where Scripture is read, proclaimed, and expounded, and in which it is interpreted and applied. It provides the community which links individuals together, both within a single culture and also in a continuity across cultures and centuries.[18]

Any discussion about the relation of theology and worship inevitably spills over to consider a third factor: that of Christian living. We have the three-legged stool of *lex orandi, lex credendi, lex vivendi*, all part of the seamless robe of Christian worship, life, and reflection which function properly only when integrated as one. The ancient definition of a theologian as one who prays also would assume one whose life is marked with the grace of Christ. The later chapters in this book are all concerned with how we might address with integrity in our worshipping lives some of the issues that confront humanity today. Contrariwise, John Baldovin is eloquent in his depiction of the effect on Christian worship and witness of scandalous abusive behaviour.

In *The Bible, Theology and Faith*, Walter Moberly effectively explores the three together when he discusses in detail the story of the risen Jesus meeting the disciples on the road to Emmaus. He understands the breaking of the bread in the evening principally as being in continuity with the practices of Jesus during his earthly ministry. "If there are overtones of the Christian eucharist, then the eucharist is to be seen in that same continuity."

> Why then are the eyes of the disciples opened now? It is because the breaking of bread is an action, and a particular kind of action—sharing the basic necessity of life (bread), in continuity with the earthly practice of Jesus. Although the disciples' hearts burn at the expounding of scripture it is only when the words are complemented by action, the action of sharing that which is necessary for daily life in the manner of Jesus that the recognition of the risen Christ comes.[19]

[18] Geoffrey Wainwright, *Doxology: The Praise of God in Worship, Doctrine and Life* (London: Epworth Press, 1980), 175–76.

[19] Walter Moberly, *The Bible, Theology and Faith* (Cambridge: Cambridge University Press, 2000), 63.

Mere familiarity with the Bible, and simple enactment of the Eucharist, of themselves are not sufficient. "If the Christian eucharist is to enable genuine encounter with the risen Christ, its symbolism must represent and express action that shares with, and meets the needs of, others in a way characteristic of Jesus."[20] Van Ommen would wholeheartedly agree!

> The meal is symbolically suggestive of the kind of action through which Jesus, the Christ, welcomed people and mediated God's kingdom to them. If this is the context for seeing the risen Lord, it means that a Christian understanding is inseparable from a certain kind of "eucharistic" lifestyle and practice. It is to those who are willing to live and act as Jesus did that the way Jesus understood God and scripture is most likely to make sense.[21]

Moberly places the emphasis firmly on eucharistic *lifestyle*, not worship. But just as worship is authenticated—or otherwise—by lifestyle, so the life of an individual or a community is given shape and meaning by its ritual behaviour. Paul F. Bradshaw and Katharine Harman describe the role of ritual as symbol: "A symbolic approach asks that one look at the ritual as a means of communication. It combines the formal and the functional definition, by defining "ritual" as an activity that conveys meaning. . . . A liturgical ritual might serve to solidify a community's group identity, facilitate an individual's prayer to God, identify structures of leadership versus participants, and remember the teaching of Jesus in the gospel."[22]

Unusually, "eucharistic lifestyle" may be a phrase in which the adjective carries more weight than the noun. The lifestyle is informed and reinforced by the ritual act through which the worshipping community, repeatedly and in different ways and circumstances, celebrates the story of Jesus by receiving the broken bread and the wine. It posits both life and faith as a gift of God offered and received.

[20] Moberly, *Bible, Theology and Faith*, 63.

[21] Moberly, *Bible, Theology and Faith*, 65–66.

[22] Paul F. Bradshaw and Katharine Harman, "Ritual," in *The Study of Liturgy and Worship*, ed. Juliette Day and Benjamin Gordon-Taylor, 21–32, 25 (London: SPCK, 2013).

One certainly cannot claim that the celebration of the Eucharist is a requirement for Christian life. Indeed, two Christian traditions rightly renowned for their Christian activism and lifestyle, the Salvation Army and the Quakers, are both distinguished also by the fact that the Eucharist is not part of their worshipping tradition at all. That said, Earl Robinson emphasises the importance in the Salvation Army of discipleship as worship using Isaiah 58:6-7, including sharing food with the hungry: Here we meet current explorations of the importance of the Eucharist as food.[23] For a tradition which links eucharistic worship and service together more closely we may instance the liturgical movement with its emphasis on the Eucharist and on the corporate nature of the church as the Body of Christ. This has often been linked with the development of political activism based around an appreciation of the importance of society.[24]

I wrote earlier of tradition as "Scripture rightly interpreted." We have moved on to include Scripture rightly lived and rightly prayed. There will be countless interpretations of the details of what that involves, varying often according to culture and circumstance, but it is the quest which all Christian traditions are engaged in, the pilgrim path for everyone seeking to follow Christ. This collection of essays hopefully will lead us all to reflect on our perception of that path and our journey on it.

[23] "Worship within the Salvation Army," in *Worship Today: Understanding, Practice, Ecumenical Implications*, ed. Thomas F. Best and Dagmar Heller, 175 (Geneva: WCC Publications, Faith and Order Paper No. 194, 2004). For wider consideration of eucharistic feeding see, e.g., Mary McGann, *The Meal That Reconnects: Eucharistic Eating and the Global Food Crisis* (Collegeville, MN: Liturgical Press, 2020).

[24] See, e.g., Donald Gray, *Earth and Altar* (London: SPCK, 1986).

Index of Biblical References